Windows NT
Registry
Troubleshooting

Rob Tidrow

New Riders Publishing, Indianapolis, Indiana

Windows NT Registry Troubleshooting

By Rob Tidrow

Published by:
New Riders Publishing
201 West 103rd Street
Indianapolis, IN 46290 USA

Copyright © 1996 by New Riders Publishing

Printed in the United States of America   3 4 5 6 7 8 9 0

Library of Congress Cataloging-in-Publication Data

```
***CIP data available upon request***
```

Warning and Disclaimer

This book is designed to provide information about the Windows NT operating system. Every effort has been made to make this book as complete and as accurate as possible, but no warranty or fitness is implied.

The information is provided on an "as is" basis. The author(s) and New Riders Publishing shall have neither liability nor responsibility to any person or entity with respect to any loss or damages arising from the information contained in this book or from the use of the disks or programs that may accompany it.

Publisher	*Don Fowley*
Publishing Manager	*Emmett Dulaney*
Marketing Manager	*Mary Foote*
Managing Editor	*Carla Hall*

Acquisitions Editor
Pete Bitar

Software Specialist
Steve Flatt

Senior Editor
Sarah Kearns

Development Editor
Stacia Mellinger

Project Editor
Amy Bezek

Copy Editors
Amy Bezek
Keith Cline

Technical Editor
Raj Rajagopal

Acquisitions Coordinator
Stephanie Layton

Administrative Coordinator
Karen Opal

Cover Designer
Sandra Schroeder

Cover Illustration
©Sally Wern Comport/SIS

Cover Production
Aren Howell

Book Designer
Gary Adair

Production Manager
Kelly Dobbs

Production Team Supervisor
Laurie Casey

Graphics Image Specialists
Dan Harris
Clint Lahnen

Production Analysts
Jason Hand
Erich Richter

Production Team
Christopher Morris
Eric Puckett
Beth Rago
Elizabeth SanMiguel

Indexers
Rob Fox
Greg Pearson

About the Author

Rob Tidrow is a technical writer, Web site designer, and president of Tidrow Communications, Inc., a firm specializing in content creation and delivery. Rob has authored or co-authored over 20 books on a wide variety of computer topics, including seven books about Windows 95. He authored *Windows 95 Registry Troubleshooting*, published by New Riders, and *Windows 95 Installation and Configuration Handbook*, published by Que. He is also a contributing author to *Inside Windows 95, Deluxe Edition*; *Inside Windows 95*; *SE Using Windows 95, Platinum Edition*; *Inside the World Wide Web*; and *Windows 95 for Network Administrators*, all published by New Riders. He lives in Indianapolis with his wife Tammy and their two sons, Adam and Wesley, and can be reached on the Internet at rtidrow@iquest.net.

Trademark Acknowledgments

All terms mentioned in this book that are known to be trademarks or service marks have been appropriately capitalized. New Riders Publishing cannot attest to the accuracy of this information. Use of a term in this book should not be regarded as affecting the validity of any trademark or service mark. Windows NT and Registry are registered trademarks of the Microsoft Corporation.

Dedication

I dedicate this book to my brothers, Jack Tidrow and Bart Tidrow, and to my sister Rachel Collette.

Acknowledgments

I would like to thank New Riders for all the support they have given me over the past year, as well as providing me opportunities to contribute to their publishing goals. I would like to thank Don Fowley for showing support of this title and believing in Windows NT. I would like to thank Emmett Dulaney for believing in me and giving me the encouragement to finish this book, as well as giving me a call in the first place to write the book. I want to thank Stacia Mellinger in helping pull together the book and offering suggestions and guidance to improve the structure and vision of the book. Amy Bezek deserves a huge thank you ("THANK YOU!") for helping compile Appendix A and tediously going through my copy to improve my writing.

Contents at a Glance

Table of Contents

Introduction

Over the past two years, Windows NT has become the fastest growing segment in networking, Internet and intranet services, and enterprise-wide environments. When Microsoft released Windows NT 3.5 in December of 1994, many users and industry pundits finally sat up and noticed the advanced features of Windows NT. Companies that previously adopted Windows 3.1, Windows 3.11 for Workgroups, or OS/2, started migrating to Windows NT Workstation. Windows NT was chosen for many reasons, including Windows NT's built-in networking, its true multitasking and multiprocessor environment, NT's stability, and its ease of use.

With Windows NT 4, the momentum created by Windows 3.5 and its upgrade 3.51 continues. Even with Microsoft's release of Windows 95 in August 1995, sales of Windows NT continue to increase. In fact, many large corporations held off upgrading to Windows 95 for Windows NT Workstation 4.

One of the most powerful features of Windows NT is the Registry database. The Registry contains configuration information for your Windows NT system. It is a replacement for the various INI (initialization) files, AUTOEXEC.BAT, CONFIG.SYS, and other configuration files found in earlier versions of Windows. (Windows 95 also includes the Registry, but it is not compatible with the one in Windows NT.)

After Windows 3.1 had been out on the market for several months, users started discovering the various INI files that Windows and Windows applications used. Further, many experienced users became adept at opening INI files, searching for a line that didn't quite make sense, and editing it until a problem was solved or a feature worked better.

Along with this newfound knowledge of modifying INI settings comes some problems. One of the major problems with INI files is that they can reside anyplace on your machine, creating a problem when you need to edit them, remove them, or update them. Network administrators also have very little control over the end-user's workstation because INI files are not designed to reside on servers or in any kind of distributed environment. Updating software and network-wide applications sometimes take much longer because of errant INI settings on a user's machine.

Now, however, INI files have been shelved by Microsoft (although they are still used by vendors for compatibility reasons), requiring that users learn new techniques for optimizing and troubleshooting their systems. Furthermore, network administrators have to understand how to "get under the hood" to work out system-wide problems or how to disable certain workstation features.

What's All the Fuss about the Registry?

The Registry is Microsoft's solution to the INI file mess. The Registry is the central database for all Windows NT configuration information. You can use the Registry to perform the following functions:

- ◆ Manage device driver configuration

- ◆ Store configuration data for applications and systems management tools

- ◆ Customize startup features

- ◆ Troubleshoot various configuration problems

- ◆ View installed system components

- ◆ Enable user profiles and system policies

The Registry is designed to replace the need for INI files, although it still supports them for backward compatibility. The Registry database keeps track of OLE operations between applications, stores all the information about the hardware on a computer, and contains information that is specific about users.

Fortunately for users of Windows NT, the Registry works in the background, performing its tasks without any involvement for the end user. If a setting needs to be changed or adjusted, a Control Panel application is usually used to make the change. On a day-to-day basis, the user doesn't have to worry about the Registry. For most users, they will never know the Registry even exists, even if they encounter serious system problems. But for some users, such as system administrators, learning how to use and manage the Registry is almost a job requirement to maximize the performance of Windows NT and troubleshoot many of its problems.

Why Have a Book about the Registry?

There are two main answers to this. The simplistic answer to this question is because one is needed. Microsoft's technical support line does not answer questions that pertain to the Registry. They claim that users should not attempt to modify the Registry in any way because it can possibly corrupt their machine. They are correct about that, and you'll see warnings to that effect throughout this book. The second answer is that the Registry is difficult to understand. You might already know this if you have opened the Registry Editor (REGEDT32.EXE) and have taken a look at the Registry. If you don't know what each of the items are in the Registry, it's very difficult to get a grasp of how the Registry stores and handles configuration information.

Tip   Although Microsoft support does not answer Registry questions, Microsoft does provide many Knowledge Base articles that require you to modify the Registry. The Microsoft Knowledge Base is a library of troubleshooting, reference, and other information published by the various product groups at Microsoft. You can find the Knowledge Base on the World Wide Web at http://www.microsoft.com/kb. You also can see Appendix C, "Finding More Information," for more sources of the Knowledge Base.

The real issue with the Registry is not that it can damage your system if you try to edit it (although that is certainly true), but that many problems can be solved only by modifying or adding entries to the Registry. Sometimes there is no way around editing the Registry to make something work or to optimize its performance. This book aims to make sure you are ready for those times.

Other Ways to Modify Settings

Before you run out and start modifying the Registry just to modify it, you should understand that other tools exist in Windows NT that are easier to use and don't cause serious problems if you set something wrong. The main utility for configuring Windows 95 and hardware on your computer is the Control Panel. The Control Panel includes the Add/Remove Programs utility, the Network application, and other tools that help you configure Windows NT. You also can use the tools in the Administrative

Tools (Common) folder, such as the User Manager for Domains. You should first try to correct any problems you might have by using these utilities. Most of your problems can be solved this way.

Another utility you can use to view (but not edit) system configuration information is the Windows NT Diagnostics utility. This utility can be run by selecting Start, Run, and entering *%SystemRoot%***WINMSD.EXE** in the Run field. The Windows NT Diagnostics properties dialog box displays (see fig. I.1), showing you information about your system, including hardware devices, graphics data, resource handling, and environment settings.

Figure I.1

You should use the Windows NT Diagnostics tool when you want to view system information.

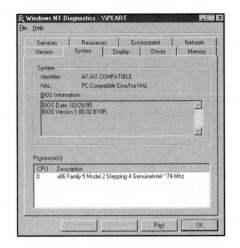

You should turn to the Registry as the last resort to solve a problem. If you make the Registry your first choice, you run the risk of damaging settings on your computer and even forcing you to reinstall Windows if you corrupt it too much. And besides, using the Control Panel options is much easier.

When to Modify the Registry

You'll come to some point, however, when you just have to modify the Registry. When this time comes, use this book to help you isolate and solve your problems. If you have a great deal of experience with INI files, you should feel somewhat comfortable with the Registry.

You'll find that many of the same skills you developed editing INI files can be used to edit the Registry. If you spent a great deal of time in INI files, you probably felt you had a "sixth sense" for sniffing out the correct setting to either tweak or delete in order to make your system run smoother. You'll need this sixth sense and more when dealing with Registry problems. The main difference is that the Registry is much more complicated, contains different types of data (including binary and text formats), and is a lot larger than INI files.

You'll learn, with the help of this book, how the Registry is set up to help you hunt down a setting or value you're looking for and to make the required changes. Some of the changes, such as changing the name of your Recycling Bin, are fairly easy to do. Others, such as starting an application at boot time, are not as self-explanatory and require a little more information to solve. Many times you need to provide binary information for a Registry setting. In these cases you need exact settings from Microsoft, the hardware vendors, or software authors. This book provides an expansive listing of these types of solutions for you to use.

Table I.1 gives you an idea of how to decide when it is best to use the Registry Editor and other tools to modify Registry information. You might want to refer to it at times to see which tool is the best for your situation.

TABLE I.1
Tools to Use to Modify the Registry

Type of Editor	Advantages	Disadvantages
Registry Editor	Designed for editing the Registry. Can edit all Registry entries. Can do remote Registry edits. Has a view only option.	Potential for serious errors. No feedback to indicate errors.
Control Panel, Administrative Tools (Common) Utilities, My Computer, Network Neighborhood	Microsoft recommended way of updating Registry.	Debugging is difficult for tough problems. Many Registry settings cannot be modified using these tools.
System Policy Editor	Better GUI and intuitive. Can provide some feedback as you edit settings. Can edit remote Registries.	Not all entries can be edited. Requires you to use system policies on your system, which can increase administration tasks at times.
WordPad, Notepad, or other text editors using exported data	Good for fast searches.	Potential for getting out of synchronization with the Registry if not careful. Not suitable for remote Registry edits.

Who Is this Book For?

For the most part, system administrators responsible for managing a Windows NT network or domain, as well as Windows NT end users, will benefit from using this book. This includes network administrators, technical support personnel, and, for a lack of a better term, power users who enjoy tweaking or customizing their operating system. For most of the settings, it doesn't matter if you are running Windows NT Server 4 or Windows NT Workstation 4 on your local machine. The information you learn in this book can be used for either operating system.

For network administrators, this book includes chapters about networking concerns, such as how to use the Registry in remote settings, how to use the System Policy Editor, and how to isolate and correct Registry problems on a network.

If you are a technical support person, having *Windows NT Registry Troubleshooting* at your side will sometimes make the difference between fixing the problem yourself or hiring an outside consultant to come in.

Power users benefit from this book because it finally gives them the much-needed documentation they've been looking for about the Registry. Many newsgroup posts and CompuServe messages pertain to the Registry. Without documentation, it has been tough to answer many of the questions that are presented.

How this Book Is Structured

You'll find this book to be structured much the same way you learn any new concept or procedure, from the general to the specific.

The first part of the book discusses what the Registry is, how it changes the role of INI files, how Windows NT components use the Registry, and how the Registry is structured. You then learn how to use the Registry Editor and System Policy Editor to make changes to the Registry. Next, networking topics are covered to help system administrators address issues with the Registry that they need to resolve. Finally, specific Registry problems are covered. A chapter on administering remote Registries is included as well, to help those who must administer Windows 95 clients on their networks.

The following describes each of the chapters in more detail.

Chapter 1, "Introducing the Windows NT Registry," is structured to give you Registry background so that you understand what the Registry is and how it behaves. You are shown how the Registry has evolved from INI files in Windows 3.x to what it is now in Windows NT and Windows 95. An examination of the relationship between the Registry and Windows NT components is provided. You'll want to start out in this chapter to get a good foundation of Registry knowledge before venturing too far.

Chapter 2, "Understanding the Windows NT Registry Structure," is designed to give you a detailed understanding of the Windows NT Registry structure, including what Registry keys, hives, value entries, and values are. You also learn the Windows NT Registry hierarchy.

Chapter 3, "Understanding the Role of Initialization Files in the Windows NT Registry," reviews the roles of INI files and how Windows NT uses them. Topics such as how INI files coexist with the Registry and which INI settings migrate to the Registry during installation are covered. You might feel compelled to skip this chapter at first. But unless you work in a "clean" environment with no INI files on your system, you should at least read the section about how Windows NT still has a few INI files floating around on its system.

Chapter 4, "Using the Windows NT Registry Editor," is a hands-on discussion about learning how to use the Registry Editor. The Registry Editor is the application you use to edit the Registry. You learn how to search for a specific key or value in the Registry, how to alter a specific key or value in the Registry, how to import and export Registry settings, and how to run a DOS version of the Registry Editor. You also are shown how to use the Windows 95 Registry Editor to edit Windows 95 Registry values.

Chapter 5, "Examining Network Settings in the Windows NT Registry," includes a discussion about the various settings that are added to the Registry when you install networking components. You learn about specific network Registry keys, how dependencies are set up, and how to find out information about the adapter and device driver you have installed. Also included in this chapter are various networking Registry value entries, as well as specific troubleshooting tips on making your Windows NT network environment perform better.

Chapter 6, "Using System Policy Editor to Modify Registry Data," is written for system administrators who want to create policies for their users. You learn about the relationship between the Registry and System Policy files. You also are shown how to use the System Policy Editor and how to troubleshoot System Policy settings.

Chapter 7, "Administering Remote Registries from Windows NT," shows you how to administer Registry information on Windows 95 clients. You learn about user profiles in Windows, how to use the Windows 95 System Policy (which is similar, but not identical or compatible with the Windows NT version), and how to create System Policy templates.

Chapter 8, "Troubleshooting Specific Problems Using the Windows NT Registry" is full of specific Windows NT problems you can solve by editing the Registry. Each problem is described and walked through so that you can quickly and easily make the same changes on your machine if you encounter a problem.

Appendix A, "Windows NT Registry Values," includes many Windows NT Registry value entries and where they are located.

Appendix B, "About the Software on the CD-ROM," shows you how to install and use the programs provided on the *Windows NT Registry Troubleshooting* CD.

Appendix C, "Finding More Information," includes references to other sources that can help you take care of your Registry problems. You'll find listings and descriptions for other books, CD-ROM sources, Internet and World Wide Web spots, and more.

Appendix D, "Troubleshooting Specific Windows 95 Problems in the Registry," includes many troubleshooting and customization tasks you can use if you have Windows 95 clients on your system. If you do not use Windows 95 or have Windows 95 clients on your network, rip out this appendix and give it to a friend to use. He or she might appreciate it.

Conventions Used in this Book

Throughout this book, certain conventions are used to help you distinguish the various elements of Windows, DOS, their system files, and sample data. Before you look ahead, you should spend a moment examining the following conventions:

◆ Information that you type is in **boldface**. This applies to individual letters and numbers, as well as to text strings. This convention does not apply to special keys, such as Enter, Esc, or Ctrl.

◆ New terms appear in *italics*.

◆ Text that is displayed on-screen, but which is not part of Windows or a Windows application—such as DOS prompts and syntax lines—appears in a `special typeface`.

Notes, Tips, and Stops

Windows NT Registry Troubleshooting features special sidebars, which are set apart from the normal text by icons. Three different types of sidebars are used—Notes, Tips, and Stops.

Note Notes include extra information that you should find useful, but which complements that discussion at hand instead of being a direct part of it.

Notes might describe special situations that result from unusual circumstances. These sidebars tell you what to expect or what steps to take when such situations occur. Notes also might tell you how to avoid problems with your software and hardware.

Tip Tips provide you with quick instructions for getting the most from your Windows system. A Tip might show you how to conserve memory in some setups, how to speed up a procedure, or how to perform one of many time-saving and system-enhancing techniques.

Stop Stops are warnings telling you when a procedure might be dangerous; that is, when you run the risk of losing data, locking your system, or even damaging your hardware. Stops generally tell you how to avoid such losses or describe the steps you can take to remedy them.

These sidebars enhance the possibility that *Windows NT Registry Troubleshooting* will be able to answer your most pressing questions about Windows use and performance. Although Notes, Tips, and Stops do not condense an entire section into a few steps, these snippets will point you in new directions for solutions to your needs and problems.

New Riders Publishing

The staff of New Riders Publishing is committed to bringing you the very best in computer reference material. Each New Riders book is the result of months of work by authors and staff who research and refine the information contained within its covers.

As part of this commitment to you, the NRP reader, New Riders invites your input. Please let us know if you enjoy this book, if you have trouble with the information and examples presented, or if you have a suggestion for the next edition.

Please note, though—New Riders staff cannot serve as a technical resource for Windows NT or for questions about software- or hardware-related problems. Please refer to the documentation that accompanies Windows NT or to the applications' Help systems.

Also, the Windows NT Registry is a critical part of your Windows NT setup. When you decide to modify it based on information in this book or from other resources be sure to back up the Registry files (see Chapter 1, "Introducing the Windows NT Registry," for details) in case you encounter problems.

If you have a question or comment about any New Riders book, there are several ways to contact New Riders Publishing. We will respond to as many readers as we can. Your name, address, or phone number will never become part of a mailing list or be used for any purpose other than to help us continue to bring you the best books possible. You can write us at the following address:

New Riders Publishing
Attn: Publishing Manager—Networking
201 W. 103rd Street
Indianapolis, IN 46290

Or, visit us on the World Wide Web at http://www.mcp.com/newriders

If you prefer, you can fax New Riders Publishing at (317) 817-7448.

You can also send electronic mail to New Riders at the following Internet address:

smelling@newriders.mcp.com

 Tip   I would like to hear from you about this book. Please feel free to send me electronic mail at rtidrow@iquest.net with your comments, suggestions, and any tips you have. If you have a Registry troubleshooting item that can be used for future versions of this book, send them as well. I'll be happy to give you credit for it! Thanks.
—Rob Tidrow

New Riders is an imprint of Macmillan Computer Publishing. To obtain a catalog or information, or to purchase any Macmillan Computer Publishing book, call (800) 428-5331.

Thank you for selecting *Windows NT Registry Troubleshooting*!

Introducing the Windows NT Registry

The Windows NT Registry is a centralized database of system, device, and application settings. The Registry is similar to the various INI files and AUTOEXEC.BAT and CONFIG.SYS files you were used to in the past. The Registry contains information on all the hardware, software, operating system, and network settings for your computer.

To help you get your feet wet, this chapter introduces the Registry with a thorough overview. It explores how the Registry relates to the INI files and offers a brief introduction to the actual structure of the Registry. In particular, this chapter covers the following:

◆ The history of the Registry

◆ What the Registry replaces

◆ How Windows NT components work with the Registry

◆ What other applications can be used to modify Registry settings

◆ How to back up the Registry

This chapter starts out with a brief explanation of the Registry's role in your Windows NT operating system.

Understanding the Role of the Windows NT Registry

Although the Registry is nothing short of painfully difficult to decipher and manipulate, it is a crucial part of Windows NT and one that any power user and network administrator needs to understand and manage.

In short, the Registry is the central database of all Windows NT configuration data. The Registry stores information about the hardware, Windows NT system configuration, all your applications (including 16-bit and MS-DOS based applications), and user preferences set up on your computer. It stores information about all Object Linking and Embedding (OLE) system information, file associations, all information about applications that support drag and drop and OLE, network configuration information, and user profiles. In short, if it's on your computer, or if it affects your computer in any way, the Registry more than likely knows about it.

Reviewing the History of the Registry

The Registry is not a new concept with Windows NT 4. The Registry was introduced in Windows NT 3.1 in 1993 and was a huge step towards making all system configurations controlled by one source, the Registration database (see fig. 1.1). (The Registry is probably a shortened term for Registration database, although this is not published by Microsoft anyplace.) It is designed to be the foundation of all system, network, and user management for Windows NT. For desktop users, Windows 95 (released in August of 1995) included the Registry to enable centralized management, plus the added benefit of supporting Plug and Play hardware devices.

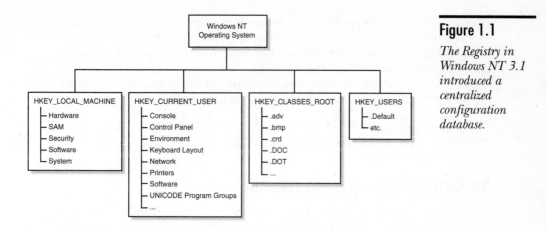

Figure 1.1

The Registry in Windows NT 3.1 introduced a centralized configuration database.

Not only is there a need to store configuration information in one place, there also is a need to keep individual user settings stored in a common place. The Registry allows users to use their own settings (called *user profiles*) regardless of the computer on which they log in. Administrators can copy user profiles to other workstations on which a user might work or allow users to roam from workstation to workstation, downloading individual user profiles from the server. In departments, studios, and other workgroup areas in which users share computing resources, this feature is invaluable. If one user prefers to have a spreadsheet application launch each time Windows NT boots, she can have that application launch on any computer regardless of where she logs into the network. On the other hand, a training classroom might need different configurations based on the course being taught. Administrators can create a different user profile for each class (such as Word, Excel, Visual Basic, and so on) and then download that user profile during system bootup.

The Registry enables administrators to set *system policies* to control a computer's configuration and what a user can access on the computer or network. A concern of network administrators has always been the diverse ways end users can configure their individual workstations. The ways in which Windows enables users to customize the desktop to suit their needs becomes a problem when a LAN has several hundred or thousand end users using different themes, screen savers, wallpaper images, and other customizable features. As administrators upgrade an installation or provide troubleshooting services, these configurations require the administrator to become familiar with all desktops on the network. This might not be a problem with networks of only a dozen or so workstations, but when sites grow to over 20 or 30 seats, becoming familiar with each computer and user configuration is unrealistic.

Companies must think about how much time is required by the administrator to learn about an individual's PC before actually fixing the problem. By using system policies to control users' environments, NT administrators finally have a way to centrally manage workstations and know what to expect when approaching a workstation. The administrator might not know the exact cause of a problem, but he can start diagnosing the problem by eliminating problems due to user customization.

The next sections go into more detail about how the Registration database has matured from INI files to the Registry now used in Windows NT 4.

So What's Wrong with INI Files?

The main source of initialization and configuration duties in Windows 3.x (do not mistake this with Windows NT 3.1 or later) fell on INI files. INI files, or initialization files, are ASCII files that contain system, application, and device settings. One of the biggest hassles and complaints about INI files was managing them. The primary Windows INI files (including WIN.INI, SYSTEM.INI, PROGMAN.INI, CONTROL.INI, and WINFILE.INI) were easy enough to manage, but as you installed applications on your system, then deleted them, your system filled with more and more INI files. They either got in your way because they were outdated, or they became spread over your system in so many directories that you had to guess where one was before you could edit it. Imagine having this type of organization for every PC on a LAN with thousands of users!

Note   INI files could be placed anywhere on your system and applications could write information to your standard INI files. This made it difficult to find every INI file or setting relating to an application when you wanted to remove the application (uninstall it) from your system. One of the requirements for gaining the distinction of being a Windows NT-compliant application is to offer uninstall capabilities. Uninstalling applications is not a new thing to working with PCs, but providing an easy way to uninstall them is. Having configuration data stored centrally in the Registry makes uninstalling applications a breeze in Windows NT. For the most part, you no longer need to go searching through your files looking for information that pertains to that application.

The Windows NT Registry takes control of the problem of diverse and numerous INI files and provides a simple solution—put all these settings in a centralized storage area. The Registry uses a handful of files to store Registry information, including SECURITY.LOG, SAM.LOG, DEFAULT.LOG, and SYSTEM.ALT to name a few. To make editing of these files easy, the Registry Editor displays all of these files in one interface. Instead of looking all over your hard drive for the right INI file to edit, you can simply open up Registry Editor to view and edit the Registry.

Note See Chapter 4, "Using the Windows NT Registry Editor," for in-depth coverage of this Registry feature.

The following are some of the concerns Microsoft addressed when deciding to replace INI files with a centralized configuration database:

◆ **What should be part of a system INI file.** One problem with INI files is the lack of control over where initialization information is stored, either in proprietary INI files or system INI files. As stipulated in the Microsoft Windows Programmers Reference, application developers were encouraged to use system INI files (such as WIN.INI and SYSTEM.INI) only for those settings that affect the system or affect more than one application. In reality, applications were written that dumped application-specific settings in system-wide INI files. Over time, many users' WIN.INI and SYSTEM.INI files grew larger with extraneous information that should have been saved to application-specific INI files. With Windows NT, developers must adhere to Win32s development for placing entries in the Registry.

◆ **Where initialization files should be stored.** Another problem users encountered was where application developers installed INI files on their hard drives. Some applications placed INI files in the user's *%SystemRoot%* folder, while others placed them in the root directory of the main partition, in the application's folder, or in other diverse places. With Windows NT and applications that use the Win32 programming environment, you know the system settings are going to be placed in the Registry.

◆ **How to decrease the likelihood of conflicting information.** Some older applications (and even some wily newer ones for that matter) have the tendency to overwrite crucial data in system INI files. One example of this is placing instructions in the WIN.INI to load specific applications during system bootup. In some cases, the SHELL= line was changed to a new setting instead of instructing Program Manager to launch as the user's shell. In other cases, some programs placed settings in the LOAD= line in order to run at startup time. Another example is forcing an application association from the currently configured one to a new one. In the Registry, the likelihood of conflicting information or data being deleted is decreased by built-in checks done by the system. In Windows NT 4, when an association is changed, for example, many times you are prompted to make sure you approve of this new configuration.

◆ **How to remove initialization settings.** As users remove applications and devices from their systems, initialization settings and files remain on their systems. To get rid of these settings, users must go through the slow process of manually locating and deleting each one. For applications to pass Microsoft's rigid Win32 application specifications now, however, the application must use the Registry to store configuration data and provide an uninstall routine to clean up the Registry when users uninstall an application.

Although Microsoft has done away with INI files, it still needs to support them for legacy hardware and older applications. For this reason, when you install Windows NT on systems that have a previous version of Windows 3.x, the Registry uses data from the INI files to help build your Windows NT environment. Settings such as desktop preferences, sound events, graphics resolutions, and supported setup routines you used in your previous installation are carried over to your Windows NT installation. You learn in Chapter 3, "Understanding the Role of Initialization Files in the Windows NT Registry," more about how the Windows NT Registry uses information from INI files.

Examining the Registry in Windows 3.x

For more experienced Windows 3.x users and administrators, the Registry shouldn't be a startling new discovery. If you are a user who enjoys troubleshooting problems or is responsible for managing several PCs at your site, you probably used the Registration database in Windows 3.x. This database is the source OLE applications use to retrieve information about OLE server applications (see fig. 1.2).

Figure 1.2

The Registration database in Windows 3.x includes OLE settings for OLE-compliant applications, such as Microsoft Word and Excel.

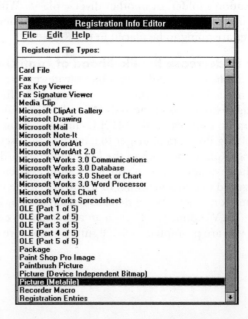

In Windows 3.x, you could view the Registry database using two different applications. The primary way used the Reg Edit by activating the REGEDIT.EXE program. This is shown in figure 1.2. Reg Edit pulled information from the REG.DAT file, which was the Registration database file stored in your Windows directory.

Reg Edit displayed all the registration file types on your system. For the most part, you didn't have to interact with this database unless one of the applications you were using didn't register itself for some reason.

The other way to view the Registration database in Windows 3.x was to run REGEDIT.EXE /V. The /V switch activated a more advanced version of Reg Edit, which is shown in figure 1.3. As you can see from this view, Microsoft already was experimenting with a hierarchical structure for displaying registration information, which is the way Windows 95 and Windows NT Registry use information. Notice the trees, branches, and key names shown in this illustration. The information was displayed in trees, with each branch displaying a key name. The key name was then associated with text strings to help provide more information about the key.

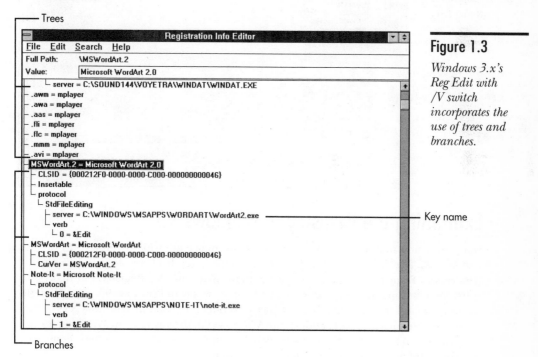

Figure 1.3

Windows 3.x's Reg Edit with /V switch incorporates the use of trees and branches.

The Registration database in Windows 3.x enabled users to modify how different objects behaved when embedded or linked in DDE- and OLE-compliant applications. It also was a way for users to quickly view the list of applications currently registered under Windows. This was important when troubleshooting linking and embedding problems, such as when a known OLE-compliant application did not show up in a list of object types in an application (see fig. 1.4). The normal procedure for adding items to the Registration database during installation of the application sometimes did not work, resulting in the object not being available.

Figure 1.4

Microsoft Word is a Windows application that displays the objects available to it in the Object dialog box.

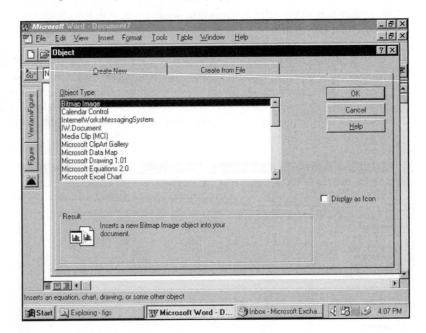

Examining the Registry in Windows 95

Many users now migrating to Windows NT 4 cut their teeth with Windows 3.11 or Windows 95. For this reason, it's important to take a step back and look at how the Windows 95 Registry looks and compare it to the Windows NT Registry. For many end users, the first time they encountered the Registry was with Windows 95. Even though Windows NT 3.1 included the basic Registry architecture used in Windows NT (including versions 3.5, 3.51, and 4) and Windows 95, the majority of Windows users had Windows 3.x (such as Windows for Workgroups 3.11) installed on their computers, which did not use the centralized Registry database.

At first glance, the Windows 95 and Windows NT Registries appear to be the same. For instance, compare figure 1.5, which shows the Windows 95 Registry format, with the Windows NT Registry shown earlier in figure 1.1. You can see their basic framework is similar, including keys, handles, and values (you learn all about the Registry structure in Chapter 2, "Understanding the Windows NT Registry Structure"). As you begin digging deeper into the Windows 95 Registry, however, you notice that it differs in many ways from the Windows NT Registry. One of the primary differences is that the Windows 95 Registry relies on two files, USER.DAT and SYSTEM.DAT, to hold all the Registry data. In Windows NT, the same information is stored in *hives*—Registry values that contain top-level Registry keys and subkeys beneath them, and usually contain pertinent information for part of the Windows NT system—and can include many separate files (some systems have over 14 of these files). The USER.DAT file in Windows 95 contains configuration information specific to a user, such as preferred desktop settings, startup options, screen saver choices, and the like. SYSTEM.DAT contains configuration information specific to a computer, such as application settings, hardware configurations, Plug and Play device settings, and similar settings.

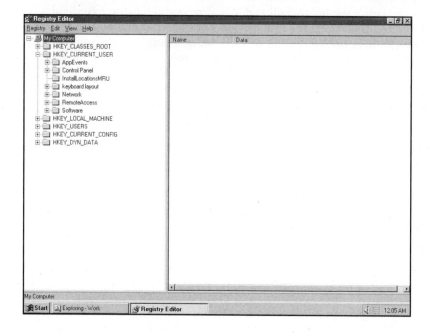

Figure 1.5

The Windows 95 Registry contains all the configuration information for your Windows 95 system.

A fundamental role of the Registry in Windows 95 is to hold hardware-specific information for the hardware-detection phase during system setup and startup. It is also the central database for Plug and Play system components. When you install a piece of hardware, the Windows 95 Registry probably already has information about it. This information is used to help you automatically configure the hardware device.

Windows 95 uses a hardware enumeration process that checks the hardware device and identifies it during the bootup process. During the bootup, the device's name and type (such as CD-ROM or network adapter) are identified. As you boot up your PC after you install a new device, the system checks the Registry to find out what resources have been used and what resources are available on your machine. These resources include I/O addresses, DMA channels, and IRQs, and are checked to make sure you don't encounter a hardware conflict with the new device.

The Registry is designed to eliminate many of the burdens placed on system integrators and users during hardware installations. The method used in Windows 3.x was to place system and application information inside INI files. SYSTEM.INI, for instance, held all your system information, including device drivers and hardware configuration information. Individual hardware components further complicated hardware installation by including dip switches and jumpers to set, as well as requiring you to configure various batch files to invoke hardware device drivers. The result for many users was that a hardware conflict kept the device from working or caused another device to quit working. In extreme, but not uncommon, cases entire systems quit working or data loss occurred during these hardware upgrades.

The configuration manager is the "traffic cop" of device configurations (see fig. 1.6). New in Windows 95, the configuration manager is instrumental in configuring Plug and Play devices. Its purpose is to make sure that all your devices are located, that the devices are set up on the hardware tree, and that each device is allocated sufficient resources. The configuration manager, for instance, makes sure that when you have two or more types of devices sharing a single bus, sufficient resources are available for each. You might, for instance, have a CD-ROM and hard disk use the same SCSI bus.

When you boot up your computer, the configuration manager sends and receives device configuration data with the Registry. When the configuration manager locates a device on bootup, it "asks" the Registry if that device is configured for this computer and, if so, what are the configuration settings for it. If the device is not registered in the Registry, the configuration manager tries to configure the device (this works very well for Plug and Play devices) or warns the user that a hardware devices was found and that the user needs to configure it, which in turns adds configuration data to the Registry for that device.

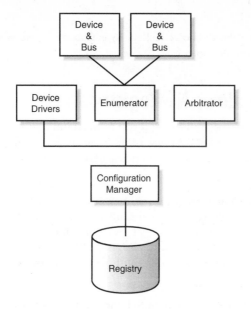

Figure 1.6

The component model of the configuration manager shows its relationship to the Registry.

Note What is the hardware tree? The *hardware tree* is the hierarchical representation of all the buses and devices on your PC. In Windows 95, the record in RAM of the current system configuration is stored in the hardware tree. This information is based on the configuration information for all the devices on your PC in the hardware branch of the Registry. In the Registry, you'll find this information in the HKEY_LOCAL_MACHINE\Hardware key. Windows 95 builds a hardware tree every time you start Windows 95 or when you make a change to your system configuration.

Not only does the configuration manager set up and configure hardware devices upon bootup, it also monitors the PC for any changes made during a session. If a device is added or removed, or if a new type of device is added during a session, the configuration manager reconfigures the devices. The configuration manager communicates these changes to applications that are running and places the information in the Registry. This is one of the real strengths of Windows 95's subsystem, and you really notice it as a mobile user who uses a docking station. With Windows 95, you can connect a laptop to a docking station without the need to shut down and reboot the system. The configuration manager can update the Registry dynamically as you connect the laptop to the docking station (this is known as *hot docking*).

Note You learn more about the Windows 95 Registry in Chapter 7, "Administering Remote Registries from Windows NT."

Examining the Windows NT Registry

Because most of this book is devoted to helping you understand and master the Windows NT Registry, you get a short overview of the Registry here. Chapter 2, "Understanding the Windows NT Registry Structure," explains it in greater detail, including a breakdown of each of the Registry root keys.

Windows NT was the first operating system from Microsoft to include the centralized Registry as now used in Windows NT 4 and used similarly in Windows 95. When Windows NT 3.1 (the first release of Windows NT) was introduced, the Registry was a key part of its underlying architecture. With the Registry, Windows NT could become a powerful and flexible environment to handle multiple users, networking responsibilities, and powerful administrative tools.

In the future, Windows NT is planned to include Plug and Play hardware support and be an object-oriented operating system; both are technologies that will rely on the Registry to handle a great deal of the configuration and communication responsibilities. The Registry also enables administrators to set up user profiles and system policies to make administering and controlling users on local and wide area networks (LANs and WANs) much easier.

The makeup of the Windows NT Registry differs from that of Windows 95 in that Registry information is stored in hives. Hives are Registry values that contain top-level Registry keys and subkeys beneath them and usually contain pertinent information for part of the Windows NT system. Figure 1.7 shows an example of a Registry hive in Windows NT. This hive is named HKEY_CURRENT_USER. Each hive stores its information in files that do not have extensions, such as SECURITY or SYSTEM. Each hive (except for the system hive) also has a LOG file that keeps track of changes to the hive. Instead of using a LOG file for the system hive, Windows NT stores any transaction to the system hive (HKEY_LOCAL_MACHINE\SYSTEM) in the SYSTEM.ALT file. See table 2.1 in Chapter 2, "Understanding the Windows NT Registry Structure," for details about which files store Registry hive data.

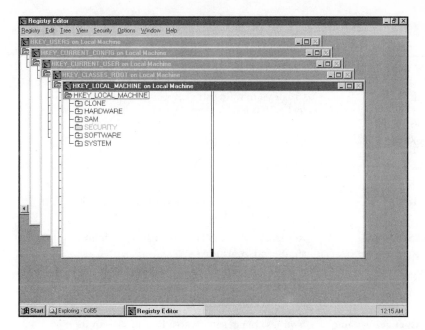

Figure 1.7

Windows NT Registry hives contain information about your Windows NT system.

One of the problems right now with the Windows NT and Windows 95 Registries is that they are not compatible with each other. You might encounter this for the first time when you install Windows NT over Windows 95. If you do this, you are required to reinstall all your applications because the two Registries are not compatible with one another. Although the two operating systems use the same Win32 API, the way the two operating systems use the API differ. Table 1.1 lists the Win32 API functions that are used to access the Registry and shows which ones are not used by Windows 95.

Note In table 1.1, API names ending with Ex, such as RegCreateKeyEx, are not used by Windows 3.1 applications. An equivalent API function is used for Windows 3.1 compatibility.

TABLE 1.1
Registry API Functions

API Name	Description
RegCreateKey	Creates a new Registry key and is used for compatibility for Windows 3.1 applications.
RegCreateKeyEx	Creates a new Registry key.
RegCloseKey	Closes a Registry key.
RegDeleteKey	In Windows NT, deletes a key that has no subkeys. In Windows 95, deletes a key and all its subkeys.
RegGetKeySecurity	Retrieves a Registry key's security description. Not supported by Windows 95.
RegLoadKey	Creates a Registry subkey under the HKEY_USER or HKEY_LOCAL_MACHINE and stores a specific file's information in that subkey.
RegNotifyChangeKeyValue	Notifies changes made to a Registry key or its content. Not supported by Windows 95.
RegOpenKey	Opens a specified key and is used for compatibility for Windows 3.1 applications.
RegOpenKeyEx	Opens a specified key.
RegQueryInfoKey	Retrieves information about a Registry key.
RegQueryMultipleValues	Retrieves type and data for multiple Registry value names.
RegQueryValue	Retrieves Registry value of a specific key and is used for compatibility for Windows 3.1 applications.
RegQueryValueEx	Retrieves Registry value of a specific key.
RegReplaceKey	Replaces the file of a key and all its subkeys with one you specify.
RegRestoreKey	Copies Registry information from one file over a specified Registry key. Not supported by Windows 95.
RegSaveKey	Saves a Registry key, subkeys, and values.
RegSetKeySecurity	Configures the security of a Registry key. Not supported by Windows 95.
RegSetValue	Specifies a value for a Registry key and is used for compatibility for Windows 3.1 applications.
RegSetValueEx	Specifies a value for a Registry key.
RegUnloadKey	Removes a specified Registry key from the Registry.

The Windows NT Registry relies on several Windows NT components to gather data from and to communicate with. These components include the Recognizer (NTDETECT.COM), the Windows NT kernel (NTOSKRNL.EXE), administration tools, device drivers, and the setup program. Some of these components work with Registry to send data to it, while others send and receive data to and from the Registry. To understand how the Registry works with the various Windows NT components, see the section "How Components Use the Registry," later in this chapter.

Examining the Relationship between NT Components and the NT Registry

One way to get a grasp on the Windows NT Registry is to understand the Windows NT operating system architecture and how the Registry fits into that architecture. The Windows NT architecture is called a *modular* operating system because it has layers of components. These layers comprise the Hardware Abstraction Layer (HAL), the Kernel, the Executive, and the environment subsystems. Each of these layers communicates with the Registry at some point during a Windows NT session.

The following sections provide an overview of the Windows NT module architecture and a description of how the components therein interact with the Registry.

 Tip   The following discussion about the Windows NT architecture is a brief overview of the features of the Windows NT subsystem. To get an in-depth look at this architecture, see the *Windows NT Server 4 Professional Reference* (ISBN: 1-56205-659-X), written by Karanjit Siyan and published by New Riders.

Windows NT Modular Architecture Overview

Older operating systems (such as MS-DOS) used to be designed as one large software program. This was called a *monolithic* operating system, in which the operating system was one part and did not include separate parts for different functions (such as I/O, hardware detection, and application support). As users became more sophisticated and their computing needs increased, so did their operating systems. One way to make operating systems more powerful was to make them modular in nature. A *modular* setup (a setup made up of separate and distinct parts) enabled software designers to modify parts (modules) of the operating system instead of changing the entire operating system for performance or feature enhancements. Each module in the operating system can also be specialized to perform specific tasks to its maximum, much like special team members on a football team are designed to perform certain duties during a kick off or punt return. Figure 1.8 shows you the Windows NT modular architecture.

Figure 1.8

Windows NT is built on a modular operating system architecture.

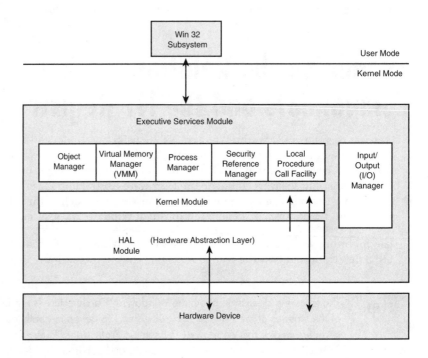

The Windows NT architecture includes two modes—the user mode and the kernel mode. The *user mode* includes the Windows NT subsystems (such as the POSIX, security, and OS/2 subsystems), logon processes, and the application level. The *kernel mode* controls the scheduling of the computer processor activities. These modes include the Hardware Abstraction Layer (HAL), the Kernel, the Executive Services, and the Environment Subsystems modules. These are explained in the following list:

◆ **Hardware Abstraction Layer (HAL).** The HAL consists of a layer of code between the CPU and the kernel that translates stack operations, input/output handling, and interrupt controller functions from the CPU so that the kernel can understand them. In most cases, the kernel communicates with the HAL for hardware information. In some special cases, however, the kernel bypasses the HAL to communicate directly with the hardware. The HAL dynamic link library (Hal.dll) is relatively small. The Windows NT 4 HAL for Intel processors is only 52 KB in size. In large part, the HAL makes it possible for Windows NT to be portable from one processor to another, because it (the HAL) makes the hardware interaction transparent from the rest of the operating system.

◆ **Kernel.** In many discussions, the kernel is the heart of the operating system. In Windows NT, the Kernel layer manages the most interaction with other layers, managing events such as thread dispatching, hardware exception handling, and processor synchronization when Windows NT runs on a system with multiple processors. The Kernel layer ensures that Windows NT threads are running most efficiently and that the processors are kept busy. The Kernel manages two types of objects, the dispatcher objects and control objects. *Dispatcher objects* include objects such as events, mutants (controlling mutual exclusive access to a resource), mutexts (same as mutants but not available in the user mode), and threads. *Control objects* include objects such as interrupts, processes, and profiles (recording the amount of time threads spend in a block of code).

◆ **Executive Services.** Provides a set of common services that all environment subsystems can use. The HAL and Kernel are part of the Executive Services module, but they are distinct modules within it. The Executive Services include a number of components, including the object manager, security reference monitor, process manager, virtual memory manager (VMM), local procedure call (LPC), and the I/O manager. Each of these components have individual responsibilities as described in table 1.2.

◆ **Environment Subsystem.** Enables many different types of applications to run on the Windows NT graphical user interface. Users can run applications written for OS/2, Windows 3.x, MS-DOS, and Windows 95, as well as applications written for the POSIX API.

TABLE 1.2
Executive Services Components

Name	Description
Object Manager	Creates objects to represent system resources, such as files, hardware devices, and shared memory. Object Manager performs the following functions on an object: create the object, protect the object, monitor who uses the object, and monitor the resource that uses the object. Object Manager manages objects during their lifetime and deletes the object when it's no longer needed.
Security Reference Monitor (SRM)	Implements basic security features, such as tracking user account privileges, managing Access Control Lists (ACLs), auditing, protecting objects, and limiting access to system resources. When a user logs onto Windows NT, a Security Access Token (SAT) is created for that user, which contains the SID (Security Identification) for the user and groups to which the user belongs. As the user accesses objects, the SRM checks to make that the user has a SAT that matches an access control entry on the ACL for that object.
Process Manager	Responsible for process objects and thread objects. Processes comprise virtual address spaces, sets of threads in a process, and resources owned by the process. Threads are scheduled events that have their own registers, kernel stacks, and environment blocks.
Virtual Memory Manager (VMM)	Implements virtual memory capabilities of the operating system, such as allocating virtual memory to the processes when there is not enough physical memory (RAM) in the computer to handle the process. The VMM maps virtual address space to pages (4 KB of memory) in the computer's memory. As more memory is needed, the least recently used pages (called the LRU) are swapped to the hard disk by the VMM to create a virtual memory space.

Name	Description
Local Procedure Call (LPC)	Enables communication between applications and protected subsystems. LPC is a localized version of the Remote Procedure Call (RPC) feature of Windows NT.
I/O Manager	Handles all input/output functions of Windows NT, including file system, network driver, device driver, and cache manager functions. Each of these drivers is a separate component, which gives application and hardware developers an easier way to replace drivers without adversely affecting other I/O devices.

Tip   See the *Windows NT 4.0 Resource Kit* (published by Microsoft Press) for specific information on the types of applications Windows NT supports.

How Components Use the Registry

The Windows NT Registry comprises several thousand settings, many of which change or update each time you boot the system, run a service, launch an application, and use a device. Because the Registry is the main database to store configuration settings, each Windows NT operating system layer sends information to the Registry. In some cases, the Registry sends data back to a service or application.

The following list summarizes the Windows NT components that modify the Registry:

◆ **Device drivers.** Device drivers use the Registry to store and retrieve configuration and to load parameters. The Registry provides a centralized storage area for system resource information about IRQ settings (hardware interrupts), DMA channels (direct memory access), and configuration settings for device drivers. This is the same information you might normally see in the DEVICE= lines in the CONFIG.SYS file under Windows 3.x or MS-DOS. A device *driver* is a piece of software that allows a hardware device to communicate with the operating system, in this case Windows NT (see fig. 1.9). When Windows NT 3.1 was introduced, Microsoft required that all device drivers be rewritten to work under Windows NT. Because device driver programming is one of the most difficult programming tasks, many hardware manufacturers decided not to upgrade their device drivers to work with Windows NT. This resulted in many legacy hardware devices not being compatible with Windows NT.

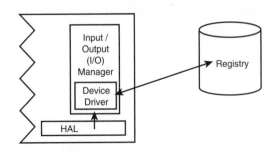

Figure 1.9

Device drivers interact between the device and the operating system.

Tip   Windows 95 introduced the concept of universal device drivers to make it easier for many of the legacy devices already installed to work with Windows 95. Universal device drivers are included for certain devices and contain most of the code necessary for a device to work with Windows 95. Universal device drivers, for example, are available for printers and modems to work with the printing and communications subsystems in Windows 95. One of the reasons Microsoft developed universal device drivers was to eliminate many of the complexities in developing device drivers for hardware devices. Manufacturers of hardware can use the universal driver and mini-driver architecture built into Windows 95 to create their drivers. Mini-drivers are small device drivers that contain any additional programming code or instructions for a specific device. Future versions of Windows NT may include universal device drivers, but probably only for devices now compatible with Windows NT 4 and above versions.

◆ **Hardware.** When you install hardware devices under Windows NT, configuration and setup information is stored in the Registry. Windows NT uses the Hardware Recognizer to send hardware configuration data to the Registry at NT startup time. Unlike other configuration information, the hardware devices list is re-created in the Registry every time NT is rebooted and is hence a volatile list.

◆ **Applications.** Applications store information and settings in the Windows NT Registry much the same way INI files stored application settings in Windows 3.x. A difference between INI files and the Registry is that application developers can take advantage of the Win32 API programming environment not available in Windows 3.x. Also, the Registry can store binary data, which INI files cannot. (See Chapter 3, "Understanding the Role of Initialization Files in the Windows NT Registry," for more information on the role of INI files in Windows NT.)

◆ **Network protocols.** The Registry keeps track of a number of network protocol values, many of which are listed in Chapter 5, "Examining Network Settings in the Windows NT Registry."

◆ **Configuration files.** In theory, the Registry replaces the need for all INI, AUTOEXEC.BAT, and CONFIG.SYS. When you upgrade from a system that previously ran a version of MS-DOS or Windows 3.x, many of the settings from the following configuration files are placed in the Windows NT Registry:

  ◆ AUTOEXEC.BAT

  ◆ CONFIG.SYS

  ◆ WIN.INI

  ◆ SYSTEM.INI

  ◆ CONTROL.INI

  ◆ PROTOCOL.INI

  ◆ All application INI files

The Registry can be thought of as the central nervous system for your Windows NT system. All components directly or indirectly communicate with the Registry. In turn, the Registry communicates with some of the components. This two-way interaction is one of the strongest features of the Registry. It enables the Registry to feed data back to the Windows NT kernel about CPU detection and load control issues. The Registry communicates with device drivers about configuration settings, resource usage data, and load parameters. Finally, the Registry sends data to the various administrative tools you use to watch Windows NT and the network (see fig. 1.10). Figure 1.11 shows how information is sent to the Registry and how the Registry disseminates it to various services.

Figure 1.10

The Registry sends data to the Windows NT administrative tools, such as the Event Viewer.

```
Event Viewer - System Log on \\PEART                                    _ 8 X
Log  View  Options  Help
Date       Time          Source        Category   Event   User   Computer
● 9/25/96   12:10:24 AM   BROWSER       None       8015    N/A    PEART
● 9/25/96   12:10:20 AM   BROWSER       None       8015    N/A    PEART
● 9/25/96   12:07:52 AM   EventLog      None       6005    N/A    PEART
● 9/25/96   12:09:08 AM   Dhcp          None       1003    N/A    PEART
● 9/24/96   3:41:51 PM    BROWSER       None       8033    N/A    PEART
● 9/24/96   3:41:51 PM    BROWSER       None       8033    N/A    PEART
● 9/24/96   3:01:45 PM    BROWSER       None       8015    N/A    PEART
● 9/24/96   3:01:41 PM    BROWSER       None       8015    N/A    PEART
● 9/24/96   2:59:14 PM    EventLog      None       6005    N/A    PEART
● 9/24/96   3:00:30 PM    Dhcp          None       1003    N/A    PEART
● 9/24/96   2:57:31 PM    BROWSER       None       8033    N/A    PEART
● 9/24/96   2:57:31 PM    BROWSER       None       8033    N/A    PEART
● 9/24/96   12:50:34 PM   BROWSER       None       8015    N/A    PEART
● 9/24/96   12:50:30 PM   BROWSER       None       8015    N/A    PEART
● 9/24/96   12:48:04 PM   EventLog      None       6005    N/A    PEART
● 9/24/96   12:49:19 PM   Dhcp          None       1003    N/A    PEART
● 9/22/96   8:04:05 PM    BROWSER       None       8033    N/A    PEART
● 9/22/96   8:04:03 PM    BROWSER       None       8033    N/A    PEART
● 9/22/96   8:00:42 PM    RemoteAccess  None       20065   N/A    PEART
● 9/22/96   7:53:19 PM    BROWSER       None       8015    N/A    PEART
● 9/22/96   7:53:15 PM    BROWSER       None       8015    N/A    PEART
● 9/22/96   7:50:47 PM    EventLog      None       6005    N/A    PEART
● 9/22/96   7:52:04 PM    Dhcp          None       1003    N/A    PEART
● 9/22/96   7:49:03 PM    BROWSER       None       8033    N/A    PEART
● 9/22/96   7:49:03 PM    BROWSER       None       8033    N/A    PEART
● 9/22/96   7:43:21 PM    RemoteAccess  None       20065   N/A    PEART
● 9/22/96   7:40:26 PM    BROWSER       None       8015    N/A    PEART
● 9/22/96   7:40:22 PM    BROWSER       None       8015    N/A    PEART
● 9/22/96   7:37:54 PM    EventLog      None       6005    N/A    PEART
● 9/22/96   7:39:11 PM    Dhcp          None       1003    N/A    PEART
● 9/22/96   7:36:10 PM    BROWSER       None       8033    N/A    PEART
● 9/22/96   7:36:10 PM    BROWSER       None       8033    N/A    PEART

Start   Exploring - Col95      Registry Editor      Event Viewer - Syste...              12:16 AM
```

Figure 1.11

Windows NT components use the Registry to store configuration data.

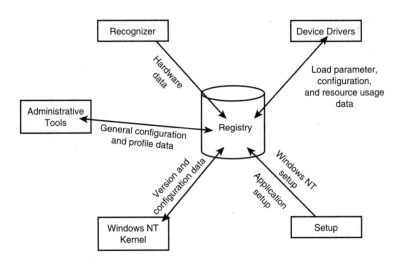

The first time the Registry receives data is when you run the Windows NT Setup program. Upon Setup, the Registry is created and begins mapping values found in initialization files on your system from previous operating systems.

Mapping is a two-part process. In one part, mapping retrieves data from an INI file and places it in the Registry. In another part, mapping places new data in the INI file. This procedure is done for system INI files and application-specific INI files. As you learn in Chapter 3, "Understanding the Role of Initialization Files in the Windows NT Registry," however, not all settings from system files are mapped to the Windows NT Registry. In these situations, Windows NT is instructed to continue using the INI settings instead of using a Registry setting. This is a good thing to keep in mind when you encounter a problem you can't seem to fix, regardless of how much time you spend altering Registry settings or using Control Panel options. The answer might reside in a long forgotten INI file on your system.

After the Registry is created, each time you run an application installation program, modify configuration settings, or change network settings, settings are placed in the Registry. When you add an application that uses a sound event, such as chimes to indicate a new e-mail message has arrived, that setting is included in the Registry. Again, if the application does not use the Registry (such as a Windows 3.1 application), Windows NT will point to the INI file for that application to enable it to run. Also, as you add hardware devices to your system, Windows NT stores configuration data in the Registry.

Tip   Not all legacy applications and hardware devices work with Windows NT 4. For more information, consult the Microsoft Windows 4.0 Hardware and Software Compatibility Lists available on the World Wide Web at http://www.microsoft.com/backoffice.

Understanding When to Modify the Registry

For many of your configuration duties, you won't need to manually modify the Windows NT Registry. You should usually use system configuration tools in Control Panel or the Administrative Tools (Common) applications to make changes to your environment. When you use these tools, you are indirectly modifying the Registry. Also, if you need to change settings in a supported device's or application's INI file, that INI setting may or may not be placed in the Registry the next time you boot the machine.

As a rule, you will want to use these tools in the Control Panel or Administrative Tools (Common) folder to alter your system (that is, alter the Registry) before attempting to alter the Registry directly with the Registry Editor. It is much easier to injure your system by affecting the Registry directly than it is by using these other system tools to make changes. Some of these "safer" tools you can use to configure Windows NT (modify Registry) include the following:

- ◆ **Add/Remove Programs.** Located in the Control Panel, you use this application to walk you through setting up Windows NT components as well as installing new software. If you want to remove an item from your Windows NT installation, use the Add/Remove Programs application as well. When the uninstall program runs, it removes all of the specified application's system files and Registry settings.

- ◆ **Network.** Located in the Control Panel, you use this application to help you add network protocols, services, and adapters to your system.

- ◆ **Tape Devices.** Located in the Control Panel, you use this application to install tape device drivers under Windows NT.

- ◆ **Sounds.** Located in the Control Panel, you use this application to change or preview system sounds for system events.

- ◆ **Disk Administrator.** Located in the Start, Programs, Administrative Tools (Common) folder, you use this application to manage disks. You can create and delete partitions (except on disks where the *%SystemRoot%* resides), format and label volumes, change drive-letter assignments, and more.

- ◆ **System Policy Editor.** Located in the Start, Programs, Administrative Tools (Common) folder, you use this application to modify the Registry (on a local or remote computer), as well as set up and modify system policies under Windows NT. Chapter 6, "Using System Policy Editor to Modify Registry Data," discusses this application in more detail.

- ◆ **User Manager for Domains.** Located in the Start, Programs, Administrative Tools (Common) folder, you use this application to add, modify, remove, view, and audit users and groups on a Windows NT network.

◆ **Windows NT Diagnostics (WINMSD.EXE).** Launch WINMSD by selecting Start, Run, entering **WINMSD**, and pressing Enter. This displays the Windows NT Diagnostics dialog box for the current computer. Although not a configuration tool, the WINMSD diagnostic tool provides a display of the Registry data in an easy-to-read format (compared to the Registry Editor).

Before you begin modifying the Registry directly using the Registry Editor, use one of the preceding tools to make configuration changes to your system. One reason to start with these tools is that they usually keep you from making changes to a setting or series of settings that will adversely affect your system.

As an example, when you configure TCP/IP options in the Network Control Panel application, you must provide specific information about IP settings or Windows NT will not accept your changes. If you use the Registry Editor to make TCP/IP changes (or any other changes for that matter), you can make changes that might result in your computer not starting, or at the least, make the TCP/IP protocol useless until you correct them. Much like INI files, you can add anything to the Registry, but that doesn't mean the setting is correct.

Backing Up the Registry

Another thing you should do before modifying the Registry is make a backup copy of it. This ensures you always have a good copy of the Registry in case you add a setting to the Registry that Windows NT does not understand or support, causing your system to not boot properly, a device to fail, or an application to run in an unexpected way. When you make a backup of your Registry, you can only save those Registry keys or hives that are not volatile. *Volatile* hives are ones that change from session to session and are not saved when you exit Windows NT.

You can use three methods to back up your Registry. These are explained in the following list:

◆ Boot the current machine into an operating system other than Windows NT, such as Windows 95, MS-DOS, or Windows NT 3.51. Open the *%SystemRoot%*\system32\config folder and copy everything there to a backup device. You can, for instance, save these files to a tape backup, a CD-R disc, or network server drive.

Note Don't expect to backup your entire Registry to a single floppy disk. Since the Registry includes every configuration setting, application settings, network settings, and more, the Registry files can grow rather large. On systems that run just Windows NT Server or Windows NT Workstation with only a handful of applications and users connected, the Registry file can easily exceed 5 MB of hard disk. Also, as you remove objects from your Windows NT system, some settings remain in the Registry, causing your Registry to grow even as you reduce or limit the activity on the computer. Even if you use the uninstall feature of the Add/ Remove Program applications in the Control Panel, you are not assured that all Registry settings are removed during the uninstall process.

A time in which you might accumulate a ton of spare or forgotten Registry settings is if you participate in Beta testing new software. Because these programs by nature are unfinished, you can't assume all the features are in place to use the Registry most effectively. In some cases, software developers actually use both INI files and Registry settings during the Beta testing period to check to make sure certain user interface and user features are working before migrating all settings to the Registry. This means you might have settings in many different sections of the Registry that might be left over after you finish the Beta review process. Unless you make a copy of the Registry before you install Beta software and compare it to the Registry after the software installation, you might never know where all the settings have been placed.

◆ Boot the current machine into Windows NT 4, open the Registry Editor (you must use the REGEDT32.EXE program), and save each Registry subkey of HKEY_LOCAL_MACHINE and HKEY_CURRENT_USER to a file. Name each subkey by a filename that matches the subkey, such as \BACKDIR\SYSTEM for the SYSTEM subkey.

◆ Launch the Backup application from the Start, Programs, Administrative Tools (Common) folder. Select Operations, Backup and select the Backup Local Registry option. This instructs Windows NT to save a copy of the Registry from the local machine to a backup set. Then, you can use the Restore Local Registry option from the Operations, Restore command when you need to restore your copy of the Registry. You must have a tape backup device installed on Windows NT to start the Backup application.

Tip

The *Windows NT 3.51 Resource Kit* included a program called REGBACK.EXE that enables you to backup Registry files. One key feature of REGBACK.EXE is that it enables you to backup Registry keys and hives that are currently open. One downfall to the REGBACK.EXE program is that it is a command-line only application, requiring you to run it from a DOS window. With REGBACK.EXE you can backup Registry data to a floppy disk or hard disk. If the Registry key or hive is too large to fit on a single floppy disk, run REGBACK.EXE and save the file(s) to your hard drive. Next, run the BACKUP.EXE program and save the file(s) to multiple floppy disks.

As this book went to the printer, it was not known whether REGBACK.EXE or another Registry backup utility would be included in the *Windows NT 4.0 Resource Kit*.

Repairing the Windows NT Registry

You usually can repair the Windows NT Registry by using the emergency repair disk (ERD) that Windows NT creates when you setup Windows NT. Before you run off and do this, however, keep in mind that this repairs the hive files of the Registry to their original state at the time you set up Windows NT. If you have added or reconfigured Windows NT in any way (such as adding software or other components) since you installed Windows NT, the Registry on the emergency repair disk does not include these changes. For instructions how to use or update the ERD, see the Windows NT Help topic called emergency repair disk.

Another mechanism to recover from bad changes to the Registry is to boot NT with the last known good configuration by pressing the spacebar during boot up. This, of course, is applicable only if there was a good configuration with which NT was booted previously on the machine. More details on this are covered in Chapter 2, "Understanding the Windows NT Registry Structure."

Summary

This chapter introduced you to the Windows NT Registry and gave you a little history of the Registry database. The Registry is a centralized storage area for all configuration and device management resources installed on Windows NT. You also read how the architecture of the Windows NT operating system is modular and how each of its components interact with the Registry. The chapter covered information about when and the "best" ways to modify the Registry, as well as the importance of backing the Registry up. The next chapter continues the introduction of the Windows NT Registry and delves a little deeper into how each Registry hive is constructed.

Understanding the Windows NT Registry Structure

Before you can fully comprehend how to work with the Registry, you must first understand its hierarchy.

When you view the Registry with the Registry Editor (see Chapter 4, "Using the Windows NT Registry Editor"), the Registry looks similar to how folders, subfolders, and files appear in Windows NT Explorer. For that reason, you will read in this chapter how the Registry structure resembles a file system structure. Don't confuse "resemble," however, with how the Registry actually works. It does not work like a file system. For simple comparison, though, a file system offers a solid starting point for discussing how the Registry is structured.

This chapter explores the general structure of the Registry and the makeup of data therein, then details each of the Registry keys and contents. Specifically, this chapter covers the following items:

◆ Understanding Registry keys, subkeys, and value entries

◆ Examining the hierarchy of the Registry

Examining Registry Data and Organization

The Registry contains four types of objects: root keys, keys, subkeys, and value entries. These are the primary building blocks for the Registry. When you first look at the Registry, you might let out an involuntary shriek because of its complexity and size. The Registry contains a lot of information, more than you probably thought was necessary for an operating system. Some of the information is even duplicated in two or more places.

The true power of the Registry, however, is really only seen when you work in a networked environment or in an environment in which several users share a single computer or workstation. Only then you can see how the complexity works to help system administrators manage and optimize the servers and workstations on their LAN. But before you start chipping away and editing the Registry, you best know what you're doing, and the best way to start is to understand the Registry hierarchy and the components that make up the hierarchy—the keys, the subkeys, and the value entries.

Understanding Registry Keys

At the top of the Registry hierarchy are the Registry *root keys*, sometimes called the *subtrees*. Root keys are similar to bracketed headings in an INI file in Windows 3.x and contain keys, subkeys, and value entries about the computer and user accounts set up on the Windows NT computer. Root key names have the prefix HKEY_ to specify that they are *handles* (which are identifiers of system objects) that software developers can use to reference that resource in a computer program. Windows NT has five root keys, which are explained in the second main section of this chapter, "Breaking Down the Registry Hierarchy." Figures 2.1 and 2.2 show each of these items in their respective applications, the Registry and an INI file. Note how the Registry root key also can have several keys and subkeys beneath it, whereas INI headings cannot. This feature is known as *nesting* and is a powerful feature of the Windows NT Registry.

Keys can contain one or more other keys, subkeys, and value entries (see the next section on value entries). Each key and value must have a unique name within a key or subkey. As with the Windows NT file system, keys are case-aware but are not case-sensitive. That is, if you enter a name for a key as GraphicsControl, it will appear with the G and C in uppercase spelling. But references to this key do not have to adhere to the correct upper- and lowercase spelling. This means you cannot use the same name within a key or subkey even if the case is different. GraphicsControl and graphicscontrol are regarded as the same name in the Registry.

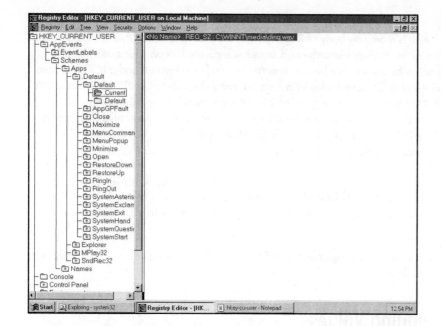

Figure 2.1

This is a key in the Windows NT Registry.

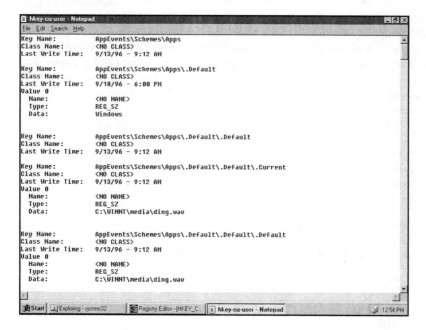

Figure 2.2

This is a bracketed heading in an INI file.

Note A *hive* is a discrete body of Registry keys, subkeys, and values that is rooted at the top of the Registry hierarchy and stored in separate files on your system. A hive is backed by a single file (which does not have a file extension) and a LOG file. Some of the hive files found on a Windows NT system include SECURITY.LOG, SECURITY, SAM.LOG, and SAM. In general, hive files are stored in the *%SystemRoot%* system32\config or *%SystemRoot%*\profiles*users* folders. Most hive files, such as DEFAULT, SAM, SECURITY, and SYSTEM, are stored in the *%SystemRoot%* system32\config folder. Hive files can be moved from one computer to another.

A key name can contain any visible characters—including spaces, underscores, and symbols—but cannot have backslashes (\). Backslashes are used by the Registry as delimiters in the hierarchy path, much as you use backslashes in a DOS path name.

 Note Chapter 4, "Using the Windows NT Registry Editor," shows you how to modify and create keys.

Understanding Values

The next part of the Registry that you need to learn about is values. Keys can include *values*, which contain instructions for how specified applications, devices, or Windows NT should perform, look, or behave. One simple example of a Registry value that Windows NT uses is the Registered Owner value, which lists the name of the owner of the selected computer. Some keys might not have values. Values comprise three parts: the data type of the value, the name of the value, and the value (or data) itself. Each value data type is displayed in the Registry Editor by an icon (see Chapter 4, "Using the Windows NT Registry Editor," for more information about these icons).

If you think in terms of the file system analogy, you can think of values as the files on a system. (Keys and subkeys are the folders and subfolders.) Just as each file on your system must have a name, all values must be named as well. The following is an example of the structure of a Registry value:

```
Value_Name: Data_Type: Value_Entry
```

Values can have one of the following six data types (each of which is explained in detail in the next section):

◆ REG_MULTI_SZ

◆ REG_BINARY

◆ REG_SZ

◆ REG_DWORD

◆ REG_EXPAND

◆ REG_FULL_RESOURCE_DESCRIPTOR

As you see in the next section, these data types give the Registry its flexibility and power to provide configuration data to hardware, software, and other resources connected to your PC.

Understanding Data in a Registry Value

The third part of a Registry value is its data. Continuing the file system analogy, the data in the Registry is similar to the data that makes up a file. Value data can be edited by double-clicking the value in the Registry Editor, invoking the appropriate editor to change the data. (You will read in Chapter 4, "Using the Windows NT Registry Editor," which editors are used for which value type.) One of the major differences between the Registry and INI files is the data types contained in the Registry. INI files can contain only text strings, whereas Registry data types can contain binary data, strings, and executable code. See Chapter 3, "Understanding the Role of Initialization Files in the Windows NT Registry," for more information about how Registry information differs from INI settings.

Registry data is always contained in a value. The following list describes each of the acceptable data types in Windows NT:

◆ **REG_MULTI_SZ.** Characters that make up a list of multiple string values. String values usually are readable (such as text entries), instead of containing binary data that most humans cannot read. The string values in the list or multiple string are separated by null characters (ASCII 0), such as in the following example:

AttachedComponents: REG_MULTI_SZ: Root\LEGACY_ATAPI\0000 Root\ LEGACY_DISK\0000...

◆ **REG_BINARY.** Data that is stored in binary format, such as hardware component information. Although some developers and administrators have experience writing binary code, this type of data is best left untouched in the Registry. Usually, if you are going to edit this type of data, you will have specific information or documentation from the vendor about which values to enter. An example of REG_BINARY data is the DiskPeripheral data in the following key:

HKEY_LOCAL_MACHINE\HARDWARE\DESCRIPTION\SYSTEM\Multifunction Adapter\2\DiskController\0\DiskPeripheral\O

The value for this setting is similar to the following:

```
ComponentInformation: REG_BINARY: 60 00 00 …
```

Note Another way to view this kind of data is to run Windows NT Diagnostics (WINMSD.EXE) and view the data in a graphical user interface (GUI) (see fig. 2.3). Although you can't make changes using WINMSD, you do get an idea of the data stored for individual components in the Registry.

Figure 2.3

Many times, the Windows NT Diagnostics tool should be used instead of viewing or editing hardware information directly in the Registry.

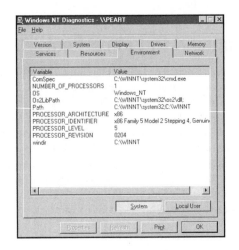

◆ **REG_SZ.** A string of data that is usually easy to read and can be modified easily in most cases. One example of this is the RegisteredOwner value found in the following key:

HKEY_LOCAL_MACHINE\SOFTWARE\Microsoft\Windows NT\CurrentVersion

For this setting, you usually have the name of the system administrator or company representative, such as the following:

```
RegisteredOwner REG_SZ: Rob Tidrow
```

Tip Windows NT stipulates that some data types are reserved for specific uses. Data types from 0x80000000 to 0xffffffff are reserved for applications, while 0 to 0x7fffffff are reserved for the system.

◆ **REG_DWORD.** Data that is 4 bytes long is sometimes referred to as double word (DWORD). This data type can be viewed in binary, decimal, or hexadecimal format in the Registry Editor (see fig. 2.4). Values usually in this data type include device parameters, memory addresses, service values, and interrupt settings. An example of REG_DWORD data is the following:

```
NumberOfButtons: REG_DWORD: 0x2
```

This example lists the number of buttons on a bus mouse installed. When you see a REG_DWORD value with the 0x prefix, you know the value is listed in hexadecimal format, which is the most common way to show REG_DWORD values.

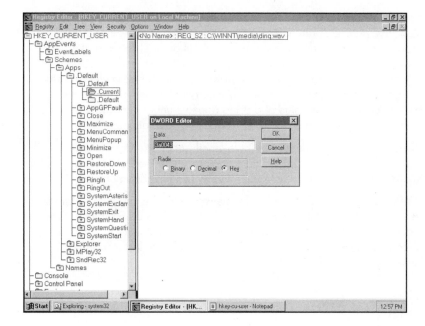

Figure 2.4

REG_DWORD data is edited and modified using the DWORD Editor in the Registry Editor.

◆ **REG_EXPAND_SZ.** Expandable data containing variables that are replaced when accessed by an application. One of the most familiar REG_EXPAND values is the %SystemRoot% variable, which is replaced by the root directory of where Windows NT is installed. An example of this is in the LicenseService subkey, which has the following value:

```
ImagePath: REG_EXPAND_SZ: %SystemRoot%\System32\llssrv.exe
```

In the preceding example, the llssrv.exe application is being referenced by the ImagePath value.

◆ **REG_FULL_RESOURCE_DESCRIPTOR.** Includes hardware device configuration data. REG_FULL_RESOURCE_DESCRIPTOR values set the hardware device settings that are stored in the HKEY_LOCAL_MACHINE\HARDWARE\ Description key. These settings are established at startup and written to the Registry by the Windows NT system. To change most of the information in these settings, you should use the appropriate application in Control Panel, such as the modem application to change modem settings.

Note If you administer Windows 95 clients on your network, note that Windows 95 has only the following three Registry data types (as opposed to five in NT):

- **String.** A string is a variable length, null-terminated set of characters, such as words, phrases, path names, or any other text. String values usually provide you a great deal of information about an application and its configuration. These values are most similar to the text-only INI settings of Windows 3.x. The name given to your Recycle Bin, for example, is in string format. You can change this name by modifying the string data of the Recycle Bin's key. The value of a string appears under the Data heading of the Registry Editor and is always surrounded by quotation marks.

- **Binary.** A binary value is a variable-length set of hexadecimal digits (0–9 and A–F). Hexadecimal information appears under the Data heading of the Registry Editor. Each byte is represented by two hexadecimal digits.

- **DWORD.** A DWORD value (or double-word value) is a single 32-bit value (8 hexadecimal digits) and appears in the Registry as an 8-digit hexadecimal number. DWORD values appear under the Data heading in the Registry Editor. The hexadecimal number 13 (decimal 19), for instance, is represented as 0x00000013(18).

Setting Registry Size

Registry value entries can have values up to 1 MB, making it likely that your Registry will grow as your network and services grow. The maximum size of the Registry depends on the paged pool size. The paged pool, which is saved in the PAGEFILE.SYS file, is the virtual memory file to which Windows NT swaps information. By default, Windows NT is set up to allow the Registry to get as large as 25 percent of the paged pool, which is usually between 22 MB and 72 MB. Windows NT uses paged pools, along with your computer's random access memory (RAM), to enable you to run more applications than you could otherwise with only your system RAM.

You can view the size of your paged pool and the maximum size of the Registry on your system using the System icon in Control Panel. To do so, use the following steps:

1. Start Control Panel and double-click the Systems icon.

2. In the System Properties dialog box, click on the Performance tab.

3. Click on the Change button to display the Virtual Memory dialog box (see fig. 2.5).

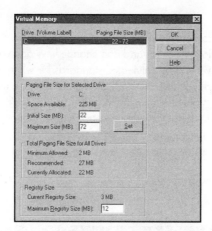

Figure 2.5

In most cases, you shouldn't need to increase the maximum size of your Registry unless you have several thousand user accounts set up on your server.

4. View the Paging File Size (MB) and Registry Size values in the Virtual Memory dialog box. To change these values, modify the settings in the Initial Size (MB) and Maximum Size (MB) fields.

5. Click on OK, then click on Close in the System Properties dialog box to save your settings.

6. Restart Windows NT.

You can view the Registry size limits and maximum size of the Registry by viewing the value of HKEY_LOCAL_MACHINE\SYSTEM\Current\ControlSet\Control\Registry SizeLimit and HKEY_LOCAL_MACHINE\SYSTEM\CurrentControlSet\Control\ Session Manager\Memory Management\PagedPoolSize.

Breaking Down the Registry Hierarchy

If you've taken a look at the Registry already, you know it can be a little confusing at first. In the Registry Editor, you can see the Registry is divided into five main keys (usually called the *root keys*) that display in separate windows. This section discusses these keys and the subkeys within them. Because it is impossible to show all the possible subkeys in the Registry, this section describes the root keys, some of the important subkeys, and some example keys to show what types of information is stored in the Registry.

Note The Registry contains thousands of keys with values that change as you use Windows NT. Applications also can add and change keys and values in the Registry. Microsoft, however, has delineated standards for when and how applications should modify the Registry. As a result, a complete list of keys and their possible values is impossible to document. In fact, if you try to document your own Registry settings, you'll find that they change each time you boot your system and make any alterations to the configuration. Appendix A, "Windows NT Registry Values," contains many of the values that are present when Windows NT installs.

The Registry has five root keys (see fig. 2.6).

Figure 2.6

The Registry contains five root keys.

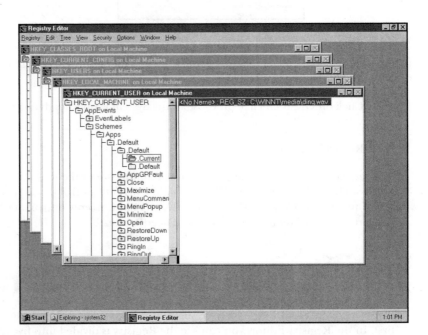

Each of these keys has its own function, as follows:

◆ **HKEY_CLASSES_ROOT.** Provides backward compatibility with Windows 3.x for Object Linking and Embedding (OLE) and Dynamic Data Exchange (DDE) support. This is where you can find file association and OLE information. If you are puzzled about a file extension of one your files on your system, many times you can examine these listings to get an idea of what that file type is. You normally set file associations using the File, Associate command in Windows 3.x, or the View, Options, File Types command in Windows NT Explorer.

◆ **HKEY_CURRENT_USER.** Includes user profile information about the user currently logged on. This data ensures that Windows NT, applications, and the user's interface operate the same for a user from session to session and from other machines on which they log on to the network. This key points to the HKEY_USERS key for the most current data, and includes information for desktop settings, printer settings, application preferences, and network connections.

◆ **HKEY_LOCAL_MACHINE.** Stores non-user–specific hardware and software configuration information for the local computer. This information is specific to the machine regardless of who logs on to it.

◆ **HKEY_USERS.** Contains all the profile information for the current user, including HKEY_CURRENT_USER, as well as profile information for other users who have previously logged on to the current computer. The .DEFAULT subkey is included for those users who log on to the company without using an established profile. Many times, system administrators set up .DEFAULT profiles that include bare minimum access privileges. You can see how to do this in Chapter 6, "Using System Policy Editor to Modify Registry Data."

◆ **HKEY_CURRENT_CONFIG.** Includes hardware profile information used at startup by the local machine. Entries include device driver settings and display settings.

 Note The Windows 95 Registry includes an additional root key called HKEY_DYN_DATA. This key holds information that must be stored in RAM at all times and should never be altered.

The following sections take a closer and expanded look at each of these keys. For best results, run the Registry Editor to look at these keys as you go through them here. Chapter 4, "Using the Windows NT Registry Editor," shows how to run and use the Registry Editor if you aren't sure how to use it.

HKEY_CLASSES_ROOT

The HKEY_CLASSES_ROOT provides backward compatibility with Windows 3.x for OLE and DDE support. It also contains OLE and DDE information specific to Windows NT, such as shell extension keys and values. This key actually points to the HKEY_LOCAL_MACHINE\SOFTWARE\Classes subkey; they both contain the same information. By having this pointer available, applications and Windows NT can access the information easier, and it allows for compatibility with Windows 3.x applications.

All the subkeys under the HKEY_CLASSES_ROOT key refer to document types associated with the applications installed on the system. The exception to this is the * subkey, which is associated with all application document types. The file extension subkeys point to document description subkeys, which in turn point to class ID subkeys. These trails of keys contain OLE, DDE, shell, and shell extension information. They also include file locations of the OLE servers that support the document type.

To help you become more familiar with how document types are registered, this section shows how a specific file type is registered, namely a hypertext markup language (HTML) file. Under the HKEY_CLASSES_ROOT key in the Registry Editor (see Chapter 4, "Using the Windows NT Registry Editor"), locate the htmlfile subkey. If you don't have this entry, you can look at another entry, such as WORDPAD.Document.1 for files associated with Microsoft WordPad. Under htmlfile (see fig. 2.7), you can see what the default icon is that displays for all files of type HTML (under the DefaultIcon subkey), as well as shell actions. For htmlfile, one of these actions is open. Under the open subkey is the following value entry, which instructs Microsoft Internet Explorer 3.0 to start when an HTML file is encountered:

```
REG_SZ: "C:\Program Files\Plus!\Microsoft Internet\IExplore.exe"
```

Figure 2.7

The Shell extension for the htmlfile subkey is an example of a document type listed in the Registry.

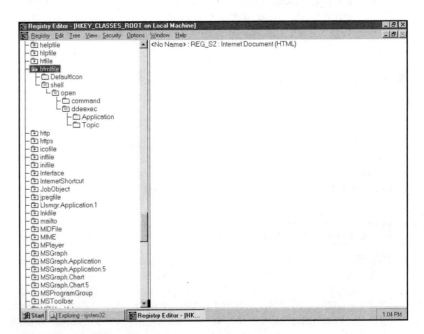

The following four sections describe each of the subkeys found in the HKEY_CLASSES_ROOTS subkey.

Wild-Card Keys

The first subkey of HKEY_CLASSES_ROOT is a wild-card key (*). The Windows NT shell extensions use a special key. Shell extensions are OLE servers (usually in DLL files) that provide extra user interface functionality to Windows NT. The wild-card key specifies shell extensions that apply to all applications, not just a single application. This means, for instance, that you can add information to the context menus of all icons, or you can add property pages to all property sheets shown in a shell.

File Extension Subkeys

Windows NT begins searching for information associated with a document type by looking for the key name that matches the file extension. The main purpose of these keys is to indicate another key in HKEY_CLASSES_ROOT that describes the document type in greater detail. The default value of the key is the name of the document definition subkey.

Document Definition Subkeys

The subkeys of the document definition subkey provide most of the OLE, DDE, and shell extension attributes of the document type. The default value is a text string that gives a one-line description of the document type.

Some document definition subkeys point to a CLSID subkey, for which the default value is a long string of numbers. These are OLE class identifiers, which match the class ID subkeys under the HKEY_CLASSES_ROOT\CLSID key.

CLSID Subkey

All subkeys underneath HKEY_CLASSES_ROOT\CLSID are OLE class identifiers. (CLSID stands for class identifier.) The class identifier for a particular document type is guaranteed unique across all PCs in the world. The default value of the key is a description of the OLE class. The location of the file that contains the OLE implementation for that class is usually located in the InProcServer32 subkey (for a DLL file) or LocalServer32 (for an EXE file). If the document is supported by older 16-bit OLE applications, the location might also be in InProcServer or LocalServer subkeys.

HKEY_CURRENT_USER

HKEY_CURRENT_USER points to the HKEY_USERS key for the user currently logged on to the PC. This user-profile information assures that Windows NT, the individual application setup, and the user interface all operate identically on whichever machine the user works. For this reason, administrators need to make sure the user's profile is available on every PC on which that user works.

Note See Chapter 7, "Administering Remote Registries from Windows NT," to see how users can store their profiles to use other PCs on the network.

When a users logs on to Windows NT, the user's computer environment is created based on the profile established in the HKEY_USERS*SID* key, to which HKEY_CURRENT_USER is mapped. The *SID* parameter is the security ID for the user who is logging in, and looks something like the following:

S-1-5-21-837503847-2108432355-1468256709-400

When a user ID cannot be found for a user who is logging on, the information in the HKEY_USERS\.DEFAULT subkey is used.

HKEY_CURRENT_USER has the following subkeys:

◆ **AppEvents.** Subkeys that contain paths to current and past sound files that play when a system event occurs, such as when you maximize a window or receive an error message.

◆ **Console.** Contains subkeys for cursor size, font family name, windows size, screen colors, and the color table. You also see the CommandPrompt setting if you modify the Windows NT command prompt window.

◆ **Control Panel.** Subkeys that contain information set when you use the Control Panel. Much of this information was stored in WIN.INI or CONTROL.INI in Windows 3.x and is in REG_SZ format, with many values containing the RGB (Red Green Blue) color coding for Windows NT.

◆ **Environment.** Includes environment variables, such as TEMP and TMP locations. Use the System icon in Control Panel to set most of your environment settings. You can do this by selecting the Environment tab on the System Properties dialog box, as shown in figure 2.8.

◆ **Keyboard Layout.** Contains information about the current keyboard configuration as established by using the Keyboard icon in Control Panel.

◆ **Printers.** Contains information about the installed printers for the user currently logged on. Printer connection information is stored in the Connections subkey under the Printers subkey. You should use the Printers folder in My Computer if you want to change printer properties or options.

◆ **Network.** Subkeys that define the current state of network components, including drives for the current user. This subkey is present only if you have a networking component installed.

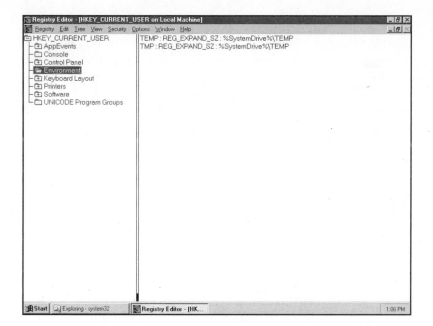

Figure 2.8

*Environment
settings are easier
to set using
Control Panel
settings than in
the Registry
Editor.*

◆ **Software.** Includes a pointer to HKEY_LOCAL_MACHINE\SOFTWARE. The
subkeys describe settings and options for the current user's installed software.
The subkey for Notepad, for instance, includes data about the appearance of
Notepad. This application-specific information was previously stored in WIN.INI
or application-specific INI files under Windows 3.x.

◆ **UNICODE Program Groups.** Contains subkeys for the program groups for
the currently logged in user. You can find program group definitions in
HKEY_LOCAL_MACHINE\SOFTWARE\ProgramGroups.

◆ **Windows 3.1 Migration Status.** Includes data about Windows 3.1 Groups
and INI files that migrated to Windows NT during setup. In some cases, this
subkey appears only in the HKEY_LOCAL_MACHINE\SOFTWARE\Windows 3.1
Migration Status subkey.

Most applications should place Registry information for this key under the
HKEY_CURRENT_USER\Software (see fig. 2.9) or HKEY_USER\DEFAULT\ Software
subkeys. The purpose is for these keys to contain information formerly placed in the
INI files of specific applications.

Tip　When identical information exists between HKEY_CURRENT_USER and
HKEY_LOCAL_MACHINE, the information in the HKEY_CURRENT_USER takes
precedence, ensuring that the user logged in is using his or her profile, not that
determined solely by the machine.

Figure 2.9

The HKEY_CURRENT_USER\ Software subkey is where most applications store their Registry information.

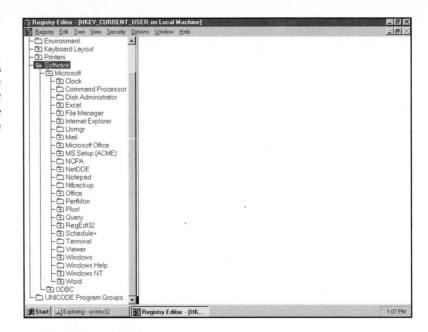

HKEY_LOCAL_MACHINE

This key contains computer-specific information about hardware and software configuration for the local PC. The information contained here applies to the computer, regardless of the user who logs on to it. HKEY_LOCAL_MACHINE has four called hives, as listed in table 2.1. See the earlier section "Understanding Registry Keys" for more information on hives.

TABLE 2.1
Windows NT Hives and Associated Files

Hives	Files in %System32\Config Folder
HKEY_LOCAL_MACHINE\SAM	SAM.LOG and SAM
HKEY_LOCAL_MACHINE\SECURITY	SECURITY.LOG and SECURITY
HKEY_LOCAL_MACHINE\SOFTWARE	SOFTWARE.LOG and SOFTWARE
HKEY_LOCAL_MACHINE\SYSTEM	SYSTEM.ALT and SYSTEM

Note Windows NT also includes two other hives—HKEY_CURRENT_USER and HKEY_USERS\DEFAULT. HKEY_CURRENT_USER has USER*nnn*, USER.LOG, ADMIN*nnn*, and ADMIN*nnn*.log as its associated files. The associated files for HKEY_USERS\DEFAULT include DEFAULT.LOG and DEFAULT. The files with LOG and ALT extensions contain backup data, while the files without extensions contain current data. If Windows NT needs to use the last best boot configuration, it uses the information in the LOG and ALT files to set up the Registry.

The following list details the hives in the HKEY_LOCAL_MACHINE:

◆ **HARDWARE.** Contains *volatile* (that which is re-created each time Windows NT boots) information about the configuration of the hardware. This includes BIOS data, hardware abstraction layer information, SCSI adapter settings, video information, and more. When the Windows NT Diagnostic program displays, it grabs information from this key to display. The data in this key is mainly in binary, so if you are going to change it using the Registry Editor, make sure you have specific data from vendors. Under the HARDWARE key are the following subkeys:

  ◆ **DESCRIPTION.** Includes data about the hardware recognized by NTDETECT.COM and the Windows NT Executive.

  ◆ **DEVICEMAP.** Includes data used by device drivers.

  ◆ **OWNERMAP.** Includes data provided by manufacturers for some device settings, such as video devices.

  ◆ **RESOURCEMAP.** Includes data about how device drivers should use hardware resources.

◆ **SAM.** Includes domain (for Windows NT Server) or workgroup (for Windows NT Workstation) information for user and group accounts. This information is controlled by the User Manager for Domains and is mapped to the HKEY_LOCAL_MACHINE\SECURITY\SAM subkey.

◆ **SECURITY.** Includes security policy and user rights information used by the Windows NT security subsystem.

◆ **SOFTWARE.** Includes information about the software installed on the computer. See the section "The Classes Subkey" for information on the Classes subkey.

- **SYSTEM.** Includes information about how the operating system starts and behaves, including the LastKnownGood setting, device driver loading, and Windows NT services startup. The System subkey contains information relating to system startups that must be stored on the system. This is in contrast to information that gets created during the boot-up process. Not surprisingly, this is the type of information that has always been stored in AUTOEXEC.BAT and CONFIG.SYS files in previous Windows 3.x systems. The System subkey theoretically eliminates the need for these two startup files to exist on your machine for Windows NT to run properly. Particularly, device drivers and services loaded with Windows NT are controlled from this subkey.

The following sections highlight some of the subkeys found in the preceding keys. Although you should use other tools (such as WINMSD) to troubleshoot system configuration problems before attempting to edit the Registry, the following subkeys are some of the most common ones you run into as you modify Registry settings.

The Classes Subkey

The HKEY_LOCAL_MACHINE\SOFTWARE\Classes subkey is identical to the HKEY_CLASSES_ROOT key that was discussed a few pages back. It simply points to that key, which has a sole purpose of providing compatibility with the Windows 3.x registration database.

The Classes subkey contains two kinds of subkeys:

- **Class-definition keys.** These keys specify shell and OLE properties of a class of documents. Applications that support DDE have shell subkeys that contain Open and Print subkeys defining DDE commands. These subkeys instruct Windows NT on how to print and open these files.

- **Filename-extension subkeys.** These keys specify the class-definition association with files that have the selected extension.

 Note   The Classes subkey is used by Windows NT to locate application- or device driver-specific files so that it doesn't have to link to the Explorer. You will not affect the Explorer display if you change these listings in the Registry.

The SYSTEM Subkey

Under the SYSTEM subkey is information about multiple configurations for a computer, such as one configuration for an administrator and another one for a user. One setup is used when you log into the computer as an administrator, while the other configuration is used when you log in as a user. You can create new hardware configurations by using the System icon in the Control Panel and accessing the Hardware Profiles tab (see fig. 2.10).

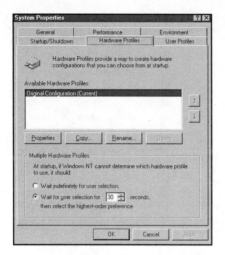

Figure 2.10

*When you use the
Hardware Profile
tab, you modify
the Registry
information in
the HKEY_
LOCAL_
MACHINE\
SYSTEM subkeys.*

Subkeys for those configurations are listed under the \ControlSet*nnn* subkeys, such as
\ControlSet001, and so on. The user-defined name for a new configuration is placed
under the HKEY_LOCAL_MACHINE\System\Current\ControlSet*nnn*\Control\
IDConfigDB\Hardware Profiles subkey. The name you create for the new hardware
configuration is then reflected in the Registry at the end of this subkey, as shown in
figure 2.11. In that example, the name of the hardware configuration is Original
Configuration.

How are these settings established during a session? When you boot your computer,
Windows NT checks the hardware configuration and runs through the following
items:

◆ Usually, the system configuration ID is mapped to a unique configuration and
Windows selects the correct one automatically. Settings in the Config subkey for
that machine determine the system configuration.

◆ In the case of multiple configurations for the same machine, the user is
prompted upon boot-up to choose which configuration he or she wants to use.

The SYSTEM subkey is used during the boot process to supply hardware-specific
information to Windows NT. This key also contains references to the display, disk
partitions, OS loader path, and any printers you have set up.

Tip   You can find information about your network settings in the \ControlSet*nnn*\
Services\Netlogon and \ControlSet*nnn*\Services\NetDetect subkeys.

Figure 2.11

You can view the user-defined hardware configuration setting in the Registry.

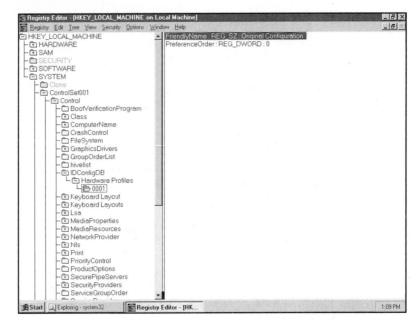

The layout of the System subkey looks like this:

```
SYSTEM
      |
      |
      Clone
      |
      ControlSetnnn
               |
               Control
               Enum
               Hardware Profiles
               Services
      CurrentControlSet
               |
               Control
               Enum
               Hardware Profiles
               Services
      DISK
      Select
      Setup
```

Nested within ControlSet*nnn* and CurrentControlSet are the following subkeys:

◆ **Control.** Controls the system startup, such as the subsystems that need to start, the computer name, type of file system, the keyboard layouts and so on.

◆ **Enum.** Provides enumeration for the hardware installed in your PC. Bus enumerators are software devices in Windows NT that are designed to do the following:

  ◆ Build a hardware tree in Windows NT.

  ◆ Assign a unique ID to each device on the bus.

  ◆ Retrieve configuration information for that device from the Registry or from the device itself.

The subkeys underneath the Enum subkey list classes of devices and configuration information for those devices. An example is shown in figure 2.12. Depending on the devices you have installed on your system, you might see separate keys for some hardware devices in the Enum subkey. You can, for example, see subkeys for IDE hard drives and floppy drives.

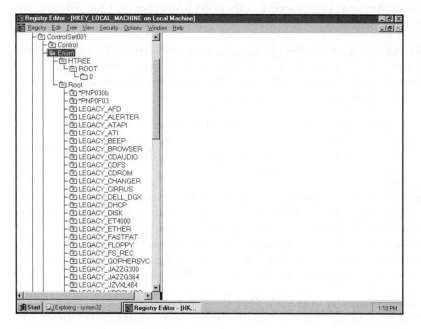

Figure 2.12

The Windows NT Enum subkeys in the Registry.

- ◆ **Hardware Profiles.** Includes information about the video controller.

- ◆ **Services.** Controls the way drives, file systems, and other services are loaded and configured at bootup.

Each of these subkeys contains numerous other subkeys that monitor and control how your system boots. Many of these subkeys are discussed in the following paragraphs.

In the Control subkey, several subkeys exist that, by their name, you shouldn't have problems understanding their roles. These include ComputerName (set by using the Network tool in Control Panel), FileSystem, KeyboardLayouts, and TimeZoneInformation. Others, which are listed here, need a little more explanation to be understood:

- ◆ **IDConfigDB.** This subkey shows the identification for the current system configuration. By default, this is named Original Configuration and is created using the System utility in Control Panel. You can create different hardware configurations from which to select at bootup time to instruct Windows to load certain drivers for certain configurations.

- ◆ **MediaProperties.** Describes the multimedia properties for your system, such as joystick and MIDI devices.

- ◆ **MediaResources.** Lists descriptions and driver information for multimedia components. Looking through these subkeys will give you some idea of the built-in multimedia support in Windows NT. You might also be able to update drivers and rename values of devices if necessary.

- ◆ **Nls.** Includes information and configuration data for national language support. Not only are languages listed, but also locale preferences are included, such as English (United States), English (British), English (Australian), English (Jamaican), English (Caribbean), and so on.

- ◆ **Print.** Although this subkey is basically self-explanatory, it contains a few subkeys that you might want to know about. The Print subkey includes information about current printers and the printing environment. The Environment subkey includes subkeys for print processes and drivers for specific operating systems. The Monitors subkey has subkeys with configuration data for network priority monitors, including the Microsoft Fax Monitor.

  Another subkey under Print is the Printers subkey. This subkey shows Printer parameters for all the printers on your system. The Providers subkey under the Print subkey contains additional subkeys for network print services and their associated DLLs. The Microsoft Network Print Provider, for example, lists the MSPP32.DLL entry.

◆ **SessionManager.** Contains some interesting information for those responsible for troubleshooting problems. This subkey has global variables (such as DLLs) maintained by Windows, a list of applications that do not run well under Windows NT, folders and file names of all session manager DLLs, and DLLs whose number should be checked.

The SessionManager subkey includes the following keys:

   ◆ **AppPatches.** Defines specific applications and fixes for common problems.

   ◆ **DOS Devices.** Includes settings for DOS devices.

   ◆ **Environment.** Includes environment settings, such as command prompt settings, number of processors on the computer, processor type (such as x86 or RISC), and more.

   ◆ **Executive.** Displays information about the Windows NT Executive.

   ◆ **FileRenameOperations.** Shows File Rename settings.

   ◆ **KnownDLLs.** Includes a listing of known 32-bit DLLS and their file names.

   ◆ **Memory Management.** Includes information about memory configurations in Windows NT, including paged pool size, system pages, and system cache.

   ◆ **SubSystems.** Lists information about Windows NT subsystem, including POSIX, the Windows object directory, and so on.

◆ **Update.** The Update subkey shows if your Windows NT installation is installed over an earlier version of Windows. If the value UpdateMode 01 exists, you know your system was upgraded. Knowing this can help you isolate problems with devices that were set up previously for Windows 3.x and are still using older device drivers under Windows NT.

Control Sets

As you've seen, Windows NT has several control sets, named ControlSet*nnn*. Also available is the CurrentControlSet. When you install Windows NT, you typically have the following control sets:

ControlSet001

ControlSet002

CurrentControlSet

Clone

The differences between ControlSet001 and ControlSet002 may be minor. In many cases, ControlSet001 may be the set used by Windows NT to boot into your current session. ControlSet002 probably contains the information for your last known good boot and is used if Windows NT cannot boot properly and needs to resort to the last best boot to bring up Windows NT. The CurrentControlSet points to one of the ControlSet*nnn* subkeys. When you boot your computer using the kernel initialization process, the Clone subkey is created and is a copy of the ControlSet*nnn* used to boot Windows NT.

To tell which control set is used to boot Windows NT, look in the Select subkey. The Current, Default, Failed, and LastKnownGood entries show you which control set is selected for each task. If, for instance, the Current setting is REG_DWORD: 0x1, then ControlSet001 was used to boot up Windows NT during the current session. The LastKnownGood setting usually points to the highest ControlSet*nnn* subkey listed under the SYSTEM key.

If you make any changes to a control set, stay away from the one listed in the LastKnownGood entry. That way, if you modify a setting and Windows NT doesn't respond well to your new setting, you can always revert to the last known good boot to start Windows NT by pressing the spacebar during system bootup. In general, you should make any modifications to the CurrentControlSet because it is usually the correct control set.

The Failed entry specifies the control set that was replaced if the LastKnownGood control set was used to start the system and can be used to identify which control set has problems.

HKEY_USERS

The HKEY_USERS root key contains all user profiles of users logged on to the computer (see fig. 2.13). This key contains the .Default subkey and SID subkeys. The SID subkeys are unique security IDs for each user who logs on to the computer. Each user is assigned a SID to be used when the user wants to access a service or device on the computer or network. The SID entry in the Registry (which is a long string of numbers) contains the configuration settings for the user assigned to that SID.

The main item of interest in the HKEY_USERS root key is the .Default subkey. The .Default subkey is used to create a user profile for users who log on to the computer who don't already have a user profile. The period (.) in the subkey name, .Default, indicates that it is the default settings. If you leave off the period, the Registry interprets "Default" as a user name like "JSMITH." Unless your name is Default, as in "Default Washington" or something, don't delete the period. Without a .Default setting, Windows NT will not know what to do.

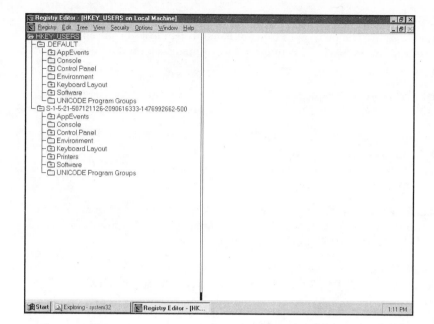

Figure 2.13

The HKEY_USERS root key contains information about users and default users for the local computer.

Tip   The time to rename the .Default subkey is when you want to restrict people from booting up a computer and starting it with default settings. This is a good way to provide one layer of security on machines you don't want used without proper log-on rights.

Any edits you make to the entries in the HKEY_USERS key are essentially useless. This key actually points to the HKEY_CURRENT_USER key. If you look in that key, you'll see the exact same entries. All settings in that key override any that you make to the HKEY_USERS key.

The .Default subkey includes the following subkeys:

◆ **AppEvents.** Subkeys that contain paths to current and past sound files that play when a system event occurs, such as when you maximize a window or receive an error message.

◆ **Console.** Lists desktop and other aesthetic values, including window size, font names, color table values, and more.

◆ **Control Panel.** Subkeys that contain information set when you use the Control Panel. Much of this information was stored in WIN.INI or CONTROL.INI in Windows 3.x.

◆ **Environment.** Includes environment variables, such as TEMP and TMP locations. Use the System icon in Control Panel to set most of your environment settings. You can do this by selecting the Environment tab on the System Properties dialog box.

◆ **Keyboard Layout.** Contains information about the current keyboard configuration as established by using the Keyboard icon in Control Panel.

◆ **Software.** Includes a pointer to HKEY_LOCAL_MACHINE\SOFTWARE. The subkeys describe settings and options for the current user's installed software. This application-specific information was previously stored in WIN.INI or application-specific INI files under Windows 3.x.

◆ **UNICODE Program Groups.** Contains subkeys for the program groups for the currently logged in user. You can find program group definitions in HKEY_LOCAL_MACHINE\SOFTWARE\ProgramGroups.

Notice anything familiar with these subkeys? You should. They are exactly the same as HKEY_CURRENT_USER that you read about earlier. So why have the HKEY_USERS key?

Unlike HKEY_CURRENT_USER, which is designed for only one user, the HKEY_USERS key enables you to set up several users to log in. (Notice the plural "USERS" rather than "USER.") When you have multiple users configured, the other names will appear as separate subkeys on the same level of the .Default subkey. An example of this is shown in figure 2.14.

Figure 2.14

Notice the additional users in the HKEY_USERS hierarchy.

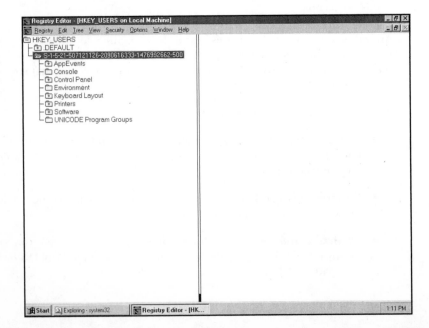

To create additional users, you should use the System Policy Editor, which is covered in Chapter 7, "Administering Remote Registries from Windows NT." Using this method is a much safer alternative than modifying the Registry directly. Plus, the System Policy Editor is much easier to use.

HKEY_CURRENT_CONFIG

The HKEY_CURRENT_CONFIG root key points to the HKEY_LOCAL_ MACHINE\ SYSTEM subkey for machine-specific information. Having the HKEY_CURRENT_ CONFIG key makes it easier for applications to access information within the HKEY_LOCAL_MACHINE\Control key.

The structure of HKEY_CURRENT_CONFIG contains two primary subkeys (although an Enum subkey contains Default entries)—Software and System. These are the same subkeys and settings discussed earlier in the HKEY_LOCAL_MACHINE\SYSTEM section.

Summary

The heart of Windows NT is the Registry database. If you do any system maintenance, management, or troubleshooting, you'll need to know what each part of the Registry does. This chapter first defined the building blocks, the components making up the structure of the Registry. It then described each of the five main root keys and devoted attention to many of the branches found in the Registry.

For the most part, you'll spend your time working in the following two subkeys:

HKEY_LOCAL_MACHINE

and

HKEY_CURRENT_USER

The other subkeys should remain untouched unless specifically advised by a support person or by the application's or device's manufacturer.

CHAPTER

3

Understanding the Role of Initialization Files in the Windows NT Registry

Just when you mastered initialization files (INI files) in Windows
3.x, Microsoft goes and changes everything. INI files contain
configuration information for Windows, hardware devices, user
settings, and application settings. No longer can you scan your
hard drive looking for INI files to make one or two slight adjustments
to fine-tune an application or get a pesky device working. You probably
even used to edit INI files in DOS-mode when something went wrong
and Windows wouldn't even boot for you.

This chapter looks at INI files and how they interact with or work
inside of the Windows NT Registry. As you troubleshoot problems with
a Windows NT system, use this information to help you isolate or
eliminate possible configuration problems that originate from INI
settings. You might, for instance, wonder why a program launches at
boot time when you have not added that application to your Startup

menu. Look in the WIN.INI file under the run= line to see if any applications are placed there to launch at bootup. Also, many INI settings are placed in the Registry to enable legacy hardware and software to work with Windows NT.

Specifically, look for the following items to be covered:

◆ Reexamining the Windows 3.x Registry and INI Files

◆ INI files and the Windows NT Registry

◆ Other INI files to note

◆ Administering INI Mappings in Windows 95 Clients

Reexamining the Windows 3.x Registry and INI Files

The Windows NT Registry promises a lot for the overall performance and power of Windows NT, and promises the system administrator a way to remotely administer PCs for which they are responsible. But you will probably still run into some INI problems every once in while. Now they just happen to be the second place you tend to look for a resource or application problem. (The first place you look is usually the Control Panel or the Registry.) The reality, however, is that more problems (such as device drivers not loading correctly, sound events not playing correctly, and so on) are due to old INI files or INI file settings that map to the Registry than most Windows NT users know and than Microsoft is willing to admit. For this reason, you should continue looking at INI settings for the source of some of the problems you encounter with a device, application, or a Windows NT setting.

The main source of initialization and configuration duties in Windows 3.x (do not confuse this with Windows NT 3.x; instead, this was for MS-DOS–based Windows, such as Windows 3.1 and Windows for Workgroups) was INI files. INI files, or initialization files, are ASCII files that contain system, application, and device settings. An example of what you might find in an INI file includes the following:

```
device=Epson Stylus Color IIs,EPMJ5C,LPT1:
```

That setting defines a printing device with the name Epson Stylus Color IIs to use the EPMJ5C and LPT1 port settings. Windows 3.x INI files contain sections of data made up of a few different types of punctuation along with alphanumeric characters. This made INI files relatively easy to edit once users and administrators got comfortable with them. Usually INI files contain square brackets, equal signs, commas, and semicolons.

Compared to the Registry format, the INI format was a very simple way of presenting configuration data. In general, the ease of use of INI files was certainly an upside to using INI files. The downside, of course, was that INI files are "flat" and cannot contain nested (hierarchical) configuration details to make them useful for powerful operating system features such as Plug and Play, hardware configuration, and more advanced OLE capabilities. INI files also cannot contain binary data that Registry files can contain.

Configuration management problems with INI files under Windows 3.x include the following:

◆ INI files are text based and limited to only 64 KB in size.

◆ APIs allow for only get/write operations.

◆ Information is stored in several locations, including standard INI files (see the next section, "Role of INI Files in Windows 3.x") and application-specific INI files.

◆ Information in INI files is non-hierarchical and supports only two levels of information—key names broken up by section headings.

◆ INI files have no way to store user-specific information that they can roam with, such as with user profiles in Windows NT and Windows 95 clients.

◆ Some INI switches and entries are complicated to configure or are used only by operating system components.

◆ There is no specialized editor for INI files.

◆ INI files can only be modified locally; Registry files enable administrators to remotely access the Registry.

The following sections dig a little deeper into INI files, showing you how to edit them and which settings are common to many Windows systems. If you are already intimate with INI files, you might want to skim these sections or skip to the section called "INI Files and the Windows NT Registry" to read about how Windows NT uses INI files.

Editing INI Files

For those not intimate with INI files or those who have forgotten how to edit INI files, here is a short overview. To gain a basic understanding of INI files, you need to understand how they look in general. The following is an example from a SYSTEM.INI file:

```
[boot]
shell=progman.exe
network.drv=
mouse.drv=mouse.drv
language.dll=
sound.drv=mmsound.drv
comm.drv=rhsicomm.drv
keyboard.drv=keyboard.drv
SCRNSAVE.EXE=(None)
```

INI files are divided into sections, with each section containing a certain number of settings that apply to particular options or categories of options. Each section has a section header as the first line of the section, with the section name contained in square brackets. In the preceding listing, the section name is [boot].

Settings in each section usually consist of a setting followed by an equal sign (=). On the right side of the equal sign is the value associated with the setting. In the preceding listing, the value shell=program.exe details the application name for the Windows 3.x program shell, which in this case is Program Manager. The value of a setting depends on the type of setting. Settings can be alphanumeric, numeric, and Boolean. Boolean settings are settings that are either On or Off, 1 or 0, or True or False. In general, a value of 1 or True is the same as On; a value of 0 or False is the same as Off.

To edit an INI file, you can use a text editor that saves files as ASCII text. You also can use a utility that comes with Windows 3.x called System Configuration Editor. It is stored in the Windows 3.x SYSTEM directory under the file name SYSCON.EXE. After you modify the INI file, you need to save the file and restart Windows NT for the changes to take effect because INI files do not flush the system as the Registry does.

Note   Before you make changes, you should consult a reference that details the various switches and setting value for a specific setting. If you still have Windows 3.x installed on your system, you can probably find the following text files that list setting changes you can make:

- ◆ **WININI.WRI.** Contains settings for the WIN.INI file.

- ◆ **SYSINI.WRI.** Contains settings for the SYSTEM.INI file.

- ◆ **NETWORKS.WRI.** Contains INI settings and other configuration data for Windows for Workgroups (WFWG or WFW) that might come in handy if you have WFWG in your workgroups.

- ◆ **MAIL.WRI.** Contains INI settings and other configuration data for WFWG's electronic mail application. Again, these settings can rescue you during those configuration nightmares you might have at times.

Role of INI Files in Windows 3.x

The primary INI files in Windows 3.x are WIN.INI, SYSTEM.INI, PROGMAN.INI, CONTROL.INI, and WINFILE.INI. By understanding these main INI files, you get a grasp on the performance and configuration of your system. When you upgrade to Windows NT from Windows 3.x, the SYSTEM.INI, WIN.INI, and WINFILE.INI files still remain in your Windows NT *%SystemRoot%* folder for compatibility reasons and device driver settings. Even though these files still remain on your system, all their settings are mapped to the Registry in the following key:

HKEY_LOCAL_MACHINE\SOFTWARE\Microsoft\Windows NT\ CurrentVersion\IniFileMapping

In this chapter's section called "INI Files and the Windows NT Registry," you see which settings from a few other INI files are actually sent to the Registry when you upgrade to Windows NT.

Note If you administer Windows 95 clients on your Windows NT network, look at the section "INI Files and the Windows 95 Registry" later in this chapter for information on how INI files are mapped in the Windows 95 Registry.

WIN.INI

The WIN.INI file contains settings that control Windows 3.x at an operating level. That is, WIN.INI primarily controls the way Windows appears and interacts with the user. Typical settings in WIN.INI define the fonts that are installed, the colors used on the desktop, port settings, document and program file associations, and other services.

Table 3.1 shows the default WIN.INI sections.

TABLE 3.1
Default WIN.INI Settings in Windows 3.x

Section Name	Function
[Windows]	Contains entries that Windows automatically launches upon start up, such as a custom shell application. Also has settings that control keyboard, mouse, and sound items.
[Desktop]	Contains wallpaper settings, as well as entries that control the spacing of icons and visual attributes of the interface.
[Extensions]	Contains file extensions that Windows recognizes as being associated with specific applications.
[intl]	Contains settings that specify the way items are displayed based on the country setting. This section controls time, date, currency values, and other settings.
[ports]	Contains all the I/O ports available on your system.
[fonts]	Shows the screen font files that are loaded by Windows. If you add new font files to the system, this entry can be used to load the new files automatically.
[fontsubstitutes]	Lists fonts that are recognized by Windows as being interchangeable. This feature was not fully used in Windows 3.x as it is in many Windows NT applications.
[TrueType]	Contains options that determine how TrueType fonts are used and displayed.
[mci extensions]	Shows file types associated with multimedia devices.
[networks]	Contains network settings and previous network connections.
[embedding]	Specifies client server associations for OLE activities.
[Windows Help]	Contains settings that control colors used by Help text, window size, and window position.
[sounds]	Contains lists of associated system events and associated sounds.

Section Name	Function
[PrinterPorts]	Shows the printers and ports you have installed. You can find the default values in the [Windows] section.
[devices]	Is used only by Windows 2.x applications and is almost identical to the [PrinterPorts] section. If you're still using Windows 2.x applications, you should invest in a newer application or newer version of the application to take advantage of recent advancements in Windows NT. Also, review the Windows NT Hardware Compatibility Guide to see if your hardware runs with Windows NT.
[programs]	Contains entries for additional paths that Windows searches in addition to the system path. This is used so Windows 3.x can locate program files when you open an associated document file.
[colors]	Contains listings for colors used to display the Windows screen interface.
[WinPopup]	Includes settings that specify the characteristics of a popup message.
[WinSetup]	Includes settings used by Windows Setup.

The WIN.INI file controls the appearance of Windows and its use of resources, such as the color of the desktop. The SYSTEM.INI file, on the other hand, defines the system resources used by Windows, such as which video device driver to use. The SYSTEM.INI file is covered in the following section.

SYSTEM.INI

SYSTEM.INI is another system INI file found in Windows 3.x. (Windows NT 4 also uses the SYSTEM.INI for compatibility to older software and hardware devices.) Settings in the SYSTEM.INI file include many that define the hardware drivers Windows uses, others that control hardware configuration, and many that control the way Windows performed in either Standard mode or 386 Enhanced mode.

Table 3.2 shows the standard sections in SYSTEM.INI.

TABLE 3.2
Default SYSTEM.INI Settings in Windows 3.x

Section Name	Function
[boot]	Contains list of device drivers and program modules that Windows 3.x uses to configure itself each time you boot.
[boot.description]	Contains list of the devices you can change when using the Windows Setup program.
[drivers]	Contains list of alias names that are assigned to installable driver files.
[keyboard]	Contains configuration information about the keyboard, including entries to identify nonstandard keyboards and different keyboard configurations.
[Network]	Contains settings that affect how your computer interacts with the network.
[Network Drivers]	Contains information used for running the real-mode network drivers to connect to the network.
[Password List]	Contains settings that specify the location of the password-list files for each user who logs on to your computer. The password-list file contains a list of the passwords you use to connect to password-protected resources.
[mci]	Contains list of Multimedia Command Interface (MCI) device drivers.
[NonWindowsApp]	Contains setup information that is used by DOS applications when you run them in Windows.
[standard]	Contains list of settings that Windows uses when running in Standard mode, such as memory-management settings.
[386Enc]	Contains settings that Windows uses when running in 386 Enhanced mode.

You'll see in the section called "INI Files and the Windows NT Registry" later in this chapter how Windows NT modifies and adds to the SYSTEM.INI file.

WINFILE.INI

In Windows 3.x, the WINFILE.INI file stores information relating to the File Manager, including two main sections, [Addons] and [Settings]. The [Addons] section lists any add-on utilities that work with File Manager, such as the ever-popular WinZip application. The [Settings] section includes information about the behavior of File Manager, such as whether Windows 3.x prompts you for confirmation on deleting or copying files. In Windows 3.11 for Workgroups, it also includes toolbar placement information.

PROGMAN.INI

PROGMAN.INI stores information about the Windows 3.x Program Manager. The settings in PROGMAN.INI control the size and position of Program Manager's window, store some of its operating options, specify the name of the Startup group, define the groups that Program Manager displays, and include options to restrict Program Manager's features. If you upgrade from Windows 95 to Windows NT and don't have an existing version of PROGMAN.INI on your system, you might not have settings for PROGMAN.INI mapped to the Windows NT Registry.

The sections that appear in PROGMAN.INI are listed in table 3.3.

TABLE 3.3
Default PROGMAN.INI Settings in Windows 3.x

Section Name	Function
[settings]	Contains settings to define the position and size of Program Manager's window, to set Program Manager options, and to define the name of the Startup group.
[groups]	Contains the program groups that Program Manager displays.
[restrictions]	This is an optional group in which you can control settings that limit Program Manager. Some of the restrictions include disabling Exit Windows, Run, and Save Settings on Exit commands on the File menu (similar to some of the features you can limit with system policies in Windows NT).

CONTROL.INI

Finally, the CONTROL.INI file in Windows 3.x stores information relating to Control Panel settings. These settings include color schemes, background patterns, descriptions of drivers installed, and other items. When you first install Windows NT, it adopts color schemes from your previous Windows 3.x installation by migrating CONTROL.INI settings (see fig. 3.1) to the following subkey:

HKEY_LOCAL_MACHINE\SOFTWARE\Microsoft\Windows NT\CurrentVersion\ IniFileMapping\control.ini subkey

Figure 3.1

Some of the CONTROL.INI settings originally from Windows 3.x are mapped to the Windows NT Registry.

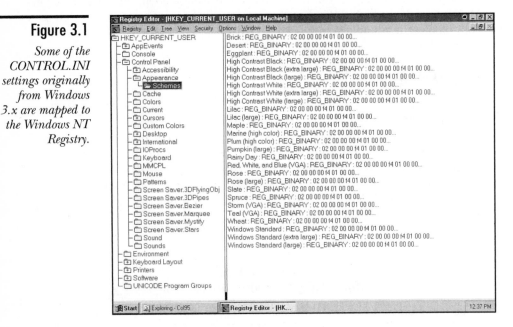

You can find out the color schemes settings, for example, that mapped from CONTROL.INI by looking for the Color Schemes: REG_SZ: #USR:Control Panel\Color Schemes entry in the preceding subkey. The value that Windows NT uses for the current user is found in a different location, however, as you learned in Chapter 2, "Understanding the Windows NT Registry Structure." You can find this information in HKEY_CURRENT_USER\Control Panel\Appearance\Schemes. The settings from the CONTROL.INI file when you upgrade from Windows 3.x are mapped to a default setting for new users that are added to the local machine. This is denoted by the # symbol that precedes the #USR: value.

INI Files and the Windows NT Registry

Although the majority of configuration tasks you need to perform are done through the Windows NT Control Panel, setup applications, the Registry, and applications, you still might need to edit INI files to make an application function properly. The more you replace older Win16 applications with Win32 applications, however, the less you need to worry about this.

The way in which Windows NT decides whether an application uses the Registry or an INI file is a simple process. For Win32 applications that want to meet the Microsoft specifications for Windows NT-compliant software, the Registry Application Programming Interfaces (APIs) must be used instead of creating INI files. Many applications being developed now are moving away from the INI settings and are using the Registry APIs. Some application programmers, however, still rely on the INI file as they create initial builds of software and distribute code as Beta software. As the application nears completion, the code is usually modified to use the Registry.

For Win16 applications installed under Windows NT, the story is a little different. These applications do not write to the Registry because they cannot use the Registry APIs for Win32. Win16 applications, therefore, must use INI files stored on the Windows NT system.

Regardless of the type of application you run, Windows NT always looks in the Registry first to see if a setting is mapped there for the application. When an application launches, Windows NT looks under the HKEY_LOCAL_MACHINE\SOFTWARE key for mapping information. The system first looks for a mapping of the initialization file, such as msmail32.ini, in the IniFileMapping subkey. If a match is found, the system looks under the mapped key for the specific application name and a variable name. If a variable name is given, the system looks for keys whose value entries are the variable names. The system then reads and writes the contents of the key to run the application. If no mapping for the application name or file name is found, the system looks for an INI file to control the application.

Note   When you run MS-DOS based and 16-bit Windows applications under Windows NT, they run inside a Windows NT virtual MS-DOS machine (usually referred to as a VDM). Devices such as the mouse, keyboard, COM ports, networks, and others that are needed by the VDM use virtual device drivers (usually referred to as VDDs). VDD information is stored in the Registry in the following key and is updated by the system:

HKEY_LOCAL_MACHINE\SYSTEM\CurrentControlSet\Control\VirtualDeviceDrivers

SYSTEM.INI, WIN.INI, and application-specific INI files still exist in Windows NT for compatibility, as do CONFIG.SYS and AUTOEXEC.BAT. (Actually, only the Set, Prompt, and Path commands of the AUTOEXEC.BAT file are used by Windows NT itself.) Win16 APIs that manipulate and use INI files still work under Windows NT. Win32-based applications, however, use the Registry APIs to store their application information. Many existing Win16-based applications will look for and sometimes modify the WIN.INI and SYSTEM.INI files to load drivers and set configuration parameters. When Windows NT boots, it still looks for any INI files called for by applications or hardware devices.

The following sections detail which INI files and INI settings are mapped to the Windows NT Registry. Because not all settings map to the Registry, you might find that some settings remain in the INI file instead of mapping to an equivalent Registry setting. These sections highlight the most common INI files on users' computers, including SYSTEM.INI, WIN.INI, CONTROL.INI, WINFILE.INI, and PROGMAN.INI.

Migrating SYSTEM.INI Entries to the Registry

As you read earlier, in Windows 3.x the SYSTEM.INI file was responsible for storing and maintaining many of Windows' configuration options. In Windows NT, this is handled primarily by the Registry. When you upgrade your Windows 3.x system to Windows NT, the Setup routine migrates many of the settings in SYSTEM.INI to the Registry.

When Windows NT migrates settings to the Registry, it uses special symbols to control how an INI setting is used. These symbols are described in table 3.4.

TABLE 3.4
Symbols Placed in Mapped INI Settings

Symbol	Explanation
USR:	Maps setting to the HKEY_CURRENT_USER key. Settings after the USR: symbol are relative to that key, such as USR:Software\Microsoft\Mail.
SYS:	Maps setting to the HKEY_LOCAL_MACHINE\ Software key. Settings after the SYS: symbol are relative to that key, such as SYS:\Microsoft\Windows NT\CurrentVersion\ Network\SMAddOns.
@	Instructs Windows NT not to read data from the associated INI file if the data is not found in the Registry.
#	Sets the Registry value for a new user to the same value set in the Windows 3.x INI file on system a that had Windows 3.x previously installed.
!	Instructs the Registry to write data to both the Registry and associated INI file.

As you learned earlier, the SYSTEM.INI files are mapped to the following Registry key:

HKEY_LOCAL_MACHINE\SOFTWARE\Microsoft\Windows NT\
CurrentVersion\WOW

Figure 3.2 illustrates this mapping.

Figure 3.2

SYSTEM.INI settings are mapped to the Windows NT Registry.

Table 3.5 lists all SYSTEM.INI sections and the Registry path to which they are mapped.

TABLE 3.5
Mapped SYSTEM.INI Settings in Windows NT

Section	Mapped Registry Path	Common Values or Keys
[boot]	HKEY_LOCAL_MACHINE\ SOFTWARE\Microsoft\Windows NT\CurrentVersion\WOW\bool	comm.drv, display.drv, drivers, fixedfon.fon, fonts.fon, keyboard.drv, language.dll, mouse.drv, network.drv, oemfonts.fon, shell, sound.drv, system.drv

continues

TABLE 3.5, CONTINUED
Mapped SYSTEM.INI Settings in Windows NT

Section	Mapped Registry Path	Common Values or Keys
[boot.description]	HKEY_LOCAL_MACHINE\ SOFTWARE\Microsoft\ Windows NT\CurrentVersion\ WOW\boot.description	display.drv, keyboard.typ, language.dll, mouse.drv, network.drv, system.drv
[keyboard]	HKEY_LOCAL_MACHINE\ SOFTWARE\Microsoft\Windows NT\CurrentVersion\WOW\keyboard and	keyboard.dll, subtype, type
	HKEY_CURRENT_USER\ KeyboardLayout	\Preload and \Substitutes subkeys
[mci]	HKEY_LOCAL_MACHINE\ SOFTWARE\Microsoft\Windows NT\CurrentVersion\MCI and	AVIVideo, CDAudio, Sequencer, WaveAudio
	HKEY_LOCAL_MACHINE\ SOFTWARE\Microsoft\Windows NT\CurrentVersion\MCI Extensions	AVI, MID, RMI, WAV
[mci32]	HKEY_LOCAL_MACHINE\ SOFTWARE\Microsoft\Windows NT\CurrentVersion\MCI32	AVIVideo, CDAudio, Sequencer, WaveAudio
[NonWindows Apps]	HKEY_LOCAL_MACHINE\ SOFTWARE\Microsoft\Windows NT\CurrentVersion\WOW\Non WindowsApps	CommandEnvSize
[standard]	HKEY_LOCAL_MACHINE\ SOFTWARE\Microsoft\Windows NT\CurrentVersion\WOW\standard	(Windows NT handles all memory management for standard and 386 enhanced MS-DOS applications)

Migrating WIN.INI Entries to the Registry

Similar to the way Windows NT migrates some of the settings in SYSTEM.INI, the same is true with the WIN.INI file. The WIN.INI file contains many of the display, keyboard, and mouse configuration parameters for Windows 3.x. When you upgrade your system, Windows NT assumes you want many of the same settings you had in the previous Windows installation. It can do this by migrating some entries from WIN.INI over to the Registry during the Windows NT Setup stage. Table 3.6 lists those settings that migrated from WIN.INI to the Registry.

TABLE 3.6
Many WIN.INI Settings are Mapped to the Windows NT Registry.

Section	Mapped Registry Path	Common Values or Keys
[colors]	HKEY_CURRENT_USER\ Control Panel\Colors	(See figure 3.3 for list)
[compatibility]	HKEY_LOCAL_MACHINE\ SOFTWARE\Microsoft\ Windows NT\CurrentVersion\ Compatibility	AMIPRO, CCMAIL, CORELPNT, DESIGNER, EXCEL, MCOURIER, MYST, PACKRAT, and more
[desktop]	HKEY_CURRENT_USER\ Desktop	AutoEndTask, CoolSwitch, CoolSwitchColumns, IconSpacing, IconTitleSize, Pattern, and more; added \WindowMetrics subkey, with BorderWidth value
[extensions]	HKEY_CURRENT_USER\ SOFTWARE\Microsoft\ Windows NT\CurrentVersion\ Extensions	BMP, CRD, GRA, INI, PCX, REC, SET, TRM, TXT, WRI, WTX
[fonts]	HKEY_LOCAL_MACHINE\ SOFTWARE\Microsoft\ Windows NT\CurrentVersion\ Fonts	Values for all fonts
[fontSubstitutes]	HKEY_LOCAL_MACHINE\ SOFTWARE\Microsoft\ Windows NT\CurrentVersion\ FontSubstitutes	Helv, Helvetica, MS Shell Dlg, Times, Tms Rmn
[intl]	HKEY_CURRENT_USER\ Control Panel\International	iCountry, iCurrDigits, iDate, Locale, sCountry, sShortDate, and more; adds \Sorting Order subkey
[mci extensions]	HKEY_LOCAL_MACHINE\ SOFTWARE\Microsoft\ Windows NT\CurrentVersion\ MCI Extensions	AVI, MID, RMI, WAV

continues

TABLE 3.6, CONTINUED
Many WIN.INI settings are mapped to the Windows NT Registry.

Section	Mapped Registry Path	Common Values or Keys
[network]	HKEY_CURRENT_USER\ SOFTWARE\Microsoft\ Windows NT\CurrentVersion\ Network\Persistent Connections and	· SaveConnections
	HKEY_LOCAL_MACHINE\ SYSTEM\CurrentControlSet\ Control\Print	Subkeys for network printers.
[ports]	HKEY_LOCAL_MACHINE\ SOFTWARE\Microsoft\ Windows NT\CurrentVersion\ Ports	COM1, COM2, COM3, COM4, FILE, LPT1, LPT2, LPT3
[printerPorts]	HKEY_CURRENT_USER\ SOFTWARE\Microsoft\ Windows NT\CurrentVersion\ PrinterPorts	Printer names, such as HP LaserJet V
[devices]	HKEY_CURRENT_USER\ SOFTWARE\Microsoft\ Windows NT\CurrentVersion\	Device names, such as HP LaserJet V
[sounds]	HKEY_CURRENT_USER\ Control Panel\Sounds	SystemDefault
[TrueType]	HKEY_CURRENT_USER\ SOFTWARE\Microsoft\ Windows NT\CurrentVersion\ True Type	TTEnable, TTonly
[Windows Help]	HKEY_CURRENT_USER\ Software\Microsoft\ Windows Help	H_WindowPosition, M_WindowPosition, Maximized, Xl, Xr, Yd, Yu
[Windows]	HKEY_LOCAL_MACHINE\ SOFTWARE\Microsoft\ Windows NT\CurrentVersion\ WinLogin	AutoAdminLogon, AutoRestartShell, CachePrimaryDomain, LegalNoticeCaption, PowerdownAfterShutdown, System, and more

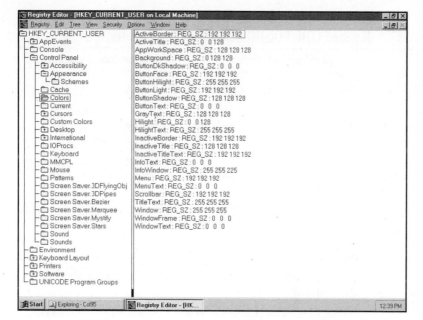

Figure 3.3

Settings from the [colors] section of WIN.INI are mapped to the Windows NT Registry.

Other INI Settings in the Windows NT Registry

Upon setup, Windows NT also maps some other INI settings of which you might want to be aware. Primarily, the CONTROL.INI, WINFILE.INI, and PROGMAN.INI files place some of their entries in the Registry. The WINFILE.INI file, for instance, places the [settings] section in the HKEY_CURRENT_USER\SOFTWARE\Microsoft\File Manager for Explorer settings. Also, the following PROGMAN.INI sections are added to the Registry:

◆ **[groups].** Moves to HKEY_CURRENT_USER\SOFTWARE\Microsoft\Windows NT\CurrentVersion\Program Manager\Common Groups.

◆ **[restrictions].** Moves to HKEY_CURRENT_USER\SOFTWARE\ Microsoft\ Windows NT\CurrentVersion\ Program Manager\Restrictions.

◆ **[settings].** Moves to HKEY_CURRENT_USER\SOFTWARE\Microsoft\Windows NT\CurrentVersion\ Program Manager\Settings

Table 3.7 lists the CONTROL.INI settings you can find in the Windows NT Registry.

TABLE 3.7
Mapped CONTROL.INI Settings in Windows NT

Section	Mapped Registry Path	Common Values or Keys
[Current]	HKEY_CURRENT_USER\Control Panel\Current	ColorSchemes
[Color Schemes]	HKEY_CURRENT_USER\Control Panel\Appearance\Schemes	Brick, Desert, Maple, Pumpkin, Slate, and more
[Custom Colors]	HKEY_CURRENT_USER\Control Panel\Custom Colors	ColorA, ColorB, ColorC, and so on
[Drivers.Desc]	HKEY_LOCAL_MACHINE\ SOFTWARE\Microsoft\ WindowsNT\CurrentVersion\ drivers.desc	Each driver has its own key and entries
[MMCPL]	HKEY_CURRENT_USER\Control Panel\MMCPL	Current MMCPL settings
[Patterns]	HKEY_CURRENT_USER\Control Panel\Patterns	(None), 50% Gray, Boxes, Critters, Scottie, Weave, and more
[Screen Saver]	HKEY_CURRENT_USER\Control Panel\Screen Saver.*nnn*	Each screen saver has its own key with its own entries
[Userinstall-able.drivers]	HKEY_LOCAL_MACHINE\ SOFTWARE\Microsoft\ WindowsNT\CurrentVersion\ Userinstallable.drivers	List of user installable drivers

Note If you run OS/2 version 1 applications, you can find their Registry entries in the following key:

HKEY_LOCAL_MACHINE\SYSTEM\CurrentControlSet\Control\Session Manager\SubSystem

You've just seen how Windows NT handles many of the INI file settings common in previous versions of Windows and in older applications and devices. Knowing to where these settings migrate is critical for anyone who must administer and trouble-shoot Windows NT. In fact, it might be several years before every Windows NT installation has rid itself of 16-bit applications that still rely on INI files.

The next section is similar to the one you just read but focuses on the Windows 95 Registry. If you work with Windows 95 workstations connected to your network, you more than likely will need to know how Windows 95 handles INI settings. This is especially true if you use Windows 95 as a client workstation because of its capability to support more legacy software and hardware. If this is the case, you'll definitely need to understand the following information for system-wide administration and troubleshooting duties.

Administering INI Mappings in Windows 95 Clients

If you administer Windows 95 clients on your network, you might need to view or alter INI mappings for a workstation. Although the Windows 95 subsystem uses the Registry in a manner similar to that of Windows NT, you do find some differences in the way INI file settings are mapped to the Registry.

One of the INI files you are likely to modify in Windows 95 is the WRKGRP.INI file. This file is similar to the WRKGRP.INI file in Windows for Workgroups, but it contains new entries for Windows 95 features and writes its data to the Windows 95 Registry. The time you usually modify this file is when you are performing custom installations on Windows 95. WRKGRP.INI contains a list of workgroups that users can join and is usually stored in the Windows directory on the server that contains the source files for Windows 95.

WRKGRP.INI contains two sections: [Options] and [Workgroups]. The [Workgroups] section is optional and can specify the workgroup that a user can select and automatically map to based on values listed in the [Options] section.

The following list describes each of the sections and valid entries for the [Options] section:

◆ **ANSI=true or false.** This setting directs Windows to convert workgroups from an OEM character set to ANSI. By default, this setting is false.

◆ **Require=true or false.** This setting either enables users to create their own workgroup name (denoted as false), or forces them to choose from the listed workgroups (denoted as true). The default is true.

◆ **ForceMapping=true or false.** If set to false, this setting enables users to change the workgroup, preferred server, and logon domain that are set by a mapping. If set to true, users cannot change these settings. The default is true.

◆ **Mapping=*network_providers.*** This setting enables administrators to specify a list of the network providers to which workgroups can be mapped. This entry is optional. The *network_providers* parameter can include one or several network providers, each separated with a comma (but no spaces). The order in which you list these providers will be the order in which values are listed in the [Workgroups] section. The Registry reads this setting to know where to store specific settings for each user.

◆ **Default=*network_providers_default.*** If a workgroup listed in the [Workgroups] section does not have a default, you can specify the default here. This is an optional setting. Like the preceding entry, you can have one or several network providers listed here, each of which is separated by commas (no spaces). You can have, for instance, a single entry to a Windows for Workgroups WRKGRP.INI file for minimal mapping functionality.

The other WRKGRP.INI setting you can include is the [Workgroups] setting. The syntax for this section looks like the following:

*workgroup=**optional_mapping***

You can include numerous *optional_mapping* values by separating each mapping with a comma (but no space). Windows 95 workgroups can be mapped to Windows NT and NetWare servers by default. Other workgroups can be included by obtaining network provider software from the network manufacturer. The following is an example of the way you might set up this line for a network with a Microsoft Network provider named MSNET1 and a workgroup named NEW_RIDERS.

```
[options]
NEW_RIDERS=MSNET1
```

For any other network providers, such as if you add a NetWare provider to this named NWARE1, it looks like the following:

```
NEW_RIDERS=MSNET1,NWARE1
```

You then can use the values in the preceding examples to denote default mappings for a Windows for Workgroups 3.11 WRKGRP.INI file you have on the network. The following line inserted into the [Workgroups] section would use the servers MSNET1 and NWARE1 as the default mapping for the WFWG network:

```
Default=MSNET1,NWARE1
```

Other changes you make to INI files, whether they are related to networking or another environment setting, are usually done case by case.

Tip   With Windows 95, you might find there are several times you have to edit INI file settings. This can become an`arduous task for installations with many networked PCs. By relying on your experience modifying INI files, you can write a MSBATCH.INF script file that includes a section to change certain configuration settings upon Setup. This script can, for instance, remove lines you don't need in a certain INI file before you even start the Setup procedure.

The next sections show the INI file settings that migrate to the Windows 95 Registry. Use this information to isolate problems with legacy applications and hardware devices.

Migrating SYSTEM.INI Settings to the Windows 95 Registry

When you upgrade your Windows 3.x system to Windows 95, the Setup routine migrates many of the settings in SYSTEM.INI to the Registry.

Tip   Another time to be aware of the SYSTEM.INI and WIN.INI files is when you have a shared installation on your network. In the machine directory, which is the directory that contains configuration files for specific computers, you'll store WIN.COM, the Registry, and SYSTEM.INI and WIN.INI. If you use a server-based setup to install Windows 95 on several machines, Setup automatically creates the machine directory and places the necessary INI files in it.

Table 3.8 shows the entries added or moved from SYSTEM.INI to the Windows 95 Registry. The column on the left shows the bracketed section from SYSTEM.INI, with the entry that is placed in the Registry in the right column. The middle column, called Event, lets you know what happens to that particular section entry. As with the INI settings in Windows NT, not all INI settings are mapped to the Windows 95 Registry.

TABLE 3.8
SYSTEM.INI Updates

Section	Event	Entry
[Boot]	Added	user.exe=user.exe
		sound.drv=sound.drv
		gdi.exe=gdi.exe
		dibeng.drv=dibeng.dll
		comm.drv=comm.drv

continues

TABLE 3.8, CONTINUED
SYSTEM.INI Updates

Section	Event	Entry
[boot]	Remain in SYSTEM.INI	386grabber=*filename* * display.drv= drivers=filename * fixedfon.fon=*filename* * fonts.fon=*filename* * keyboard.drv= language.dll=*library_name* * mouse.drv= network.drv= oemfonts.font=*filename* * shell=*filename* * system.drv=*filename* * TaskMan.Exe=*filename* *
[386Enh]	Remain in SYSTEM.INI	AllEMSLocked= AllXMSLocked= AltKeyDelay= AltPasteDelay= Device=*filename* * DMABufferSize Display= DOSPromptExitInstructions KeybdPasswd= * Keyboard= KeyPasteCRSkipCount= KeyPasteKeyDelay= KeyPasteTimeout= Local= * Local Reboot= * MaxDMAPGAddress= MaxPagingFileSize= MessageBackColor= * MessageTextColor= * MinUserDiskSpace= Mouse= NetAsyncTimeOut= * NetAsyncFallback * NetDMASize= * Paging= PagingDrive= PasteSkipCount= * ScrollFrequency=

Section	Event	Entry
[386Enh]	Added	device=*vcd device=*vshare device=*intl13 device=*dynapage
[386Enh]	Deleted	device=*serial.386 device=*configmg device=*vfd device=pagefile.386 device=lpt.386 timecriticalsection= device=isapnp.386 device=wshell.386 maxbps=
[386Enh]	Moved to Registry	Network3= Network= SecondNet= Transport= V86ModeLANAs
[drivers]	Remain in SYSTEM.INI	alias=*driver_filename* *
[Network]	Moved to Registry	AuditEnabled= AuditEvents= AuditLogSize= AutoLogon= Comment= ComputerName= DirectHost= EnableSharing= FileSharing= LANAs= LMAnnounce= LMLogon= LogonDisconnected= LogonDomain= LogonValidated= MaintainServerList= Multinet= PasswordCaching= PrintSharing= Reshare= SlowLANAs= Username= Winnet= Workgroup=

continues

TABLE 3.8, CONTINUED
SYSTEM.INI Updates

Section	Event	Entry
[mci]	Retained in SYSTEM.INI	(Entries created by application) *
[Network drivers]	Moved to Registry	DevDir= LoadRMDrivers= NetCard= Transport=
[NonWindowsApps]	Remain in SYSTEM.INI	CommandEnvSize=

* Indicates entries retained in SYSTEM.INI that are not supported in the user interface in Windows 95. All others that are retained are supported in the user interface.

Note During Windows 95 Setup, the lanabase= parameter from SYSTEM.INI is moved to the Registry. In SYSTEM.INI, this setting falls under the [nwnblink] section when you install Windows for Workgroups 3.11 with IPXODI.COM and LSL.COM support over Ethernet or Token Ring Networks. Also note that the [Password list] section does not move to the Registry or is deleted. It remains intact in SYSTEM.INI.

The entries that Windows 95 migrates from SYSTEM.INI to the Registry are stored in the HKEY_LOCAL_MACHINE subkey. You'll find many of these entries listed in table 3.9.

TABLE 3.9
Registry Subkeys for Migrated SYSTEM.INI Settings

Entry	HKEY_LOCAL_MACHINE\....
	[386Enh]
Network=	System\CurrentControlSet\Services\VxD\Vnetsetup
Transport=	System\CurrentControlSet\Services\VxD\trans-port_entry
	[Network]
Comment=	System\CurrentControlSet\Services\VxD\VxD\ Vnetsetup
ComputerName=	System\CurrentControlSet\Contro\ComputerName
EnableSharing=	System\CurrentControlSet\Services\VxD\Vnetsetup

Entry	HKEY_LOCAL_MACHINE\....
LMAnnounce=	System\CurrentControlSet\Services\VxD\Vnetsetup
LMLogon=	\Network\Logon
LogonDomain=	Network
LogonValidated=	Network\Logon
MaintainServerList=	System\CurrentControlSet\Services\VxD\Vnetsetup
Reshare=	System\CurrentControlSet\Network\LanMan*sharename*
Username=	Network\Logon
Winnet=	System\CurrentControlSet\Services\Class\ NetClient\00001\Ndir\Interfaces
Workgroup=	System\CurrentControlSet\Services\VxD\Vnetsetup
[Network drivers]	
DevDir=	Software\Microsoft\Windows\CurrentVersion\ Setup\WinBootDir
LoadRMDrivers=	Software\Microsoft\Windows\CurrentVersion\ Network\Real Mode Net
NetCard=	Software\Microsoft\Windows\CurrentVersion\ Network\Real Mode Net
Transport=	Software\Microsoft\Windows\CurrentVersion\ Network\Real Mode Net

Note When you install Windows 95 over an existing Windows 3.x installation, Windows 95 automatically converts program groups to the Start menu folder. These program groups are stored in files with the extension GRP and can be seen in the Registry subkey HKEY_CURRENT_USER\Software\Microsoft\Windows\CurrentVersion\ GrpConv\Groups.

Now that you've seen how Windows 95 handles SYSTEM.INI file settings, the following section focuses on the settings that migrate from the WIN.INI file to the Windows 95 Registry.

Migrating WIN.INI Settings during Setup

Table 3.10 shows which WIN.INI settings migrate to the Windows 95 Registry during the Windows 95 Setup.

TABLE 3.10
WIN.INI Updates

Section	Event	Entry
[desktop]	Moved to Registry	IconVerticalSpacing
[Windows]	Moved to Registry	Beep= BorderWidth= CursorBlinkRate= DoubleClickSpeed= KeyboardDelay= KeyboardSpeed= MouseThreshold1= MouseThreshold2= MouseSpeed= ScreenSaveActive= ScreenSaveTimeOut= SwapMouseButtons=
[Windows]	Retained in WIN.INI *	CursorBlinkRate= Device= DoubleClickHeight= DoubleClickWidth= DoubleClickSpeed KeyboardDelay= KeyboardSpeed= MouseSpeed= MouseTrails= SwapMouseButtons Load and Run= **
[WindowMetrics]	Moved to Registry	BorderWidth= CaptionHeight= CaptionWidth= MenuHeight= MenuWidth= MinArrange= MinHorzGap= MinVertGap= MinWidth= ScrollHeight= ScrollWidth= SmCaptionHeight= SmCaptionWidth=
[embedding]	Retained in WIN.INI	*object* **
[fonts]	Retained in WIN.INI	*font_name* *

Section	Event	Entry
[FontSubstitute]	Retained in WIN.INI	*font_name=font_name* **
[ports]	Retained in WIN.INI	*port_name* *
[Intl]	Retained in WIN.INI *	iCountry= iCurrDigits= iCurrency= iDate= iDigits= iLZero= iMeasure= iNegCurr= iTime= iTLZero= s1150= s2350= sCountry= sCurrency= sLanguage= sDecimal= sList= sShortDate= sLongDate= sThousand= sTime=
[Mail]	Retained in WIN.INI	MAPI= **
[mci extensions]	Retained in WIN.INI	*extensions* **
[PrinterPorts]	Retained in WIN.INI	*device_name*

* Indicates entries retained in WIN.INI that are supported in the user interface.
** Indicates entries retained in WIN.INI that are not supported in the
   user interface in Windows 95.

Note Regardless of the system under which you are operating, Setup adds the entry
ATMWorkaround=1 to the [Pscript.Drv] section. This entry is for the Adobe Type
Manager for Windows.

The way the WIN.INI entries are dispersed in the Registry is much more compact
compared to how SYSTEM.INI entries end up in the Registry. For the most part, the
entries in the [desktop] and [Windows] sections show up in the following Registry
hierarchy:

HKEY_CURRENT_USER\Control Panel\Desktop

For the [sounds] section in WIN.INI, Windows 95 migrates your settings to the HKEY_CURRENT_USER\AppEvents\Schemes\Apps*event*\current. An example of this branch is shown in figure 3.4.

Figure 3.4

An example of the [sounds] settings after migrating to the Registry.

The *event* subkey includes the .Default key, Explorer, Multimedia Player, Sound Recorder, and other system events you have installed. Under the .Default key you'll find the list of system events on your machine. This list is fairly long even when you don't customize the list using the Sounds icon in the Control Panel.

Other INI Files To Note

Two other INI files are of interest to administrators and support people. These are the PROTOCOL.INI and NETDET.INI files.

PROTOCOL.INI

PROTOCOL.INI contains information about network protocols used by Windows 95 and, if a network is previously installed, used by Windows for Workgroups. In fact, the PROTOCOL.INI file in Windows 95 is in the same format as that for WFWG. Entries in PROTOCOL.INI describe the settings for specific network protocols. In the following example, the [EXP16$] section refers to the Intel EtherExpress 16 network card. The following is an example of this file:

```
[nwlink$]
DriverName=nwlink$
Frame_Type=4
cachesize=0
Bindings=EXP16$

[NETBEUI$]
DriverName=NETBEUI$
Lanabase=1
sessions=10
ncbs=12
Bindings=EXP16$

[EXP16$]
DriverName=EXP16$
transceiver=Twisted-Pair (TPE)
iochrdy=Late
irq=11
ioaddress=0x300

[protman]
priority=ndishlp$
DriverName=protman$
```

During Windows 95 Setup, Windows 95 searches your system for the PROTOCOL.INI file. Setup looks in the Windows, Windows for Workgroups, and LAN Manager directories to make sure that, if you have this file, Setup reads it and finds any network adapter settings already configured. You can look at the entry for this detection phase by looking in the hardware detection log (DETLOG.TXT) file. The following is a snippet of detection log:

```
Checking for: 3Com EtherLink 16 Network Adapter
; path to WFW protocol.INI
WFW: path=c:\wfwg\protocol.ini
; protocol.ini mac driver section
```

Once found, this data is stored in the HKEY_LOCAL_MACHINE\Enum\Network Registry subkey.

You might need to reference the PROTOCOL.INI file if you experience system problems during the Setup phase. Make sure that the file is properly formatted and that each setting is correctly set.

NETDET.INI

NETDET.INI is another INI file you might want to become acquainted with or reacquainted with when you start supporting Windows 95. NETDET.INI contains network detection settings used for network drivers and cards that are not as common as others. If you use common network drivers, such as IPX/SPX, TCP/IP, and NetBIOS/NetBEUI, you usually don't have to use the NETDET.INI file. Entries in the NETDET.INI file relate to information about the way network drivers communicate.

The following snippet of entries includes different behaviors for running with a NetWare network:

```
;;;;;; NOVELL Directory Services VLM 4.x ;;;;;;;;;
[VLM]
detection0=custom_dll
detection_dll=NETOS.DLL
detection_call=NW_IsNDSinUse
full_install0=prevent

;;;;;; IPX MONO Detection ;;;;;;;;;
[IPXMONO]
detection0=custom_dll
detection_dll=NETDI.DLL
detection_call=NW_IsIpxMonoOnlyCard
full_install0=prevent

;;;;;;;;;;; SOURCE ROUTING FOR NETWARE ;;;;;;;;;
[ROUTE]
detection0=mcb
full_install0=remove,gen_install(NWSRCR)

 [NWSRCR]
AddReg=NWSRCR.reg
UpdateInis=NWSRCR_INI

 [NWSRCR.reg]
HKLM,System\CurrentControlSet\Services\VxD\NWLINK,cachesize,,"16"
HKLM,System\CurrentControlSet\Services\VxD\NWLINK\Ndi\params\cachesize,"",,"16"

 [NWSRCR_INI]
%26%\protocol.ini,NWLINK$,,"cachesize=16"
```

```
;;;;;;; NOVELL Named-Pipes Support ;;;;;;;;;;;;;;;
[DOSNP.EXE]
detection0=mcb,mcb_nobat
protstack_install0=prevent
detection1=mcb_nobat
full_install1=prevent

;;;;;; NOVELL NETBIOS ;;;;;;;;;;;;;;;;;;
[NETBIOS]
detection0=mcb
full_install0=remove,install_devnode(NWNBLINK)

;;;;;; NOVELL Personal Netware ;;;;;;;
[SERVER.EXE]
detection0=mcb
full_install0=prevent
```

Like the PROTOCOL.INI file, you should not have to directly modify the NETDET. INI file on a normal basis. Most of its settings are determined when you install applications and hardware devices that affect it. You might, however, want to keep this file in mind if you run into problems with a network device for which Windows 95 does not have built-in support.

Summary

One of the promises of Windows NT and future Windows operating systems is to eliminate INI files and centralize configuration files. This chapter pointed out the key differences between INI files and Registry settings and also included the INI settings that are migrated to the Registry during installation. Even on a clean Windows NT installation (one that is not an upgrade to a previous MS-DOS–based Windows installation), you'll find a few INI files (namely SYSTEM.INI and WIN.INI) on your system. This chapter also showed you the INI files that migrate to the Windows 95 Registry.

CHAPTER
4

Using the Windows NT Registry Editor

he best way to discover the complexities and power of the
Registry is to run the Registry Editor and meet the Registry
face-to-face. The Registry Editor provides the capability to
view, edit, search, print, and export Windows NT Registry.

This chapter identifies how to start, run, and work in the Registry
Editor. Specifically, it covers the following:

◆ Running the Registry Editor

◆ Examining the Registry interface

◆ Searching for specific Registry data

◆ Editing Registry settings

◆ Setting security options

◆ Printing Registry keys and branches

Introducing the Registry Editor

Try this. Call Microsoft's technical support line and ask a Registry question. Not surprisingly, the support staff tells you that Microsoft does not support Registry problems and that users should not edit the Registry. Why, then, does Microsoft provide the Registry Editor, which clearly enables you to do just that (see fig. 4.1)? Further, if Microsoft did not want mere mortals like us tampering with the Registry, why is the Registry Editor so easy to use?

Figure 4.1

The Registry Editor—one of the keys to customizing Windows NT.

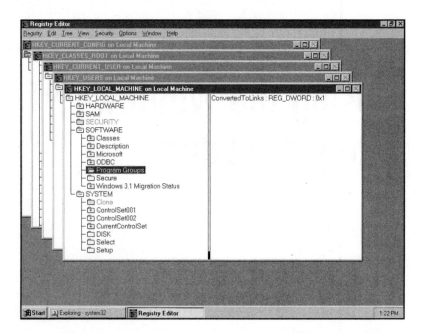

Perhaps one reason that Microsoft *does* want you to have the capability of editing the Registry is because it's the last line of defense against something really going wrong with your system. The other ways that you can troubleshoot and reconfigure Windows NT include the Control Panel applications, such as Server, System, Network, and other tools, as well as the administrative tools in the Administrative Tools (Common) folder. Microsoft doesn't want to *officially* support the Registry because users who want to customize and optimize Windows would be ringing Microsoft's phone off the hook.

Fortunately, the Registry Editor is available and actually installed by Windows NT Setup. You might need to find it on your system in the *%SystemRoot%*\system32 folder because it doesn't create a shortcut or application icon in your Start menu.

The first main section within this quick introduction into the Registry gets you started running the Registry by showing how to acquire original access to it, how to create a shortcut to it, and finally, how to create an application icon for it in the Start menu. The next main section offers a quick tour of the Registry's interface. The final main section shows how to view value entries.

Stop

As noted, the Registry Editor is quite simple to use. What isn't simple is ensuring that the edits and modifications you make to your working Registry database are the correct ones for your machine. For this reason, don't make any edits until you've read Chapter 1, "Introducing Windows NT Registry." That chapter shows you when to modify the Registry and offers some tips on making the editing process more successful. Otherwise, you might end up making changes that corrupt the configuration settings of your machine, causing it not to boot or run properly. The key is to at least make a backup of your Registry in case you need to return to it from the DOS command line.

Running the Registry Editor

Before you run the Registry Editor, you need to find it on your system. When you install Windows NT, the file REGEDT32.EXE installs in your Windows NT \system32 folder. Locate REGEDIT32.EXE on your system and double-click on it to start. You can also enter the path of your Windows NT folder and \REGEDT32.EXE on the Open line of the Run dialog box from the Start menu.

Note

Windows NT actually installs two versions of the Registry Editor: REGEDT32.EXE and REGEDIT.EXE. REGEDT32.EXE is the Windows NT version of the Registry Editor. The other version, REGEDIT.EXE is either the Windows 95 version or the Windows 3.x version of Registry Editor. The Windows 3.x version installs if you upgraded a previous version of Windows 3.x to Windows NT, or if Windows NT detects that a version of Windows 3.x is installed in a Windows 3.x folder. Otherwise, Windows NT installs the Windows 95 version of the Registry Editor. Regardless of the version that installs, it is placed in the %*SystemRoot*% folder.

If you have the Windows 3.x version of the Registry Editor installed, you can install the Windows 95 version by copying the REGEDIT.EXE, REGEDIT.HLP, and REGEDIT.CNT files from the Windows NT CD-ROM to any folder other than %*SystemRoot*%. To help you understand how to run the Windows 95 Registry Editor, see the section later in this chapter entitled "Using the Windows 95 Registry Editor."

The best way to start the Registry Editor, however, is to place it on the Start menu or create a shortcut to it on you desktop. This gives you virtually instant access to it whenever you want. Create a shortcut to it by dragging the REGEDT32.EXE file to your desktop from Explorer. To place the Registry Editor on the Start menu, however, use the following steps, which are a bit more involved than creating a shortcut:

1. Right-click on the Start menu and select Open from the context menu.

2. In the Start menu folder, select File, New, and then enter the path to REGEDT32.EXE in the Command Line box (see fig. 4.2). Use Browse to find the file if you are not sure what its path is.

Figure 4.2

The Start menu folder.

3. Click on Next. Rename the shortcut to Registry Editor and click on Finish. If you use both the Windows NT and Windows 95 or Windows 3.x Registry Editors, assign a name to the Windows NT Registry Editor that helps differentiate it, such as Registry Editor 32.

Now when you click on the Start menu, the Registry Editor icon appears at the top of the menu (see fig. 4.3).

Start the Registry Editor now so that you can begin to uncover its features and capabilities. Your screen looks similar to the one shown in figure 4.4. At first, the Registry Editor might look intimidating and complicated, but it becomes more approachable when you dissect its individual parts and understand their uses.

When the Registry Editor starts, it displays the entire Registry database all together. To get an idea of the files that make up the Registry, read Chapter 1, "Introducing the Windows NT Registry."

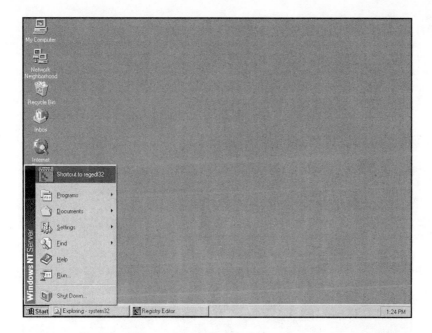

Figure 4.3

The Registry Editor can be placed on the Start menu for quick access.

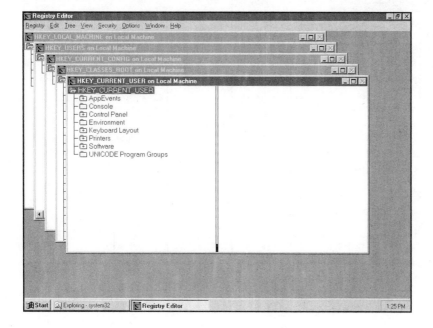

Figure 4.4

The Windows NT Registry Editor.

Examining the Registry Editor Interface

As a quick reference to using the Registry Editor, this section shows and describes each feature of the Registry Editor. Later sections describe how to use each of these features to modify or navigate your Windows NT Registry.

The Registry Editor has four main areas (see fig. 4.5):

◆ **Menu bar.** Displays the four menus: Registry, Edit, View, and Help.

◆ **Subtrees.** A window for each root key of the Registry. The root key HKEY_CURRENT_USER is displayed in figure 4.5. Chapter 2, "Understanding the Windows NT Registry Structure," describes each of these root keys in detail.

◆ **Left pane.** Displays the Registry hierarchy, organized in keys, subkeys, and values.

◆ **Right pane.** Shows the current settings of a selected entry, known as values.

Figure 4.5

The Registry Editor, with main areas shown.

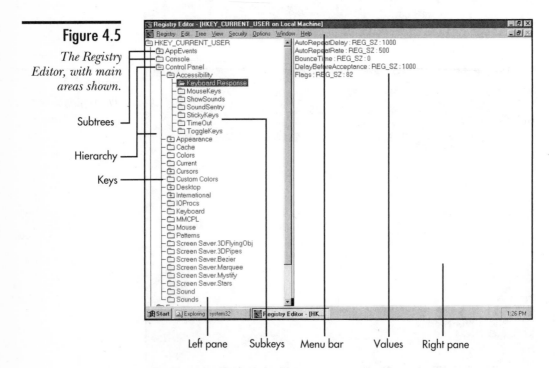

A quick review of each menu item will help you understand how to navigate and use the Registry Editor.

In the Registry menu, the Open Local command displays the Registry of the local computer. The Close option closes the displayed Registry. Load Hive and Unload Hive enables you to open and close information from the HKEY_USER and HKEY_LOCAL_MACHINE keys from another computer. Restore is used to restore a hive saved as a file. Use the Save Key command when you want to save data from a Registry key to a file. If you want to view and edit another computer's Registry from the network, use the Select Computer command (see fig. 4.6). The Print Subtree and Printer Setup commands help you print parts of the Registry. Save Subtree As is used when you want to save keys as a text file.

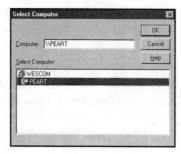

Figure 4.6

Insert the name of the remote computer to edit a remote Registry file.

As you learn in the section "Editing Registry Settings" (later in this chapter), the real power of the Registry Editor lies in your capability to make changes and add entries to your Registry database. The Edit menu contains seven options that enable you to find and modify specific Registry entries:

◆ Add Key

◆ Add Value

◆ Delete

◆ Binary

◆ String

◆ DWORD

◆ Multi String

These options enable you to add and delete keys and values and input new value entries. The last four options are available only when you have selected a value name in the right-hand pane of the Registry Editor. You are shown how to make modifications to entries in the section "Editing Registry Settings" later in this chapter.

The Delete option in the Edit menu is self-explanatory—it enables you to delete or rename a value. You can delete a value also by clicking on it and pressing the Del key.

Stop When you delete a value from the Registry Editor, don't expect to be able to undo your action. The Registry Editor doesn't contain an Undo command, so be extra careful when you want to delete a value. Be certain that you really want to delete it for good. The Confirm on Delete option in the Options menu instructs Windows NT to display a dialog box asking if you are sure that you want to delete the item. After you press Yes, there's no turning back.

The Tree Menu

The Tree menu contains options that enable you to expand and collapse the branches of the selected subtree. The Expand One Level, Expand Branch, and Expand Alloptions are used when you want to see more of the subkeys. The Collapse Branch enables you to collapse the entire subtree so that all you can see is the main root key, such as HKEY_LOCAL_MACHINE. These options, along with other ways to view information in the Registry, are covered in the section "Viewing Value Entries in the Registry Editor."

The View Menu

The View menu's Tree and Data, Tree Only, and Data Only options are helpful when you want to have only the subtrees or value entries display (see fig. 4.7). By default, the Tree and Data option is selected so that you can see both the left and right panes of information.

In between the left and right panes of the Registry Editor windows is a divider. You can slide this to the left or right, resizing the panes to fit your needs. Sometimes you will want to see all the subkeys in the left hand pane, and you might need to move the divider over to the right a little. An example of this is shown in figure 4.8. In that example, the hierarchy of the selected key is several subkeys long, making it difficult to see all of it at one time.

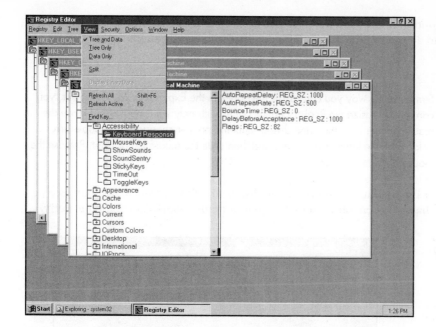

Figure 4.7

The View menu enables you to modify how the Registry Editor looks.

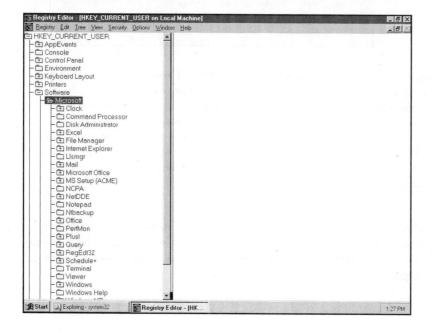

Figure 4.8

An example of viewing a long Registry subtree.

The Split option in the View menu moves the mouse pointer to the divider so that all you have to do is move the mouse left or right, find a new position for the divider, and click.

Tip Similar to the way you can resize the panes in the Explorer or My Computer, you can quickly resize the Registry Editor panes with only your mouse. Just move the mouse pointer over the pane divider until the pointer changes to a double-arrow, hold down the left mouse button, and then slide the mouse left or right. Release the mouse button when done.

The Display Binary Data option is used to display the Binary Data dialog box (see fig. 4.9). This dialog box enables you to view, but not edit, binary data of a value entry.

Figure 4.9

Use the Display Binary Data option to view binary data of a key.

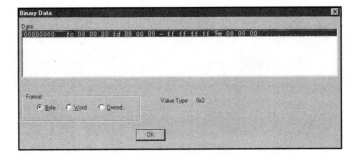

Another option on the View menu is the Refresh All and Refresh Active commands. After you make changes to the Registry, some of the changes are not immediately displayed in the Registry Editor. You need to refresh the Registry Editor by using the Refresh Active command, or by pressing F6. This refreshes the Registry Editor interface, but the change usually does not take effect until the next time you reboot the system. To refresh the entire Registry, select the Refresh All command. Some changes, such as adding system events via the Registry, take effect as soon as you refresh the Registry.

Note When you edit a remote Registry and click on the Auto Refresh command in the Options menu, the Refresh All and Refresh Active are not available. This is so you cannot refresh the Registry of the remote computer while someone is using that computer.

The Find Key command is used to locate specific keys in the Registry. This command is discussed in detail in the section entitled "Viewing Value Entries in the Registry Editor."

The Security Menu

The Security menu includes the Permissions, Auditing, and Owner options, which enable you to control who has rights to edit a Registry key. Your ability to edit keys is usually the same as you have for using administrative tools in the Administrative Tools (Common) folder. See the section "Setting Security Options" found later in this chapter for more details on this topic.

The Options Menu

The Options menu includes the Font option. It enables you to control the font, font style, and font size of the Registry Editor display (see fig. 4.10). To change a font characteristic, select it in the Font dialog box, and then click on OK.

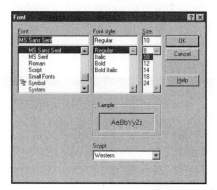

Figure 4.10

The default font for the Registry Editor is MS Sans Serif, Roman, 10 point.

The other Options menu choices are toggle commands, which you can turn on or off at your discretion. The Auto Refresh command is used when you want the Registry to update after you make a change to it. The Read Only Mode is handy when you do not want others (or yourself) to make changes to the Registry by using the Registry Editor. When this option is on, you can view, but not edit, entries. The Save Settings on Exit is used to preserve settings you have made to the Registry Editor. Changes to the Registry values are saved when you refresh the Registry, regardless of the status of the Save Settings on Exit option.

The Window and Help menus contain the same commands found on standard Windows applications.

Viewing Value Entries in the Registry Editor

Now that you have learned about the menu structure in the Registry Editor, it's time to take a look at how the Registry Editor displays each entry. The Registry Editor displays Registry subtrees, keys, subkeys, and value entries in two panes. The keys and subkeys are in the left pane, and the values are in the right pane. Keys and subkeys are denoted with folders, either open or closed depending on whether you have to click on them to view subkeys within them. These folder icons are similar to the ones visible in the Windows NT Explorer and My Computer.

When you first open the Registry Editor, each subtree displays in a separate window, with each of their subkey branches collapsed. These are the root key names and are described in detail in Chapter 2, "Understanding the Windows NT Registry Structure." Each of these root keys can display its subkeys when you click on the plus sign next to the key. This expands the key to the next level of subkeys (see fig. 4.11), much like expanding folders and subfolders in Windows NT Explorer.

Figure 4.11

You can expand branches of keys to expose nested subkeys in your Registry.

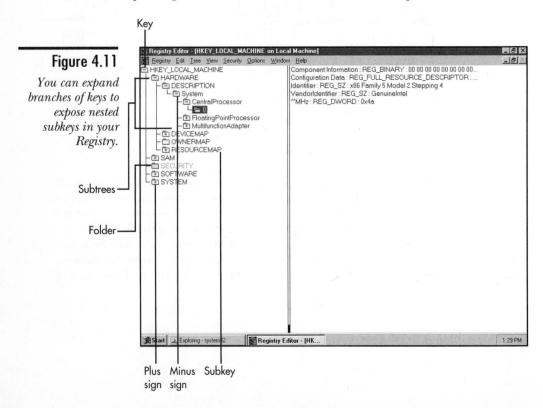

If subkeys are below that subkey, another plus sign appears to the left of the item, on which you can click to expose another layer of subkeys. This type of layering of subkeys, known as *nesting*, can go on for several layers depending on the subkey and item. This is one of the primary differences and strengths of the Registry as compared to the flat-file capabilities of the old INI files in Windows 3.x.

Upon reaching the bottom of the nesting, a minus sign appears to the left of the subkey indicating that you cannot display any more items, and can only move back up the hierarchy.

If a subkey does not have a plus sign or minus sign next to it, you know that it does not contain subkeys below it.

Table 4.1 lists the Registry Editor's shortcut keys for navigation and viewing.

TABLE 4.1
Registry Editor Shortcut Keys

Shortcut Key	Action Taken
+	Expands the selected key one level to show subkeys.
−	Collapses the selected key one level.
Up arrow	Moves you up to the next key.
Down arrow	Moves you down to the next key.
Right arrow	Expands the selected key if it has subkeys; otherwise moves you down to the next key.
Left arrow	Collapses the selected key if it's open; otherwise moves you up to the next key.
Enter	Expands one level of a selected key.
Ctrl+* (on numeric keyboard)	Expands all levels of the subtree.
* (on numeric keyboard)	Expands branch of a selected subtree.
Tab	Moves you to the next pane in the Registry Editor window.

In the right pane of the Registry Editor are the value entries (see fig. 4.12). Each value entry contains three different parts: data type, name, and value itself.

Figure 4.12

The right pane includes the values of a selected key.

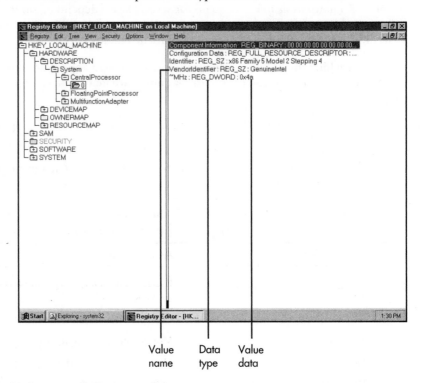

Value name   Data type   Value data

Each value can have a name, or use <No Name> to denote a value without a name. Many of the values provided by Microsoft use the name <No Name> as you will see when you start using the Registry Editor a great deal. Value names appear on the far left of the right pane. These names help you to understand the function of the value and are usually provided by application designers and hardware providers.

Next to the name is the data type and data of the value entry. This is the data that controls how the key behaves, and is the data that you edit, modify, or create to change or enhance the way a Windows NT feature works. The value entry is limited to a size of 1 MB, which in most cases is sufficient unless you include a large binary data type.

Searching for Information in the Registry

Before you start modifying the Registry, you first need to find the correct value to modify or delete. One way to do this is to scroll through the keys and subkeys until you find what you're looking for. Unless you know exactly where the entry resides, you probably don't want to exercise this approach. You will end up clicking hundreds of times on a seemingly endless bank of subkeys and folders.

The best approach is to search for the value by using the Registry Editor's Find Key option. This enables you to quickly move through the Registry until you find exactly what you need.

Another way to search through a long Registry is to export a piece of the Registry to an ASCII file and use a text editor to search for the entry. A good editor to use for this situation is Notepad or WordPad. Both of these come with Windows NT and are quick to use. The limitation of Notepad is that you cannot open files larger than 50 KB.

The next two sections show how to find what you need in the Registry by using both of these methods.

Searching with the Registry Editor

Depending on the configuration of your computer or the computer you are supporting, the Registry that loads into the Registry Editor can contain hundreds, even thousands of subkeys and individual entries. To find an entry in this mess is like finding the proverbial needle in a haystack. Fortunately, this haystack provides a powerful magnet to find just what you're looking for quickly and easily.

On the View menu is the Find Key command. When you select it, the Find dialog box appears (see fig. 4.13), in which you can describe the key you are searching for. Unlike the Windows 95 Registry Editor, you cannot search for values or data in values, or any combination of these items. Windows NT's Registry Editor enables you to search only for a key, such as the Minimize key of the HKEY_CURRENT_USER subtree.

Figure 4.13

Enter the key name in the Find what text box to begin your search.

To use the Find key command, enter the value in the Find what text box in the Find dialog box. The Match whole word only option ensures that the Registry Editor locates only complete words instead of partial words during its search. An example of this is when you search on the word *Paint*. If you have installed on your system Microsoft Paint, Microsoft Paintbrush (a relic perhaps from an old Windows 3.x installation), and another program with the word *Paint* in it (such as PaintShop Pro), the Registry Editor finds all these items during the search.

When you use the Match whole word only option, you increase the search time, which might be significant for large Registry databases.

Tip   Now that I've given you two reasons to use the Match whole string option, I'm going to give you a reason not to ever use this option.

Some key names use different types of spelling. Some use spaces in them; some use underscores; and others use continuous strings (such as Dialer10CallingCard). For this reason, you may want to search on partial words only and keep the Match whole string only check box cleared.

You can also use the Match case option to instruct Registry Editor to locate words that match the way you have the key spelled in the Find what field. This is OK if you don't mind hitting all of them to find what you need, but you might know that you want to find the Microsoft Paint program and that's all. Use the Match whole word only option to narrow your results. Conversely, if you want to find all the variations of a key, keep the Match case option cleared. This is valuable when you don't know the exact wording or spelling of an item.

To instruct Registry Editor to perform the search from top to bottom through the Registry, click on the Down radio button. For searches to begin from the bottom of the Registry to the top, click on the Up radio button.

After you fill out the Find dialog box, click on the Find Next button to start the search.

After the Registry Editor finds a match, it places a fine blue border around the item (see fig. 4.14). This helps you locate where the item resides; that is, in which key or subkey is it nested.

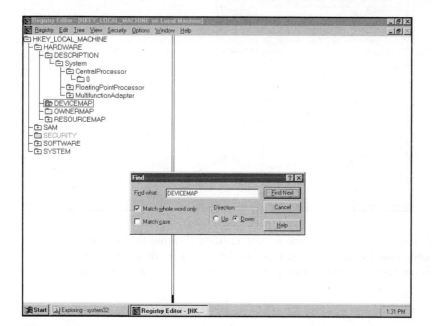

Figure 4.14

After the Registry Editor finds a match for your word or number, it highlights the item.

Tip Sometimes it's difficult to see which subkey is found. One trick you might want to use when you search for a value or value name is to look at the bottom of the screen after the search is done. Usually, but this isn't always the case, the subkey associated with the entry is near the bottom of the screen.

Figure 4.15 shows an example of a subkey found by using the Find tool, but you cannot readily tell the key to which it belongs. To find this out, you can scroll up the left-hand pane to view the folder hierarchy. This is painless, but is tedious and time-consuming in long, nested subkeys (take a look at the CLSID subkey, for example).

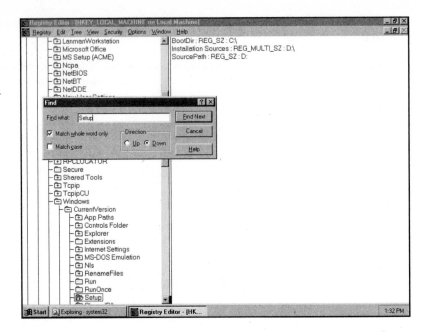

Figure 4.15

Sometimes it's difficult to determine the parent folder of the found subkey.

You can now modify the item (see the section entitled "Editing Registry Settings" later in this chapter), end the search, or just ignore the search result and continue the search. Click on the Find Next button to go to the next occurrence of the matched item.

Note   During searches, you should keep in mind that key names are not unique. Your Registry can, and probably does, contain several occurrences of the same key and value names. For this reason, it's a good idea to provide as much specific information as you can. Using the word *inbox*, for example, may result in up to ten different hits.

Searching with a Text Editor

The sheer size of the Registry database makes searching somewhat clumsy and time-consuming in the Registry Editor. To make your searches move faster and locate specific data such as value entries, you might want to dump out a portion of the Registry as an ASCII file and search using a text editor, such as WordPad or Notepad.

Tip

Because Registry files tend to get very large, you might want to opt to use WordPad to read in these files instead of Notepad. Notepad is still limited to the 50 KB file size that it can open.

To get started searching in a text editor, you need to first export a portion of the Registry. The best way is to export a branch of the Registry, such as the HKEY_CLASSES_ROOT, by clicking on it in the left pane and selecting Registry, Save Subtree As after the Export Registry Save As dialog box appears (see fig. 4.16). Input a name for the file in the File name text box. Windows does not know to give it an extension, so you can give it one yourself, such as TXT if you plan to open it in a text editor. You can store the file in any folder on your system, but you might want to store it in an archive folder other than your *%SystemRoot%* Windows NT folder. This way you can keep better track of exported Registry files.

Figure 4.16

The Registry Save As dialog box.

Note Unlike the Windows 95 Registry Editor, you cannot control the amount of the subtree saved to a text file. In Windows 95, you can use the Export range area of the Export Registry dialog box to control whether to export the entire Registry database (by using the All option) or just a portion of it (by using the Selected branch option). Unless wanting to make a backup of the Registry or share its entire contents with someone else, most users choose the Selected branch option. This is especially true if you need to work in only a portion of the Registry. With Windows NT, however, you have only the option to save the entire subtree. This is probably due to the fact that the Windows 95 Registry Editor is newer than the Windows NT Registry Editor (even REGEDT32.EXE that comes with Windows NT 4).

Click on the Save button, and the file is saved to disk. Don't wait for a prompt or message telling you that it has been saved. You don't get one in this case.

Now open the file in a text editor—both Notepad and WordPad are installed in the \PROGRAMS\ACCESSORIES folder on the Start menu—and run your search by using the search command available in that application. If you are using WordPad, for example, your display looks something like the one in figure 4.17. (This figure shows the HKEY_CURRENT_CONFIG key from my machine.) Select Search, Find, and then enter the text or numbers you want to locate in the Find what text box.

Figure 4.17

WordPad's search utility can be used to find a specific Registry setting.

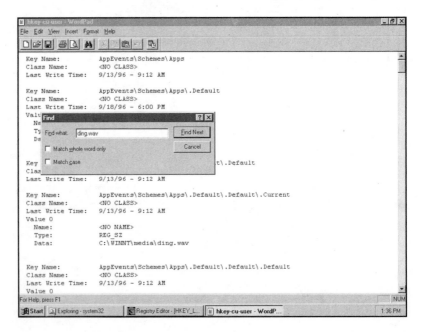

After you find the setting you're searching for, return to the Registry Editor and locate that setting in the Registry Editor. You now can edit or delete the setting as necessary.

Note   Notice that binary data from the Registry does not display when you view a portion of the Registry in a text editor. This is because the text editor doesn't know how to handle that type of data.

Editing Registry Settings

The key to using the Registry Editor is to understand how to modify Registry values. If you are familiar with the Microsoft Knowledge Base, you've probably seen several articles telling you to modify a certain value in the Registry. This is great information if you already know how to edit Registry values, but it might cause your eyes to glaze over if you're not sure how to do it.

You might, for instance, see instructions for changing the setting for the registered owner on a workstation machine. The article or document you are reading would tell you to change the RegisteredOwner value entry in the HKEY_LOCAL_MACHINE\ SOFTWARE\Microsoft\Windows NT\CurrentVersion Registry subkey. Unless you've done this a time or two, you might not have a clue as to what to do next. The following sections help you understand exactly what you need to do to change subkeys, value entries, and value settings in the Registry. You learn how to modify existing settings, delete settings, and add new ones.

Note   The Microsoft Knowledge Base is a technical support service the company makes available to users. In the Knowledge Base (also referred to as KB), you can find articles that list problems and solutions, bug reports, and other software or system updates on various Microsoft products. You can find the Knowledge Base from various sources, including the World Wide Web, the Microsoft Network, CompuServe, and the Microsoft TechNet CD-ROM service.

Modifying Registry Values and Keys

Modifying a Registry value or key is quite easy. In fact, it's so easy that you should always be cautious when opening the Registry Editor and leaving it unattended on your system. Keys or values can quickly be deleted or changed without much effort. Before going any further, make a backup of your Registry. The key is to make certain that if you make a mistake editing a value or key, you can always return to a working copy of the Registry.

To edit a value, use the following general steps:

1. If it's not open, start the Registry Editor.

2. Locate the value or key that you want to modify or delete (see the previous section on searching if you need help doing this).

3. To modify a value of a key, double-click on the value entry in the right pane of the Registry Editor window. You also can click on the value or key, and then select the Edit menu. From that menu, choose Binary, String, DWORD, or Multi String, depending on the type of value data you want to input. Change the value entry from the old setting to a new setting.

    As shown in figure 4.18, for example, the String Editor dialog box displays when you select to edit a string or multi-string setting. This shows the value of the selected subkey.

4. Click on OK when you finish editing the value.

Note For specific examples of editing the Registry, see Chapter 8, "Troubleshooting Specific Problems Using the Windows NT Registry." That chapter contains several ways to modify specific Registry values to help you troubleshoot problems you may encounter in Windows NT.

To help you understand the way all this works, the rest of this section walks you through the process of modifying a specific, existing item in the Registry—in this case, changing the name of the registered owner of Windows NT.

Figure 4.18

The String Editor dialog box displays when you select to edit a string or multi-string setting.

Find the following Registry key:

HKEY_LOCAL_MACHINE\SOFTWARE\Microsoft\Windows NT\
CurrentVersion

Double-click on the RegistredOwner value name. Now do the following:

1. In the String Editor dialog box, change the value in the String text box to something new, such as *Dave Matthews*.

2. Click on OK. The Registry Editor displays the new settings (see fig. 4.19).

3. To check the change, select Start, Run, and then type **WINVER** in the Run field to see the name that the product is licensed to. Repeat steps 1 and 2 to return the RegisteredOwner value to its original state (unless your name is Dave Matthews).

Figure 4.19

You can rename the Registered-Owner value by using the Registry Editor.

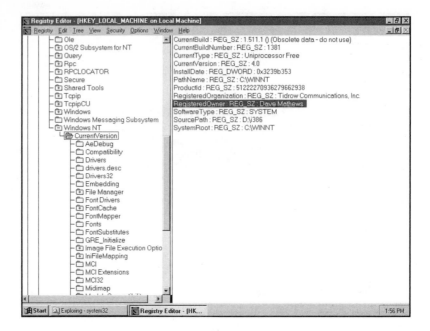

The Binary and DWORD Editors (see figures 4.20 and 4.21) enable you to select the Radix, or number system, you feel most comfortable using, including binary, decimal, or hexadecimal. When you select the binary choice, Registry Editor displays the data in base-2 number format, which uses values of 0 and 1. Decimal displays data in a base-10 format. The hexadecimal choice (shown as Hex on-screen), uses a base-16 number format, which uses the numbers 0-9, and uppercase letters A to F. Letters A-F represent the numbers 10-16 in the decimal system. The number 842647162 in decimal, for example, is displayed as 3239C67A in hex, and 110010001110011100011001111010 in binary.

Figure 4.20

The Binary Editor.

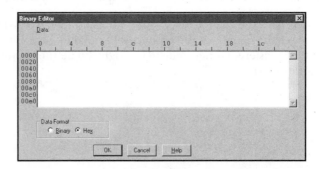

Figure 4.21

The DWORD Editor.

Stop   Unless specifically advised to, or if you are comfortable and have experience working with binary and hexadecimal data formats, do not tamper with these types of values in the Registry. You can create a major headache for yourself if you input the wrong values here.

For a value entry that uses Multi String format (that is, entries that can contain one or more string settings), you use the Multi-String Editor (see fig. 4.22). To use this editor, select Edit, Multi String. In the Data area, edit or add to the value entry. Click on OK when finished.

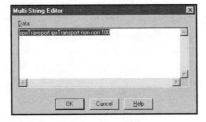

Figure 4.22

The Multi-String Editor.

Adding a Key to the Registry

The Registry Editor can be used to add a key to your Registry. You might need to do this, for example, to install a device driver that doesn't have an installation program.

Use the following steps to add a key to the Registry:

1. Select the key or subkey under which you want the new key to appear.

2. From the Edit menu, choose Add Key.

3. In the Add Key dialog box (see fig. 4.23), insert a new name for the key in the Key Name field. You can leave the Class field blank or add the data type you want to use.

4. Click on OK after you input the name.

Figure 4.23

*Adding a new key
in the Registry.*

Key names can be up to 16,000 characters (32 KB) and can be null using the format
" ". Key names cannot contain backslashes (\) and must be unique to that hierarchy.
Other subkeys at the same level cannot have the same name. That is, you cannot have
two keys using the same name under a parent key. If, for instance, you have a key
called \Display, you cannot have two keys named \Settings under it; only one subkey
can have that name. If you attempt to use the same name, the Registry Editor returns
an error message indicating that you must select a different name.

Adding a Value Entry

After you add a key to the Registry, you will more than likely want to assign a new
value entry to it. If you don't, the new key won't have a value for it and Windows NT
won't know what to do with the setting. This is like buying an ice cream cone without
getting ice cream in it. You get the cone but not the good stuff. Value entries without
settings declared are ignored by Windows NT. (Again, the material in Chapter 8,
"Troubleshooting Specific Problems Using the Windows NT Registry," deals specifically with tuning and troubleshooting items, but the following steps shows you how to
add a new value entry in general terms.)

To add a value entry, perform the following steps:

1. Select the key to which you want to assign the new value.

2. Select Edit, Add Value to display the Add Value dialog box (see fig. 4.24).

3. In the Add Value dialog box, fill in the Value Name text box with the value
   name.

4. In the Data Type drop-down list, select the data type (sometimes called a class)
   you want to use.

5. Click on OK.

6. Depending on the data type you select in step 4, that data type's editor appears,
   enabling you to enter the value entry for that value name.

7. Click on OK to save the new value to the Registry.

Figure 4.24

Use the Add Value dialog box to add a new value to a new key.

Deleting Registry Values and Keys

Values and keys you no longer need in the Registry can be deleted. Normally, you don't need to delete Registry items because Windows or an application takes care of removing items it doesn't need. One reason you might want to remove something from the Registry is if you delete a program from your system without using the Add/Remove Program utility from Control Panel. When you use this utility, Windows removes the program files plus Registry settings that the application set up when you installed the application. For programs that don't include an uninstall program, however, you need to manually remove Registry entries.

Deleting a Registry item is quick. In fact, it's entirely too easy to delete something in the Registry. It's more difficult to delete a text file in Explorer than it is to delete a vital system setting in the Registry. You can delete a key or value entry in one of two ways:

◆ Select the item to delete, and then press the Del key on your keyboard.

◆ Select the item to delete, and then choose Edit, Delete from the Registry Editor menu.

Regardless of which method you choose, Windows prompts you to confirm the file deletion. Click on Yes to delete the selected item. You can click on No if you are not certain that you have selected the correct key or value to delete. If you have the Confirm on Delete option on the Option menu turned off, you do not get a confirmation message when you delete a Registry item. For best results, keep the Confirm on Delete option turned on.

Stop   As noted earlier, deletions you make to the Registry are gone forever after you say Yes to the Windows confirmation prompt. The items you delete are not sent to the Windows Recycle Bin for later reinstatement. Further, the Registry Editor does not have an undo option to undo an action. After it's deleted, it's gone for good.

Stop One way to retrieve a key you deleted is to restart the computer in Safe Mode, and return to your previous last best boot into Windows NT.

Without trying it (that would be operating-system suicide), you might or might not be able to delete or rename the following five main root keys. In Windows 95, you are protected from accidentally deleting or renaming these subtrees (and the additional HKEY_DYN_DATA subtree). Windows NT, unfortunately, might not offer the same protection. Don't test the operating system unless you want to reinstall Windows NT.

◆ HKEY_CLASSES_ROOT

◆ HKEY_CURRENT_USER

◆ HKEY_LOCAL_MACHINE

◆ HKEY_USERS

◆ HKEY_CURRENT_CONFIG

Setting Security Options

In Windows NT, you can protect the Registry by declaring who has rights to modify part of it. Because the Registry controls the setup, configuration, and general behavior of Windows NT, you need to ensure that only authorized users have permission to access and modify it. One way to do this is to delete REGEDT32.EXE from all the workstations you administer. If you need to access that computer's Registry, open it on your local machine by using the remote Registry feature.

Tip If you use the Windows NT File System (NTFS), you can control access to the Registry hive files for user profiles by using the Security commands in Windows Explorer. If you don't have NTFS installed, you cannot set file-level security restrictions. You learn more about user profiles in Chapter 7, "Administering Remote Registries from Windows NT."

You also can control access privileges to the Registry by assigning access rights to Registry keys and by auditing who uses the Registry. The following two sections explain how to do each. The final section within this larger security section shows you how to change the ownership of a Registry key by using the Ownership option in the Security menu.

Setting Access Rights on Registry Keys

Windows NT enables you to set access rights on Registry keys for users and groups regardless of the file system you have installed (FAT or NTFS). You can set Full Control, Read, and Special Access permissions for a Registry key depending on how much security you want to grant a user or group. This is sometimes referred to as editing the Access Control Lists (ACLs) that determine who has rights to data on the Windows NT system.

Note   The Windows 95 Registry does not have the capability to set security permissions. About the only way to make certain that users do not alter the Windows 95 Registry is to use User Profiles and System Policies to disable the Control Panel and other configuration altering tools. You also should delete the REGEDIT.EXE file on workstations running Windows 95.

The following list explains each of the permissions:

◆ **Full Control.** Enables users to access, edit, and take ownership of the selected key. Assign this permission to users who have administrator privileges.

◆ **Read.** Enables users to view, but not modify, the selected key. This is helpful for users who you want to have rights to look at a Registry key(s) for troubleshooting concerns, but not have the right to edit a key.

◆ **Special Access.** Enables you to set combinations of permissions to a user or group. This permission option is more thoroughly explained later in this section.

To set permissions for a Registry key, do the following:

1. Start Registry Editor. You must be logged on as an administrator.

2. Select the Registry key you want to set permissions for.

3. Select Security, Permission.

4. In the Registry Key Permissions dialog box (see fig. 4.25), set the permissions for each user or group by using the Name area (to select a user or group) and the Type of Access drop-down list (to choose type).

Figure 4.25

The Registry Key Permissions dialog box is used to set access rights for Registry keys.

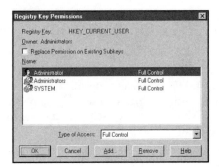

The following list explains each of the options in the Registry Key Permissions dialog box:

◆ **Registry Key.** Shows the selected Registry key, such as HKEY_LOCAL_MACHINE, Software, and so on.

◆ **Owner.** Shows the currently logged on user. This usually says Administrators.

◆ **Replace Permission on Existing Subkeys.** Assigns the permission to the selected key and its subkeys. By default, this option is not selected. This option is handy if you want to select a subtree and assign permissions throughout it. Some rights may restrict the system from making changes to the Registry as well, however, which may produce unlikely results if you install new software or a new device.

◆ **Name.** Includes the names of the users and groups who have permission to access the selected key. These names are provided by the Windows NT access control list (ACL).

◆ **Type of access.** Displays a drop-down list for you to select Read, Full Control, or Special Access as the access permission for the selected key. After you select the Special Access option, the Special Access dialog box appears (see fig. 4.26).

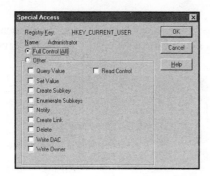

Table 4.2 summarizes the Special Access permissions you can set after you select the Special Access option and the Special Access dialog box appears (see fig. 4.26).

TABLE 4.2
Special Access Permissions

Permission	Description
Full Control (All)	Sets all rights for the selected user or group.
Query Value	Enables you to read a Registry value entry.
Set Value	Enables you to read and modify a Registry value entry.
Create Subkey	Enables you to create a new Registry subkey.
Enumerate Subkey	Enables you to read (expand) the subkeys of a Registry key.
Notify	Enables you to audit notification events of a Registry key.
Create Link	Enables you to create a symbolic link from a Registry key.
Delete	Enables you to delete a Registry key.
Write DAC	Enables you to modify a Registry key's permissions.
Write Owner	Enables you to gain ownership of a Registry key.
Read Control	Enables you to read a Registry key's security information.

♦ **Add.** Enables you to add users and groups to the Name section. When you click on the Add button, the Add Users and Groups dialog box appears (see fig. 4.27), from which you can select users and groups from the Names section.

Figure 4.27

You can modify the list of users and groups who have access rights to a Registry key by using the Add Users and Groups dialog box.

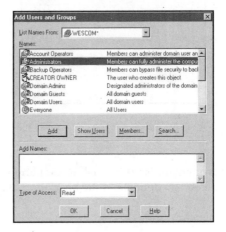

Double-click on a group name to add it to the Add Names section. To add individual users, you must click on the Members button to display the Local Group Membership dialog box, from which you add users to the Registry Key Permissions list. If a user or group is in a different domain, click on the List Names From drop-down list to obtain a list of domains from which to choose. You also can set the access type by selecting Read or Full Control from the Type of Access drop-down list. Click on OK to return to the Registry Key Permissions dialog box.

♦ **Remove.** Deletes a selected user or group from the Name section.

Tip

If a user or group has a Special Access permission already established, after you click on the Type of Access drop-down list, two Special Access choices appear. To modify the access choices from the Special Access dialog box, you must choose Special Access....

5. Click on OK when you have set permissions for all users or groups.

Stop For best results, make certain that the administrators and SYSTEM users have Full Control access rights. If you set these users to limit the changes that can be made, you run the risk of configuration changes not being saved to the Registry. If, for example, you set the SYSTEM user to have no modification rights (using the Special Access permissions and disabling the Set Value option) for a Registry key that controls application settings, that application may not run properly.

Also, after you change a Registry permission, run the auditing feature to test the system. See the following section, "Setting Auditing Features of the Registry."

Setting Auditing Features of the Registry

Windows NT enables you to audit Registry keys used by users or services. The Windows NT auditing feature is also used to monitor the usage of files and directories on the system. You can use the Registry auditing tool to help keep track of Registry keys you add that you want to test or monitor usage of. Another reason to use auditing is to troubleshoot a particular Registry key that has recurring problems. Through the auditing process, you can pinpoint which users or applications are affecting that key.

Before you use the Registry auditing feature, you must turn on auditing in Windows NT by using the User Manager for Domains tool in the Administrative Tools (Common) folder. Do this by following these steps:

1. Start Windows NT and log on as administrator.

2. Select Start, Programs, Administrative Tools (Common), User Manager for Domains.

3. From the User Manager window, select Polices, Audit. The Audit Policy dialog box displays (see fig. 4.28).

Figure 4.28

*The Windows NT
auditing feature
must be enabled
before you can set
auditing in the
Registry Editor.*

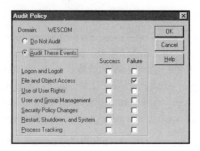

4. To display the Windows NT events you can set auditing for, click on Audit These Events.

5. For auditing Registry events, select the Failure option for the File and Object Access. You can select other events as well, but the auditing log tends to get very large if you add too many events to it.

6. Choose OK to save your changes.

Note   For more information about auditing other Windows NT events, click on the Help button on the Audit Policy dialog box.

7. Exit the User Manager window.

You now switch to the Registry Editor and set up auditing for Registry keys. The following steps show you how:

1. In the Registry Editor, select the Registry key you want to audit.

2. Select Security, Auditing. The Registry Key Auditing dialog box displays (see fig. 4.29).

3. Click on the Audit Permission on Existing Subkeys option if you want the auditing to apply to all subkeys of the selected key. By default, this is turned off.

4. To add users and groups to the Name list, click on the Add button. This displays the Add Users and Groups dialog box, similar to the one shown in figure 4.27 in the preceding section. Double-click on those users or groups you want to audit so that their names appear in the Add Names list on the Add Users and Groups dialog box. Click on OK when you finish, to return to the Registry Key Auditing dialog box.

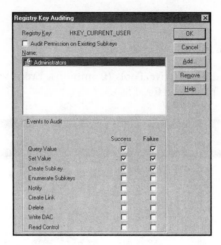

Figure 4.29

The Registry Key Auditing feature is used to view changes made to a Registry key.

5. Select the user or group name, for which you want to set auditing events, in the Name list. You can set either the Success, Failure, or both settings. In the Events to Audit list, select the events to audit. The following list describes each of the auditing events in more detail:

   ◆ **Query Value.** Audits an activity attempting to read a Registry key value entry.

   ◆ **Set Value.** Audits an activity attempting to modify a Registry key value entry.

   ◆ **Create Subkey.** Audits an activity attempting to create a new subkey under the selected Registry key.

   ◆ **Enumerated Subkeys.** Audits an activity attempting to read subkeys of the selected Registry key.

   ◆ **Notify.** Audits notification events from the selected Registry key.

   ◆ **Create Link.** Audits an activity attempting to create a symbolic link to the selected Registry key.

   ◆ **Write DAC.** Audits an activity of a user attempting to access the selected Registry key to set security permissions of the key.

   ◆ **Read Control.** Audits an activity of a user attempting to read the security permissions of the selected key.

6. Click on OK to save your settings.

To read the audit log, perform the following steps:

1. Select Start, Programs, Administrative Tools (Common), Event Viewer. The Event Viewer window displays (see fig. 4.30).

Figure 4.30

The Event Viewer is used to view auditing.

Date	Time	Source	Category	Event	User	Computer
9/20/96	2:13:58 PM	Security	Object Access	562	Administrator	PEART
9/20/96	2:13:58 PM	Security	Object Access	560	Administrator	PEART
9/20/96	2:13:58 PM	Security	Object Access	562	Administrator	PEART
9/20/96	2:13:58 PM	Security	Object Access	560	Administrator	PEART
9/20/96	2:13:58 PM	Security	Object Access	562	Administrator	PEART
9/20/96	2:13:57 PM	Security	Object Access	562	Administrator	PEART
9/20/96	2:13:57 PM	Security	Object Access	560	Administrator	PEART
9/20/96	2:13:39 PM	Security	Object Access	562	Administrator	PEART
9/20/96	2:13:39 PM	Security	Object Access	562	Administrator	PEART
9/20/96	2:13:39 PM	Security	Object Access	560	Administrator	PEART
9/20/96	2:13:39 PM	Security	Object Access	562	Administrator	PEART
9/20/96	2:13:39 PM	Security	Object Access	560	Administrator	PEART
9/20/96	2:13:39 PM	Security	Object Access	562	Administrator	PEART
9/20/96	2:13:39 PM	Security	Object Access	560	Administrator	PEART
9/20/96	2:13:39 PM	Security	Object Access	562	Administrator	PEART
9/20/96	2:13:39 PM	Security	Object Access	560	Administrator	PEART
9/20/96	2:13:39 PM	Security	Object Access	562	Administrator	PEART
9/20/96	2:13:39 PM	Security.	Object Access	560	Administrator	PEART
9/20/96	2:13:39 PM	Security	Object Access	562	Administrator	PEART
9/20/96	2:13:39 PM	Security	Object Access	560	Administrator	PEART
9/20/96	2:13:39 PM	Security	Object Access	562	Administrator	PEART
9/20/96	2:13:39 PM	Security	Object Access	560	Administrator	PEART
9/20/96	2:13:39 PM	Security	Object Access	562	Administrator	PEART
9/20/96	2:13:39 PM	Security	Object Access	560	Administrator	PEART
9/20/96	2:13:39 PM	Security	Object Access	562	Administrator	PEART
9/20/96	2:13:39 PM	Security	Object Access	560	Administrator	PEART

2. If you need to select a different computer, select Log, select Computer, and then select the computer from the Select Computer dialog box. Click on OK.

3. Select Log, Security. View the Event Viewer for auditing activities.

Note   For details about using the Event Viewer, read *Windows NT Server 4 Professional Reference*, published by New Riders.

Changing Registry Key Ownership

If you need to change the ownership of a Registry key from an administrator to another user or group, use the following steps. Unless you have specific reasons to change ownership, you probably should keep it set to the administrator so that no unauthorized users (those who should not have access to critical system settings) alter the Registry unfavorably.

1. Select the Registry key for which to change ownership.

2. Select Security, Owner, to display the Owner dialog box (see fig. 4.31).

Figure 4.31

You can change a Registry key's ownership in the Registry Editor.

3. Click Take Ownership. This changes the ownership from the one listed on the Owner line to the one currently logged on. Only those who have full control over a Registry key can grant ownership to others (see the earlier section "Setting Access Rights On Registry Keys" for more information).

4. Click on Close to abort the change.

Printing Registry Information

Having a hard copy of your Registry might be as useful as having a hard copy of your old INI files. That is not especially handy if your system tends to change often, which in most cases is each time you boot your machine.

A hard copy does come in handy when you have to diagnose a problem and want to compare settings with another system's entries. Or you might want to have a copy of a recent Registry so that you can reference it in case you have performance problems or a device that has quit working.

More than likely, you probably won't re-create an entire Registry from a hard copy, but you might want to have portions of the Registry handy that you can key in case of system problems. The Registry Editor has the capability to print out the entire Registry, or to print out just a branch of it.

Tip

One of the quickest ways to become familiar with the Registry is to print out a portion and review it. After reading through it a few times, you will start understanding how it's set up.

You probably should not print the entire Registry, however. Depending on the size of your Registry, it may be as large as 100 pages or more.

To print from the Registry Editor, use the following steps:

1. Select the Registry subtree that you want to print.

2. Choose Registry, Print Subtree. The selected key with its subkeys prints to the default printer.

To set up the printer for printing a key, do the following:

1. Select Registry, Printer Subtree. The Print Setup dialog box appears (see fig. 4.32). Click on the Properties button to change the default printer settings.

2. In the Name drop-down list, select the name of the printer to which to print.

Figure 4.32

You can set printer settings by using the Print Setup dialog box.

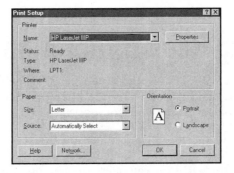

3. Select the size and source of the paper to use from the Size and Source drop-down lists.

4. See the orientation of the paper (Portrait is the default) in the Orientation area.

5. Click on OK to return to the Registry Editor.

The hard copy that prints does not look like the Registry displayed in the Registry Editor. What you see is something similar to that shown in figure 4.33. In that figure, callouts have been added to point out each item as you have already seen it in the Registry Editor.

```
Key Name:         HKEY_CURRENT_USER ─────────── Key
Class Name:       <NO CLASS>
Last Write Time:  9/19/96 - 4:59 PM

Key Name:         AppEvents ──────────────── Subkey
Class Name:       <NO CLASS>
Last Write Time:  9/20/96 - 11:57 AM
Value 0
  Name:           Migrated Schemes ────────── Value name
  Type:           REG_SZ
  Data:           1 ───────────────────────── Data


Key Name:         AppEvents\EventLabels
Class Name:       <NO CLASS>
Last Write Time:  9/19/96 - 4:59 PM

Key Name:         AppEvents\EventLabels\.Default
Class Name:       <NO CLASS>
Last Write Time:  9/20/96 - 11:57 AM
Value 0
  Name:           <NO NAME>
  Type:           REG_SZ
  Data:           Default Beep


Key Name:         AppEvents\EventLabels\AppGPFault
Class Name:       <NO CLASS>
Last Write Time:  9/20/96 - 11:57 AM
Value 0
  Name:           <NO NAME>
  Type:           REG_SZ
  Data:           Program error


Key Name:         AppEvents\EventLabels\Close
Class Name:       <NO CLASS>
Last Write Time:  9/20/96 - 11:57 AM
Value 0
  Name:           <NO NAME>
  Type:           REG_SZ
  Data:           Close program


Key Name:         AppEvents\EventLabels\EmptyRecycleBin
Class Name:       <NO CLASS>
Last Write Time:  9/20/96 - 11:57 AM
Value 0
  Name:           <NO NAME>
  Type:           REG_SZ
  Data:           Empty Recycle Bin
```

Figure 4.33

A hard copy of a branch printed from the Registry Editor.

Summary

This chapter focused on how to use the Registry Editor to modify, view, import, export, and print the Registry database. The Registry Editor is the easiest way to manage the Registry, but it's also the easiest way for you to introduce an error directly into the Registry. When you open the Registry Editor, be careful to not delete or make haphazard changes. If you change a setting, note the original setting exactly as it appears before making the change. This saves you time if you need to go back in and return the value to its original state.

Examining Network Settings in the Windows NT Registry

Windows NT is a powerful operating system in and of itself. Many users run Windows NT Server or Workstation as a stand-alone operating system, without any networking features enabled. In most cases, however, Windows NT is used as a networking operating system (NOS), connecting multiple users to a server and to shared devices across the LAN. For this reason, an entire chapter is devoted to subkeys and value entries you can modify in the Registry that affect network settings and performance.

This chapter can be broken down into two main sections. The first section consists of a number of Registry key values you can edit or change to customize or tweak a network service. The second section addresses specific networking problems you can correct by modifying Registry values.

Specifically, this chapter covers the following:

- ◆ Understanding the network Registry keys

- ◆ Reviewing network Registry values

- ◆ Troubleshooting network Registry problems

Understanding the Network Registration Keys

When you want to install a network component, such as a network interface card, a protocol, or a network service, the best method is to use the Network application found in the Control Panel. When you double-click on the Network icon in the Control Panel, the Network dialog box displays. To install a component, such as an adapter, click on the corresponding tab for that component. Figure 5.1 shows the Adapters tab selected. When you use the Network dialog box, Windows NT sets up the component and sends the configuration data for that component to the Registry. Some of the common information placed in the Registry includes device type, adapter properties, and IP information.

Figure 5.1

When you use the Network application to install networking components, the configuration data is saved to the Registry.

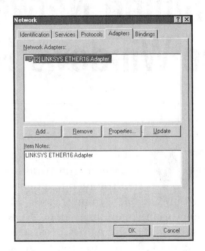

Windows NT contains the following network components:

◆ **Driver.** Specifies a software driver for a hardware device.

◆ **Adapter.** Usually specifies a network interface card (NIC). For Windows Dial-Up Networking, the adapter is not a physical NIC, but software provided by Windows NT.

◆ **Service.** Specifies software that provides capabilities to user applications. Services support the basic Windows NT networking system, such as providing file and printer sharing support or backup support.

◆ **Protocol.** Specifies a language used by the network to communicate with other computers across the network. The most common protocols used with Windows NT are NWLink IPX/SPX, NetBEUI, and TCP/IP.

◆ **Binding.** Specifies connections Windows NT establishes between adapter cards, protocols, and services installed on the computer.

When you set up a networking component, Windows NT adds several subkeys to the Registry. Subkeys for both the software and the service for a component are added to the Registry. An adapter card, for instance, has at least four related subkeys in the Registry, two for the adapter itself and two for the adapter driver. An example of the settings for a network adapter is as follows:

HKEY_LOCAL_MACHINE\SOFTWARE\Microsoft\ETHER\CurrentVersion\LINKSYS ETHER 16

HKEY_LOCAL_MACHINE\SYSTEM\CurrentControlSet\Services\ETHER\LINKSYS ETHER16

Network component information is stored in the Registry in one of two places, depending on the type of component it is. For network services, the Registry uses the following key to store the information:

HKEY_LOCAL_MACHINE\SYSTEM

On the other hand, network software components are saved under the following Registry key:

HKEY_LOCAL_MACHINE\SOFTWARE

In Windows NT, networking services can be dependent upon other services or drivers, which in turn can be dependent upon other services and drivers, and so on. This is called *dependency handling*. When Windows NT creates a dependency, the previous dependencies are deleted. You can include the OtherDependencies value entry in the network component's Linkage subkey to ensure the component is always part of a specified dependency. Windows NT can establish the following dependencies:

◆ **Specific dependencies.** These are required services and are denoted in the Registry as a value in the Use entry in the NetRules subkey. These types of dependencies are specified by the names of the services upon which a service is dependent. In one example, a client service may be dependent on another service, such as ABC, which is connected to an adapter card and its drivers. Windows NT creates a dependency between ABC and the cards, as well as a dependency between the client and the network card's drivers and ABC.

♦ **Group dependencies.** Specifies a group established that relies on another service or group of services to load before all members of the group load. If any member of the group fails to load, the rest of the group does not load. Network components can all be identified as members of a group. For example, adapter cards are part of the NDIS group. You can find group dependencies in the Use entry of the HKEY_LOCAL_MACHINE\SYSTEM\CurrentControlSet\Control\ GroupOrderList\NetRule subkey.

♦ **Static dependencies.** Specifies a required service and is not affected by the way in which Windows NT establishes bindings.

You've read how Windows NT assigns Registry information for network components you install in the HKEY_LOCAL_MACHINE\SOFTWARE and HKEY_LOCAL_ MACHINE\SYSTEM subkeys. The next discussions cover these two Registry subkeys in detail. The section "Bindings Information in the Registry" later in this chapter discusses how the Registry stores information about network bindings for components you install.

Software Component Registry Information

As you add software network adapter cards and other component types to Windows NT, the HKEY_LOCAL_MACHINE\SOFTWARE key begins to fill up with many subkeys and entries to describe your network configuration. Finding all these Registry entries can be difficult if you don't know where to start looking.

The following are the general subkeys you might look under for the software component of a network adapter, including the adapter driver:

HKEY_LOCAL_MACHINE\SOFTWARE*driver_company_name**product_name**version_number*

HKEY_LOCAL_MACHINE\SOFTWARE\Microsoft\Windows NT\CurrentVersion\ NetworkCards\netcard#

In the preceding key, the netcard# is a number beginning with 1 to denote the first network adapter installed. As you install more adapters, this number increases by one, such as 1, 2, 3, and so on.

Note You also can find Registry information about the adapter card and driver in the HKEY_LOCAL_MACHINE\CurrentControlSet\Services. In this subkey, you can find the following value entries and values:

♦ **Start.** Instructs Windows NT when to load the driver for a network card during bootup. The default setting is 0x3, which tells WindowsNT to load the driver on demand.

◆ **ErrorControl.** Specifies the way in which Windows NT should handle errors occurring at bootup. The default setting is 0x1, which tells Windows NT to handle errors in the normal way. Usually, this means continue with the boot process and display errors in the Event Viewer.

◆ **Type.** Specifies the type of service installed. 0x1 denotes a driver; 0x4 denotes an adapter.

The following is an example of the Registry settings for a Linksys Ethernet adapter card driver:

HKEY_LOCAL_MACHINE\SOFTWARE\ETHER\CurrentVersion

The following values and value entries are included in the preceding subkey:

```
Description = REG_SZ: LINKSYS ETHER16 Driver
InstallDate = REG_DWORD: 0x3239c67a
MajorVersion = REG_DWORD: 0x3
MinorVersion = REG_DWORD: 0x3
RefCount = REG_DWORD: 0x1
ServiceName = REG_SZ: ETHER
SoftwareType =REG_SZ: driver
Title = REG_SZ: LINKSYS ETHER16 Driver
```

To continue with this example, the following shows the subkey for the Linksys adapter:

HKEY_LOCAL_MACHINE\SOFTWARE\Microsoft\Windows NT\CurrentVersion\NetworkCards\2

The following values and value entries are included in the preceding subkey:

```
Description = REG_SZ: LINKSYS ETHER16 Adapter
InstallDate = REG_DWORD: 0x3239c67a
Manufacturer = REG_SZ: Microsoft
ProductName = REG_SZ: ETHER
ServiceName = REG_SZ: ETHER
Title = REG_SZ [2] LINKSYS ETHER16 Adapter
```

For every network component you install, a subkey named NetRules is added to the Registry. The NetRules subkey is used to identify the component listed in that subkey as a member of the network group.

An example of the NetRules subkey for the preceding example of the Linksys adapter card is as follows:

```
bindable = REG_MULTI_SZ: etherDriver etherAdapter non exclusive 100
bindform = REG_SZ: "etherSys" yes no container
class = REG_MULTI_SZ: etherDriver basic
InfName = REG_SZ: oemnad1.inf
InfOption = REG_SZ: ETHER
type = REG_SZ: etherSys ndisDriver etherDriver
use = REG_SZ: driver
```

Likewise, the following is an example of the NetRules subkey for the Linksys adapter card driver:

```
bindform = REG_SZ: "ETHER2" yes yes container
class = REG_MULTI_SZ: etherAdapter basic
InfName = REG_SZ: oemnad1.inf
InfOption = REG_SZ: ETHER
type = REG_SZ: ether etherAdapter
```

Table 5.1 lists and describes the NetRules subkey entries. (Note that some of the value entries in the following table are not shown in the preceding examples. This is because these entries are not used for the configuration for the Linksys adapter in this example.) For complete value entry syntax and descriptions, see the *Windows NT 4.0 Resource Kit*, published by Microsoft Press.

TABLE 5.1
NetRules Registry Subkey Entries

Entry	Data Type	Description
Bindable	REG_MULTI_SZ	Includes possible biding information and constraints. This entry is optional.
Bindform	REG_SZ	Includes the component name, if Windows NT should use binding information from the Linkage subkey, if the binding should appear in binding strings, and instructions about how binding device names are created.
Class	REG_MULTI_SZ	Enables a component to add a new class. This entry is optional.
Hidden	REG_DWORD	Instructs Windows NT not to display the adapter or network software component in the Network properties sheet when you use the Network icon in Control Panel.

Entry	Data Type	Description
Infname	REG_SZ	Includes the name of the INF file used to set up the device.
Infoption	REG_SZ	Specifies options to use in INF file.
Interface	REG_MULTI_SZ	Enables a computer to have multiple capabilities available to the network.
Review	REG_DWORD	Specifies if a component needs bindings review.
Type	REG_SZ	Defines the component type (refer to the list in the "Understanding the Network Registration Keys" section earlier in this chapter).
Use	REG_SZ	Specifies the role of the component, including driver, service, or transport. Services is the default and is for software components only.

You can use the NetRules subkey value entries to help you view network software components installed on your system. You also can use these entries to help you isolate potential network problems you might experience. You might, for instance, know that an adapter is installed on a machine but the Network properties sheet does not display it. Look for the Hidden subkey in the HKEY_LOCAL_MACHINE\ SOFTWARE\Microsoft\Windows NT\CurrentVersion\ NetworkCards*netcard*#\ NetRules. Set this value to 0 to instruct Windows NT to display it in the Network properties sheet. If you want to hide the adapter card entry from users, set the Hidden value to 1.

The following section discusses the Registry information Windows NT stores for network service components.

Service Component Registry Information

The other type of information for a network component is the service Registry information. The service information includes the location of EXE files, start parameters, and service type. In the HKEY_LOCAL_MACHINE\SYSTEM\ CurrentControlSet\Services*adapter_name* subkey, the service information controls the way network components use memory. One of the settings in the software Registry settings—ServiceName—is a pointer to the entries listed in this subkey. You can read about the software settings in the preceding section, "Software Component Registry Information."

When you look at the Registry for the service components, you might find that a component creates a set of services, each with its own Services subkey. The top-most service is usually referred to as the main service. You might, for instance, find that your network adapter's ServiceName entry (such as ETHER for a standard Ethernet card manufactured by LinkSys) defines the main service and where the driver file is located, its child services, and startup data. As you expand the ETHER subkey, you find other subkeys that contain settings and pointers for the driver. The LinkSys adapter's ServiceName entry is ETHER, and also appears as a Services subkey that points to bindings and physical parameters of the network card.

Under the HKEY_LOCAL_MACHINE\SYSTEM\CurrentControlSet\Services\ *adapter_name* subkey is the Parameters subkey. The Parameters subkey defines the various settings for an adapter card, including the I/O address, card type, DMA channel, and card speed. To set these parameters, you should not modify the Registry directly. Instead, use the Network property dialog box that displays when you double-click on the Network icon in the Control Panel to perform this task.

 Tip   One Parameters subkey you might need to modify is the BusNumber. On computers that have a PCI bus, you might need to install an ISA adapter card. If this is the case and your card is not recognized, try setting the BusNumber REG_DWORD to 0.

You can see a list of the Parameters subkeys and value entries that appear in the Registry for adapter cards in table 5.2.

TABLE 5.2
Parameters Subkey for Adapter Cards

Subkey	Type	Description
BusNumber	REG_DWORD	Specifies the bus number. This number, starting with 0, denotes the number of bus types on your system, such as ISA, EISA, or MCA.
BusType	REG_DWORD	Denotes the type of bus on the computer. The values for this include the following: 0 for MIPS bus, 1 for ISA bus, 2 for EISA bus, 3 for MCS bus, and 4 for TcChannel bus.

Subkey	Type	Description
CableType	REG_DWORD	Denotes the type of networking cable used for Proteon 1390 cards. For unshielded twisted pair, the setting is 1; for shielded twisted pair, the setting is 2.
CardSpeed	REG_DWORD	Denotes the card speed for Proteon 1390 cards. For 4 megabits/second, the setting is 0x4; for 16 megabits/second, the setting is 0x10.
CardType	REG_DWORD	Denotes the card type installed.
DMAChannel	REG_DWORD	Denotes the DMA channel configured for the adapter card. Settings for this include 5, 6, or 7.
InterruptNumber	REG_DWORD	Denotes the IRQ for the adapter card. If you have an IRQ of 6, for instance, the setting is 0x6.
IoBaseAddress	REG_DWORD	Denotes one of two parameters. For some adapter cards, denotes the card as the primary card (1) or secondary card (2). For some adapter cards, denotes the I/O port base address.
MediaType	REG_DWORD	Denotes the network type. The settings for this subkey can be as follows: Ethernet (1), IBM Token Ring (2), ARCnet (3), FDDI (4), and Apple LocalTalk (5).
MaximumPacketSize	REG_DWORD	Indicates the maximum packet size on a Token Ring adapter.
MemoryMapped	REG_DWORD	Denotes if the adapter card is memory mapped.
MemoryMapped BaseAddress	REG_DWORD	Denotes the I/O address of the adapter card, which must be one specified by the network card's manufacturer.
NetworkAddress	REG_SZ	Specifies for the adapter card's address to replace the address that the adapter card comes with from the manufacturer.
Transceiver	REG_DWORD	Denotes the transceiver value of 1 (for External) or 2 (for OnBoard).

Although you should use the Network and System applications in the Control Panel (as well as the installation software provided by your network adapters) to modify many of the settings shown in table 5.2, you can use these value entries to view how a service is configured. You might also run into a problem, such as a conflict with an interrupt number (IRQ), that you need to modify at the Registry level. This table will help you isolate the Registry value entry that causes the conflict. In this case, view the InterruptNumber value entry in the HKEY_LOCAL_MACHINE\SYSTEM\ CurrentControlSet*adapter_name*\Services\Parameters subkey and make any necessary changes to the value, such as changing the IRQ from 7 to 5.

The next section discusses how Windows NT uses the configuration information for network components to establish bindings for them.

Bindings Information in the Registry

Network bindings is a term used to describe how several different network components must be installed and establish relationships with other components. These bindings are what make networks operate. When you boot up the system, the Registry subkey HKEY_LOCAL_MACHINE\SYSTEM\CurrentControlSet is scanned for binding settings for the current network components. When bindings are located, a Linkage subkey is added to the Registry, such as the following:

HKEY_LOCAL_MACHINE\SYSTEM\CurrentControlSet*NOS*\Linkage

When the system checks the Registry for binding information, it looks at the following data:

◆ Information about the network components to be configured

◆ Types of network components

◆ Parameters of the network components, as well as their bindings

◆ Potential bindings

◆ Linkages to network components

The Linkage subkey includes entries shown in table 5.3.

TABLE 5.3
Linkage Subkey Entries

Subkey	Type	Description
Bind	REG_MULTI_SZ	Specifies the name of a Windows NT object, based on the object names denoted in the Bindform entry in the NetRules subkey (refer to table 5.2).
Export	REG_MULTI_SZ	Specifies the name to be included in the system to allow access to the corresponding object, as denoted by the Bindform entry in the NetRules subkey.
Route	REG_MULTI_SZ	Specifies the path through the binding protocol represented by the binding.

You can find the bindings for your system in the following subkey:

HKEY_LOCAL_MACHINE\SYSTEM\CurrentControlSet\Services*NOS*\Linkage

One requirement of bindings is that they must terminate at either an adapter or at a logical end-point to avoid having software components that do not have actual uses. If this happens, such as if a device drive fails for an adapter card, the other network components will load at startup, even if the network cannot be used.

Note An *adapter* is the physical adapter card. A *logical end-point* is a software component that manages all connection information.

Now that you've seen how Windows NT places network configuration data in the Registry, you can use this information to help you find settings relating to your network installation. You might want to do this if Windows NT cannot find a driver for one of your installed network adapters, or if you want to change the setting of a network device. The next section reviews many of the Registry values Windows NT has for networking components, including protocols, adapter cards, and services.

Reviewing Network Registry Values

As you become more comfortable using the Registry Editor and modifying Registry values, you will begin to acquire a sixth sense of where different Registry settings might reside. You might, for instance, know without looking it up where some of the user settings, application data, and Windows NT-specific information are stored. For other settings, you might need to do a key search to isolate the desired key. Still, in other cases, you need to reference a book such as the *Windows NT 4.0 Resource Kit* to find a value or key to modify or view.

Note See Appendix A, "Windows NT Registry Values," for other Windows NT Registry values.

The following sections discuss some of the most common network services Registry value entries and settings in Windows NT. The following "Network Registry Values" section contains several general networking values you need to know to adequately troubleshoot problems you encounter with Windows NT networks. You might, for instance, run into conflicts if you run AppleShare on your Windows NT network. What Registry values are associated with AppleShare? The next section shows you. Because some of the topics associated with Windows NT networking (including RAS, WINS, and TCP/IP) are somewhat specialized, those Registry settings are pulled out of the general networking coverage into this section and are also included in separate sections. These topics are described in the following list:

- ◆ **Server Registry values.** Windows NT includes many Registry value entries pertaining to server settings. Some of these settings include the number of users that can be logged on to a server through a single circuit, sharing violation settings, and the number of users that can be logged on to a server at one time. See the section "Server Registry Entries" later in this chapter for a complete list of these values.

- ◆ **Remote Access Services (RAS) Registry values.** Many companies running Windows NT networks install RAS to enable users to connect to a Windows NT network from a remote setting. With RAS, users can use a common phone line and dial up a Windows NT server or workstation computer to access resources on the network. The section "Remote Access Service (RAS) Registry Values" later in this chapter lists and describes the Registry value entries for RAS. Many of the entries included here will help troubleshoot server-side RAS problems, such as setting user authentication times.

- ◆ **TCP/IP Registry values.** Transmission Control Protocol/Internet Protocol (TCP/IP) is the language of the Internet as well as for the many companies running internal intranets. The "TCP/IP Registry Entries" section later in this chapter lists the Registry value entries associated with TCP/IP settings, including information about Internet database files, TCP/IP retransmission rates, and adapter card parameters for TCP/IP.

◆ **Windows Internet Naming Service (WINS) Registry values.** WINS is a naming service provided by Microsoft that aids you in setting up Internet names on your network. The section "The Windows Internet Name Server (WINS) Registry Entries," later in this chapter, includes the Registry value entries associated with WINS. You can use these settings to troubleshoot WINS problems that affect the WINS database, the WINS log file, and settings for clients accessing the WINS database.

Network Registry Values

Table 5.4 lists many of the Windows NT networking Registry value entries and where to find them. Because each value entry is covered in detail in the *Windows NT 4.0 Resource Kit* (including possible value entry data for specific hardware), that level of detail is not included here. Instead, you can use this as a reference to quickly help you find a setting you are looking for.

The table lists the type of network service in the first column. These services are the same as the ones listed on the Services tab when you run the Windows NT Diagnostics utility in Windows NT. The second column in the table lists the value entry for the service. The third and fourth columns show the data type and full Registry path for the value entry. These columns are important if you need to isolate a value already in the Registry and change its setting, or add a value to the Registry. The final column briefly describes the value entry.

TABLE 5.4
Network Services Registry Values

Service	Value Entry	Data Type	Key	Description
Alerter	AlertName	REG_MULTI_SZ	HKEY_LOCAL_MACHINE\SYSTEM\CurrentControlSet\Services\Alerter\Parameters	Includes a list of the users to whom administrators can send alerts.
AppleTalk	DefaultPort	REG_SZ	HKEY_LOCAL_MACHINE\SYSTEM\CurrentControlSet\Services\AppleTalk\Parameters	Indicates the network on which Services For Macintosh (SFM) are registered.

continues

TABLE 5.4, CONTINUED
Network Services Registry Values

Service	Value Entry	Data Type	Key	Description
AppleTalk	DesiredZone	REG_SZ	HKEY_LOCAL_ MACHINE\ SYSTEM\Current ControlSet\ Services\Apple Talk\Parameters	Indicates zone in which SFM is available.
AppleTalk	EnableRouter	REG_DWORD	HKEY_LOCAL_ MACHINE\ SYSTEM\Current ControlSet\ Services\Apple Talk\Parameters	Specifies whether routing needs to be started on the local computer and reports that to the AppleTalk protocol.
AppleTalk	AarpRetries	REG_DWORD	HKEY_LOCAL_ MACHINE\ SYSTEM\Current ControlSet\ Services\Apple Talk\Adapters\ *Adapter_Name*	For AppleTalk protocol, sets the number of AppleTalk address-resolution protocol packets to send.
AppleTalk	DdpCheck-Sums	REG_DWORD	HKEY_LOCAL_ MACHINE\ SYSTEM\Current ControlSet\ Services\Apple Talk\Adapters\ *Adapter_Name*	Specifies if AppleTalk protocol computes checksums in the DDP layer.
AppleTalk	DefaultZone	REG_SZ	HKEY_LOCAL_ MACHINE\ SYSTEM\Current ControlSet\ Services\Apple Talk\Adapters\ *Adapter_Name*	If adapter is seeding the local network, specifies the default zone for this network.

Service	Value Entry	Data Type	Key	Description
AppleTalk	Network Range-LowerEnd	REG_DWORD	HKEY_LOCAL_MACHINE\SYSTEM\CurrentControlSet\Services\AppleTalk\Adapters\ *Adapter_Name*	If adapter is seeding the local network, indicates lower network number of the network range.
AppleTalk	PortName	REG_SZ	HKEY_LOCAL_MACHINE\SYSTEM\CurrentControlSet\Services\AppleTalk\Adapters\ *Adapter_Name*	Includes name to identify AppleTalk protocol running a specific computer.
AppleTalk	Seeding-Network	REG_DWORD	HKEY_LOCAL_MACHINE\SYSTEM\CurrentControlSet\Services\AppleTalk\Adapters\ *Adapter_Name*	Specifies if AppleTalk is seeding the network (value of 1 is yes, 0 is no).
Appletalk	ZoneList	REG_MULTI_SZ	HKEY_LOCAL_MACHINE\SYSTEM\CurrentControlSet\Services\AppleTalk\Adapters\ *Adapter_Name*	If AppleTalk protocol is seeding the network, this list specifies the zones to be seeded.
DHCP	IgnoreBroadCastFlag	REG_DWORD	HKEY_LOCAL_MACHINE\SYSTEM\CurrentControlSet\Services\DhcpServer\Parameters	Instructs the DHCP server to broadcast initial DHCP offer packet to the DHCP client. Should be set to 0 if your DHCP client and server are on an Ethernet-only network or Token-Ring network.

continues

TABLE 5.4, CONTINUED
Network Services Registry Values

Service	Value Entry	Data Type	Key	Description
DNS	Bind-Secondaries	REG_DWORD	HKEY_LOCAL _MACHINE\ SYSTEM\Current ControlSet\ Services\DNS\ Parameters	Enables the Microsoft DNS server to interoperate with non-Microsoft DNS servers.
EventLog	Category-Count	REG_DWORD	HKEY_LOCAL_ MACHINE\ SYSTEM\Current ControlSet\ Services\EventLog\ *System*or *application* or *securitylogfile*\ Sources	Specifies number of categories that are supported.
EventLog	Category-MessageFile	REG_EXPAND _SZ	HKEY_LOCAL_ MACHINE\ SYSTEM\Current ControlSet\ Services\EventLog\ *System*or *application* or *securitylogfile*\ Sources	Sets the category message file path.
EventLog	Event-MessageFile	REG_EXPAND _SZ	HKEY_LOCAL_ MACHINE\ SYSTEM\Current ControlSet \Services\EventLog *System* or *application* or *securitylogfile*\ Sources	Sets the event identifier message file path.
EventLog	File	REG_SZ	HKEY_LOCAL_ MACHINE\ SYSTEM\Current ControlSet\ Services\EventLog\ *System* or *application* or *securitylogfile*	Specifies the event log path file.

Service	Value Entry	Data Type	Key	Description
EventLog	MaxSize	REG_DWORD	HKEY_LOCAL_ MACHINE\ SYSTEM\Current ControlSet\ Services\EventLog\ *System* or *application* or *securitylogfile*	Sets the maximum size of the event log.
EventLog	Retention	REG_DWORD	HKEY_LOCAL_ MACHINE\ SYSTEM\Current ControlSet\ Services\EventLog\ *System* or *application* or *security logfile*	Instructs the Event Viewer when (in number of seconds) to overwrite an event log.
EventLog	Sources	REG_EXPAND _SZ	HKEY_LOCAL_ MACHINE\ SYSTEM\Current ControlSet\ Services\EventLog\ *System* or *application* or *security logfile*	Lists the source that writes events to the event log, including applications, groups of applications, and services.
EventLog	Types Supported	REG_DWORD	HKEY_LOCAL_ MACHINE\ SYSTEM\Current ControlSet\ Services\EventLog\ *System* or *application* or *security logfile*\ Source	Shows a list of supported event type.
MacFile	LoginMsg	REG_SZ	HKEY_LOCAL_ MACHINE\ SYSTEM\Current ControlSet\ Services\MacFile\ Parameters	Indicates the message (up to 198 characters) users see at login time.

continues

TABLE 5.4, CONTINUED
Network Services Registry Values

Service	Value Entry	Data Type	Key	Description
MacFile	MaxSessions	REG_DWORD	HKEY_LOCAL_MACHINE\ SYSTEM\Current ControlSet\ Services\MacFile\ Parameters	Indicates maximum user sessions Macintosh file server can handle.
MacFile	PagedMem-Limit	REG_DWORD	HKEY_LOCAL_MACHINE\ SYSTEM\Current ControlSet\ Services\MacFile\ Parameters	Indicates the top value for the page memory for Macintosh file server usage.
MacFile	NonPaged-MemLimit	REG_DWORD	HKEY_LOCAL_MACHINE\ SYSTEM\Current ControlSet\ Services\MacFile\ Parameters	Indicates the maximum amount of RAM the Macintosh file server can use.
MacFile	ServerName	REG_SZ	HKEY_LOCAL_MACHINE\ SYSTEM\Current ControlSet\ Services\MacFile\ Parameters	Indicates the server name running SFM under Windows NT.
MacFile	ServerOptions	REG_DWORD	HKEY_LOCAL_MACHINE\ SYSTEM\Current ControlSet\ Services\MacFile\ Parameters	Indicates which Server Manager options you have selected.

Service	Value Entry	Data Type	Key	Description
MacFile	*Volume*	REG_MULTI_SZ	HKEY_LOCAL_ MACHINE\ SYSTEM\Current ControlSet\ Services\ MacFile\ Parameters	Specifies information about a Macintosh volume. You can choose from MaxUses, *Properties*, *Password*, and *Path* for the variable *Volume*.
Type_ Creators	##	REG_MULTI_SZ	HKEY_LOCAL_ MACHINE\ SYSTEM\Current ControlSet\ Services\ MacFile\ Parameters\ Type_Creators	Includes three value entries, including Creator=, Type=, and Comment=.
NBF	AddName- QueryRetries	REG_DWORD	HKEY_LOCAL_ MACHINE\ SYSTEM\Services\ NBF\Parameters	Indicates times NBF tries to send ADD_NAME_ QUERY and ADD_GROUP_ NAME_QUERY frames.
NBF	AddName- QueryTimeout	REG_DWORD	HKEY_LOCAL_ MACHINE\ SYSTEM\Services\ NBF\Parameters	Indicates time-out setting between NBF sending ADD_NAME_ QUERY and ADD_GROUP_ NAME_QUERY frames.
NBF	General- Retries	REG_DWORD	HKEY_LOCAL_ MACHINE\ SYSTEM\ Services\NBF\ Parameters	Indicates times NBF tries sending STATUS_QUERY and FIND_NAME frames.

continues

TABLE 5.4, CONTINUED
Network Services Registry Values

Service	Value Entry	Data Type	Key	Description
NBF	DefaultT1-Timeout	REG_DWORD	HKEY_LOCAL_MACHINE\SYSTEM\Services\NBF\Parameters	Indicates T1 timeout start time, which controls wait time for NBF to await a response after sending a logical link control (LLC) poll packet to resend it.
NBF	DefaultT2-Timeout	REG_DWORD	HKEY_LOCAL_MACHINE\NBF\Parameters	Time NBF waits after receiving an before responding.
NBF	DefaultTi-Timeout	REG_DWORD	HKEY_LOCAL_MACHINE\SYSTEM\Services\NBF\Parameters	Indicates the default inactivity timer (Ti).
NBF	General-TimeOut	REG_DWORD	HKEY_LOCAL_MACHINE\SYSTEM\Services\NBF\Parameters	Indicates time between NBF sending STATUS_QUERY and FIND_NAME requests.
NBF	InitAddresses	REG_DWORD	HKEY_LOCAL_MACHINE\SYSTEM\Services\NBF\Parameters	Indicates the number of initial addresses to allocate within NBF imposed memory.
NBF	Init-AddressFiles	REG_DWORD	HKEY_LOCAL_MACHINE\SYSTEM\Services\NBF\Parameters	Indicates number of initial address files to allocate within NBF imposed memory.

Service	Value Entry	Data Type	Key	Description
NBF	Init-Connections	REG_DWORD	HKEY_LOCAL_ MACHINE\ SYSTEM\Services\ NBF\Parameters	Indicates amount of NetBIOS sessions to allocate within NBF imposed memory limits.
NBF	InitLinks	REG_DWORD	HKEY_LOCAL_ MACHINE\ SYSTEM\Services\ NBF\Parameters	Indicates amount of LLLC links to allocate within NBF imposed memory limits.
NBF	MaxAddress	REG_DWORD	HKEY_LOCAL_ MACHINE\ SYSTEM\ Services\NBF\ Parameters	Indicates maximum number of addresses NBF allocates within NBF imposed memory limits.
NBF	Max-Connections	REG_DWORD	HKEY_LOCAL_ MACHINE\ SYSTEM\ Services\ NBF\Parameters	Indicates number of connections allowed within NBF imposed memory limits.
NetLogon	Change-LogSize	REG_DWORD	HKEY_LOCAL_ MACHINE\ SYSTEM\Current ControlSet\ Services\ NetLogon\ Parameters	Enables you to set the size of the change log.
NetLogon	Maximum-MailSlot-Messages	REG_DWORD	HKEY_LOCAL_ MACHINE\ SYSTEM\Current ControlSet\ Services\ NetLogon\ Parameters	Sets the number of mailslot messages that can be spooled to the Netlogon service.

continues

TABLE 5.4, CONTINUED
Network Services Registry Values

Service	Value Entry	Data Type	Key	Description
NetLogon	Maximum-MailSlot-Timeout	REG_DWORD	HKEY_LOCAL_MACHINE\SYSTEM\Current ControlSet\Services\NetLogon\Parameters	Sets the number of seconds an incoming mailslot message can exist.
NetLogon	Pulse	REG_DWORD	HKEY_LOCAL_MACHINE\SYSTEM\Current ControlSet\Services\NetLogon\Parameters	Sets the pulse frequency in seconds.
NetLogon	Scripts	REG_DWORD	HKEY_LOCAL_MACHINE\SYSTEM\Current ControlSet\Services\NetLogon\Parameters	Sets the logon scripts path.
Network Provider	Provider-Order	REG_SZ	HKEY_LOCAL_MACHINE\SYSTEM\Current ControlSet\Control\NetworkProvider\Order	When you specify the order for accessing available network providers, the ProviderOrder is placed in the Registry.
Redirector	Connect-Timeout	REG_DWORD	HKEY_LOCAL_MACHINE\SYSTEM\Current ControlSet\Services\Rdr\Parameters	Sets time redirector should wait for connection or disconnection.

Service	Value Entry	Data Type	Key	Description
Redirector	LowerSearch-BufferSize	REG_DWORD	HKEY_LOCAL_MACHINE\ SYSTEM\Current ControlSet\ Services\Rdr\ Parameters	Sets redirector byte size for small search activities.
Redirector	LowerSearch-Threshold	REG_DWORD	HKEY_LOCAL_MACHINE\ SYSTEM\Current ControlSet\ Services\Rdr\ Parameters	Sets a value that the redirector will request a search when the number of bytes falls below the LowerSearch-BufferSize. The redirector uses the UpperSearch-BufferSize value when the search size is larger than the LowerSearch-BufferSize value but lower than the UpperSearch-BufferSize value.
Redirector	StackSize	REG_DWORD	HKEY_LOCAL_MACHINE\ SYSTEM\Current ControlSet\ Services\Rdr\ Parameters	Sets redirector IRP stack size.
Redirector	UpperSearch-BufferSize	REG_DWORD	HKEY_LOCAL_MACHINE\ SYSTEM\Current ControlSet\ Services\Rdr\ Parameters	Sets redirector byte size for large search activities.

continues

TABLE 5.4, CONTINUED
Network Services Registry Values

Service	Value Entry	Data Type	Key	Description
Redirector	UseAsync-WriteBehind	REG_DWORD	HKEY_LOCAL_MACHINE\SYSTEM\CurrentControlSet\Services\Rdr\Parameters	Turns on the asynchronous option of the write-behind optimization feature.
Redirector	UseWrite-Behind	REG_DWORD	HKEY_LOCAL_MACHINE\SYSTEM\CurrentControlSet\Services\Rdr\Parameters	Turns on the write-behind optimization feature.
Replicator	CrashDir	REG_SZ	HKEY_LOCAL_MACHINE\SYSTEM\CurrentControlSet\Services\Replicator\Parameters	Specifies a folder name during a system repair that the replicator service automatically adds to the Registry.
Replicator	ExportList	REG_SZ	HKEY_LOCAL_MACHINE\SYSTEM\CurrentControlSet\Services\Replicator\Parameters	Specifies list of servers and domains to receive notices notices during an update of the export directory.
Replicator	ExportPath	REG_SZ or REG_EXPAND_SZ	HKEY_LOCAL_MACHINE\SYSTEM\CurrentControlSet\Services\Replicator\Parameters	Sets the export path for replicated files.

Service	Value Entry	Data Type	Key	Description
Replicator	GuardTime	REG_DWORD	HKEY_LOCAL_MACHINE\ SYSTEM\Current ControlSet\ Services\ Replicator\ Parameters	Sets amount of time the export folder must have no activity before its files are replicated by the import servers.
Replicator	ImportList	REG_SZ	HKEY_LOCAL_MACHINE\ SYSTEM\Current ControlSet\ Services\ Replicator\ Parameters	Sets import server replication path for export server to send replicated files.
Replicator	Interval	REG_DWORD	HKEY_LOCAL_MACHINE\ SYSTEM\Current ControlSet\ Services\ Replicator\ Parameters	Specifies when an export server looks for changes in the replicator folders.
Replicator	Pulse	REG_DWORD	HKEY_LOCAL_MACHINE\ SYSTEM\Current ControlSet\ Services\ Replicator\ Parameters	Sets last update notice repeat rate for the export server.
Replicator	Random	REG_DWORD	HKEY_LOCAL_MACHINE\ SYSTEM\Current ControlSet\ Services\ Replicator\ Parameters	Sets wait time for import servers before update request is sent.

continues

TABLE 5.4, CONTINUED
Network Services Registry Values

Service	Value Entry	Data Type	Key	Description
Replicator	Replicate	REG_DWORD	HKEY_LOCAL_ MACHINE\ SYSTEM\Current ControlSet\ Services\ Replicator\ Parameters	Sets status of replicator. For export status, set to 1; for import status, set to 2; and for both set to 3.
UPS	BatteryLife	REG_DWORD	HKEY_LOCAL_ MACHINE\ SYSTEM\Current ControlSet\ Service\UPS	Sets the UPS maximum battery life.
UPS	CommandFile	REG_EXPAND_SZ	HKEY_LOCAL_ MACHINE\ SYSTEM\Current ControlSet\ Service\UPS	Sets the name of the file to run before shutting down the UPS system.
UPS	FirstMessage Delay	REG_DWORD	HKEY_LOCAL_ MACHINE\ SYSTEM\Current ControlSet\ Service\UPS	Tells Windows NT how long to wait after UPS turns on during a power failure to send a message to users.
UPS	Message Interval	REG_DWORD	HKEY_LOCAL_ MACHINE\ SYSTEM\Current ControlSet\ Service\UPS	Tells Windows NT how to wait between power-failure messages sent to users.
UPS	Options	REG_DWORD	HKEY_LOCAL_ MACHINE\ SYSTEM\Current ControlSet\ Service\UPS	Includes Registry settings for options you can select from the UPS dialog box.

Service	Value Entry	Data Type	Key	Description
UPS	Port	REG_SZ	HKEY_LOCAL_ MACHINE\ SYSTEM\Current ControlSet\ Service\UPS	Sets the port value to which the UPS is connected.
UPS	RechargeRate	REG_DWORD	HKEY_LOCAL_ MACHINE\ SYSTEM\Current ControlSet\ Service\UPS	Sets UPS battery recharge rate.

If your network includes a NetWare server, you can manage NWLink parameters using the Registry. Well over 60 different Registry value entries are associated with NWLink, with the majority of them in the following Registry keys:

HKEY_LOCAL_MACHINE\SYSTEM\CurrentControlSet\Services\NWLinkSPX\Parameters

HKEY_LOCAL_MACHINE\SYSTEM\CurrentControlSet\Services\NWLinkNB\Parameters

HKEY_LOCAL_MACHINE\SYSTEM\CurrentControlSet\Services\NWLink

IPX\NetConfig*adapter_name*

For an in-depth listing and discussion of these keys, see Chapter 12, "Integrating NetWare withWindows NT Server," in *Windows NT Server 4 Professional Reference* published by New Riders. That chapter also gives you an excellent tutorial of how to use NetWare on a Windows NT network.

The next four sections go into detail about four of the most popular Windows NT network services—server, RAS, TCP/IP, and WINS—and show you Registry settings for each of these services.

Server Registry Entries

Windows NT stores its server information in the following subkey. You can use the value entries in table 5.5 to modify the startup parameters of the server. All of the entries in this table fall under the following Registry key.

HKEY_LOCAL_MACHINE\SYSTEM\CurrentControlSet\Services\LanmanServer\Parameters

TABLE 5.5
Server Registry Value Entries

Value Entry	Data Type	Description
AlertShed	REG_DWORD	Sets frequency rate that the server uses to check alert conditions and send alert messages.
BlockingThreads	REG_DWORD	Sets threads the server reserves for large service requests that take a long time to process.
ConnectionlessAutoDisc	REG_DWORD	Sets the time for clients using direct hosted IPX to disconnect automatically if a request has not been sent within the specified interval (in minutes).
CriticalThreads	REG_DWORD	Lists number of threads assigned for high-priority tasks.
DiskSpaceThreshold	REG_DWORD	Shows the free disk space (in percentage) available before an alert is sent.
EnableFCPopens	REG_DWORD	Enables file control blocks (FCBs) of remote MS-DOS sessions to be grouped as a single open on the server to conserve server resources.
EnableRaw	REG_DWORD	Specifies (when set to 1) that the server processes raw SMBs (Server Message Blocks).
EnableSharedNetDrives	REG_DWORD	Reshares NWCS (NetWare Client Services) drives as Windows NT shares.

Value Entry	Data Type	Description
EnableSoftCompat	REG_DWORD	Enables Window NT to map server read requests for several requests for the same file.
EnableWFW311DirectIpx	REG_DWORD	Instructs Windows NT to allow Windows for Workgroups clients running IPX to connect to the server.
ErrorThreshold	REG_DWORD	Specifies AlertSched interval error rate that can occur before an alert message is sent.
Hidden	REG_DWORD	Enables (1) or disables the announcement of the server to other computers on the domain.
InitConnTable	REG_DWORD	Shows the connection table for each server connection.
InitFileTable	REG_DWORD	Shows the file table for each server connection.
InitSearchTable	REG_DWORD	Shows the search table for each server connection.
InitSessTable	REG_DWORD	Shows the session table for each server connection.
InitWorkItems	REG_DWORD	Shows receive buffers used by the server.
IRPstackSize	REG_DWORD	Shows the server's stack locations in IRPs (I/O request packets).
LinkInfoValidTime	REG_DWORD	Sets valid interval for transport link information.
MaxFreeConnections	REG_DWORD	Sets number of free connection blocks that each endpoint can have.

continues

TABLE 5.5, CONTINUED
Server Registry Value Entries

Value Entry	Data Type	Description
MaxGlobalOpenSearch	REG_DWORD	Sets number of simultaneous server searches.
MaxLinkDelay	REG_DWORD	Sets time interval to wait for a link delay before the server disables raw I/O.
MaxNonpagedMemoryUsage	REG_DWORD	Sets nonpaged memory allocation for a server.
MaxPagedMemoryUsage	REG_DWORD	Sets paged memory allocation for a server.
MaxRawWorkItems	REG_DWORD	Sets raw work allocation for a server.
MaxWorkItems	REG_DWORD	Sets receive buffer allocation for a server.
MaxWorkItemIdleTime	REG_DWORD	Sets time that the idle queue holds a work item before it is released.
MinFreeConnections	REG_DWORD	Sets minimum number of free connection blocks that each endpoint can have.
MinFreeWorkItems	REG_DWORD	Specifies when the server starts processing blocking SMBs.
MinLinkThroughput	REG_DWORD	Sets lowest link throughput allowed for server before it disables raw locks for the connections.
MinRcvQueue	REG_DWORD	Enables you to set minimum work items for server.
NetworkErrorThreshold	REG_DWORD	Sets value (in percentage) for an alert to be sent when the AlertSched interval is passed for failed network operations.

Value Entry	Data Type	Description
NonBlockingThreads	REG_DWORD	Sets thread number that cannot be blocked for a large amount of time.
NullSessionPipes	REG_DWORD	Specifies the null session pipes that a client can access.
NullSessionShares	REG_DWORD	Specifies the null session shares that a client can access.
OpenSearch	REG_DWORD	Sets number of searches that can be open on the server for each connection.
RawWorkItems	REG_DWORD	Sets the raw work items for a server.
RemoveDuplicateSearches	REG_DWORD	Instructs the server to remove duplicate searches that are open.
RestrictNullSessionAccess	REG_DWORD	Sets the server to deny or allow null session access to clients.
ScavTimeout	REG_DWORD	Sets scavenger idle time.
ScavQosInfoUpdateTime	REG_DWORD	Sets interval for scavenger to update link information.
SessConns	REG_DWORD	Sets connections that are allowed on a server through a single virtual circuit.
SessOpens	REG_DWORD	Sets number of open files allowed on a single virtual circuit.
SesUsers	REG_DWORD	Sets number of users that are allowed on a server through a single virtual circuit.

continues

TABLE 5.5, CONTINUED
Server Registry Value Entries

Value Entry	Data Type	Description
SharingViolationRetries	REG_DWORD	Sets server delay time (in milliseconds) between each retry.
SizReqBuf	REG_DWORD	Sets server request buffer size.
ThreadPriority	REG_DWORD	Sets the server thread priority.
Users	REG_DWORD	Tells server the number of simultaneous logged on users it can have.
XactMemSize	REG_DWORD	Sets the Xactsrv service virtual memory allocation.

If you run the Windows NT Remote Access Service (RAS), the following section helps you understand where each of the RAS Registry settings are stored.

Remote Access Service (RAS) Registry Values

Windows NT's Remote Access Service (RAS) enables computers to access a Windows NT network from remote locations. RAS is invaluable to the many workers and users who must connect with the local network while in mobile environments. It also enables users to connect to the office LAN while working from home. RAS also is used to dial out from the office to other networks, including wide area networks (WANs) and the Internet. RAS includes both server-side (RAS Server) and client-side (Dial-Up Networking) components. RAS Server resides on a computer to make it a server for a Dial-Up Networking client.

When you install RAS, a number of configuration entries are added to the Windows NT Registry. The primary subkey added is the Remote Access subkey, which is placed in the following Registry key:

HKEY_LOCAL_MACHINE\SYSTEM\CurrentControlSet\Services\RemoteAccess\Parameters

Table 5.6 summarizes the RAS Registry configuration entries for the RAS Server component.

TABLE 5.6
Remote Access Service Registry Entries

Subkey	Value Entry	Date Type	Key	Description
RemoteAccess	Authenticate-Retries	REG_DWORD	HKEY_LOCAL_MACHINE\SYSTEM\CurrentControlSet\Services\RemoteAccess\Parameters	Specifies number of retries allowed for authentication process.
RemoteAccess	Authenticate-Time	REG_DWORD	HKEY_LOCAL_MACHINE\SYSTEM\CurrentControlSet\Services\RemoteAccess\Parameters	Specifies how much time a user has to authenticate with the RAS server.
RemoteAccess	AutoDisconnect	REG_DWORD	HKEY_LOCAL_MACHINE\SYSTEM\CurrentControlSet\Services\RemoteAccess\Parameters	Specifies inactivity time limit. After time limit passes, user is disconnected from RAS server.
RemoteAccess	CallbackTime	REG_DWORD	HKEY_LOCAL_MACHINE\SYSTEM\CurrentControlSet\Services\RemoteAccess\Parameters	Specifies callback time for server to call client. Callback feature must be enabled for this to work.
RemoteAccess	EnableAudit	REG_DWORD	HKEY_LOCAL_MACHINE\SYSTEM\CurrentControlSet\Services\RemoteAccess\Parameters	Turn on (1) to enable RAS auditing.

continues

TABLE 5.6, CONTINUED
Remote Access Service Registry Entries

Subkey	Value Entry	Date Type	Key	Description
RemoteAccess	Netbios-Gateway-Enabled	REG_DWORD	HKEY_LOCAL_MACHINE\ SYSTEM\ CurrentControl Set\Services\ RemoteAccess\ Parameters	Enables users to access LAN services as if RAS server is a NetBIOS gateway. Otherwise, users can access only those services on the RAS computer.
NetbiosGateway	Disable-McastFwd-WhenSession-Traffic	REG_DWORD	HKEY_LOCAL_MACHINE\ SYSTEM\ CurrentControl Set\Services\ RemoteAccess\ Parameters\ NetbiosGateway	Specifies that multicast datagrams are not sent unless there is no NetBIOS traffic.
NetbiosGateway	Enable-Broadcast	REG_DWORD	HKEY_LOCAL_ SYSTEM\ CurrentControl Set\Services\ RemoteAccess\ Parameters\ NetbiosGateway	Specifies if MACHINE\ broadcast datagrams are sent to remote computers.
NetbiosGateway	EnableNetbios-Sessions-Auditing	REG_DWORD	HKEY_LOCAL_MACHINE\ SYSTEM\ CurrentControl Set\Services\ RemoteAccess\ Parameters\ NetbiosGateway	Enables RAS auditing between the remote clients and Windows NT serversin NetBIOS environments.

Subkey	Value Entry	Date Type	Key	Description
NetbiosGateway	MaxBcastDg-Buffered	REG_DWORD	HKEY_LOCAL_ MACHINE\ SYSTEM\ CurrentControl Set\Services\ RemoteAccess\ Parameters\ NetbiosGateway	Specifies how many broadcast datagrams are sent to the buffer for a client.
NetbiosGateway	MaxDg-Buffered-PerGroup-Name	REG_DWORD	HKEY_LOCAL_ MACHINE\ SYSTEM\ CurrentControl Set\Services\ RemoteAccess\ Parameters\ NetbiosGateway	Specifies how many broadcast datagrams can be sent to the buffer per group name.
NetbiosGateway	MaxDynMem	REG_DWORD	HKEY_LOCAL_ MACHINE\ SYSTEM\ CurrentControl Set\Services\ RemoteAccess\ Parameters\ NetbiosGateway	Specifies virtual memory space for NetBIOS data for a client.
NetbiosGateway	MaxNames	REG_DWORD	HKEY_LOCAL_ MACHINE\ SYSTEM\ CurrentControl Set\Services\ RemoteAccess\ Parameters\ NetbiosGateway	Specifies number (up to 255) of NetBIOS names for a client.
NetbiosGateway	MaxSessions	REG_DWORD	HKEY_LOCAL_ MACHINE\ SYSTEM\ CurrentControl Set\Services\ RemoteAccess\ Parameters\ NetbiosGateway	Specifies number (up to 255 for all clients) of NetBIOS simultaneous sessions for a client.

continues

TABLE 5.6, CONTINUED
Remote Access Service Registry Entries

Subkey	Value Entry	Date Type	Key	Description
NetbiosGateway	MultiCast-ForwardRate	REG_DWORD	HKEY_LOCAL_MACHINE\ SYSTEM\ CurrentControl Set\Services\ RemoteAccess\ Parameters\ NetbiosGateway	Determines group name multicasting to datagrams remote users.
NetbiosGateway	NumRecv-Query-Indications	REG_DWORD	HKEY_LOCAL_MACHINE\ SYSTEM\ CurrentControl Set\Services\ RemoteAccess\ Parameters\ NetbiosGateway	Enables RAS client to have multiple network connections running simultaneously.
NetbiosGateway	RcvDg-SubmittedPer-GroupName	REG_DWORD	HKEY_LOCAL_MACHINE\ SYSTEM\ CurrentControl Set\Services\ RemoteAccess\ Parameters\ NetbiosGateway	Sets the amount of NetBIOS Receive Datagram commands each group name can submit simulta-neously.
NetbiosGateway	RemoteListen	REG_DWORD	HKEY_LOCAL_MACHINE\ SYSTEM\ CurrentControl Set\Services\ RemoteAccess\ Parameters\ NetbiosGateway	Specifies access level to a remote client for a LAN client.

Subkey	Value Entry	Date Type	Key	Description
NetbiosGateway	SizWorkBufs	REG_DWORD	HKEY_LOCAL_ MACHINE\ SYSTEM\ CurrentControl Set\Services\ RemoteAccess\ Parameters\ NetbiosGateway	Specifies work buffer size.
IP	WINS-NameServer	REG_SZ	HKEY_LOCAL_ MACHINE\ SYSTEM\ CurrentControl Set\Services\ RemoteAccess\ Parameters\IP	Specifies in a RAS server configuration to change the RAS server's WINS server to the RAS client.
IP	WINSName-ServerBackup	REG_SZ	HKEY_LOCAL_ MACHINE\ SYSTEM\ CurrentControl Set\Services\ RemoteAccess\ Parameters\IP	Specifies in a RAS server configuration to change RAS server's backup server to the WINS RAS client.
IP	WIDNSName-Servers	REG_MULTI _SZ	HKEY_LOCAL_ MACHINE\ SYSTEM\ CurrentControl Set\Services\ RemoteAccess\ Parameters\IP	Specifies in a RAS server configuration to change RAS server's backupDNS server to the RAS client.
AsyncMac	MaxFrameSize	REG_DWORD	HKEY_LOCAL_ MACHINE\ SYSTEM\ CurrentControl Set\Services\ AsyncMacn\ Parameters	Sets maximum frame size.

continues

TABLE 5.6, CONTINUED
Remote Access Service Registry Entries

Subkey	Value Entry	Date Type	Key	Description
AsyncMac	TimeoutBase	REG_DWORD	HKEY_LOCAL_ MACHINE\ SYSTEM\ CurrentControl Set\Services\ AsyncMacn\ Parameters	Sets elapse time on a NetBIOS gateway before disconnecting connection.
NdisWand	NetworkAddress ="xxxxxx"	REG_SZ	HKEY_LOCAL_ MACHINE\ SYSTEM\ CurrentControl Set\Services\ NdisWan\ Parameters	Reassigns the first 4 bytes of the 6-byte IEEE address.
NwlnkRip	NetbiosRouting	REG_DWORD	HKEY_LOCAL_ MACHINE\ SYSTEM\ CurrentControl Set\Services\ NwlnkRip\ Parameters	Specifies configuration information for the forwarding of IPX NetBIOS broadcast packets to and from the LAN.
RasMan	Logging	REG_DWORD	HKEY_LOCAL_ MACHINE\ SYSTEM\ CurrentControl Set\Services\ RasMan\ Parameters	Initiates logs to capture activity from serial ports to devices connected to them during command mode.
PPP	MaxTerminate	REG_DWORD	HKEY_LOCAL_ MACHINE\ SYSTEM\ CurrentControl Set\Services\ RasMan\PPP	Specifies amount of Terminate- Request packets to send before acknowledging that the peer cannot respond with a Terminate- Ack packet.

Subkey	Value Entry	Date Type	Key	Description
PPP	MaxConfigure	REG_DWORD	HKEY_LOCAL_MACHINE\ SYSTEM\ CurrentControl Set\Services\ RasMan\PPP	Specifies amount of Configure-Request packets to send before acknowledging that the peer cannot respond with a Configure-Ack, Configure-Nak, or Configure-Reject packet.
PPP	MaxFailure	REG_DWORD	HKEY_LOCAL_MACHINE\ SYSTEM\ CurrentControl Set\Services\ RasMan\PPP	Specifies amount of Configure-Nak packets to send before acknowledging that the configuration is not converging and cannot respond with a Configure-Ack packet.
PPP	MaxReject	REG_DWORD	HKEY_LOCAL_MACHINE\ SYSTEM\ CurrentControl Set\Services\ RasMan\PPP	Specifies amount of Config-Rejects packets to send before assuming PPP negotiation cannot converge.

continues

TABLE 5.6, CONTINUED
Remote Access Service Registry Entries

Subkey	Value Entry	Date Type	Key	Description
PPP	RestartTimer	REG_DWORD	HKEY_LOCAL_ MACHINE\ SYSTEM\ CurrentControl Set\Services\ RasMan\PPP	Specifies the number of seconds for transmission of Configure-Request and Terminate-Request packets.
PPP	Negotiate-Time	REG_DWORD	HKEY_LOCAL_ MACHINE\ SYSTEM\ CurrentControl Set\Services\ RasMan\PPP	Specifies the number of seconds for PPP negotiation to converge before disconnecting.
PPP	Force-Encrypted-Password	REG_DWORD	0 - 1	Specifies that the Crypto-Handshake Authentication Protocol (CHAP) be used on RAS servers while authenticating clients.
PPP	Logging	REG_DWORD	HKEY_LOCAL_ MACHINE\ SYSTEM\ CurrentControl Set\Services\ RasMan\PPP	Turns on PPP event logging, saving the log to the \%systemroot\ system32\ras\ ppp.log file.
PPP	Disable-Software-Compression	REG_DWORD	HKEY_LOCAL_ MACHINE\ SYSTEM\ CurrentControl Set\Services\ RasMan\PPP	Enables software compression.

Subkey	Value Entry	Date Type	Key	Description
PPP	CBCP	REG_EXPAND _SZ	HKEY_LOCAL_ MACHINE\ SYSTEM\ CurrentControl Set\Services\ RasMan\PPP	Sets Callback Control Protocol (CBCP) DLL location to negotiate callback information with the remote client.
PPP	CHAP	REG_EXPAND _SZ	HKEY_LOCAL_ MACHINE\ SYSTEM\ CurrentControl Set\Services\ RasMan\PPP	Sets CHAP DLL path.
PPP	COMPCP	REG_EXPAND _SZ	HKEY_LOCAL_ MACHINE\ SYSTEM\ CurrentControl Set\Services\ RasMan\PPP	Sets Compres- sion Control Protocol(CCP) DLL path.
PPP	IPCP	REG_EXPAND _SZ	HKEY_LOCAL_ MACHINE\ SYSTEM\ CurrentControl Set\Services\ RasMan\PPP	Sets Internet Protocol Con- trol Protocol (IPCP) DLL path.
PPP\IPCP	AcceptVJ- Compression	REG_DWORD	HKEY_LOCAL_ MACHINE\ SYSTEM\ CurrentControl Set\Services\ RasMan\PPP	Prevents IPCP from accepting IPCP Van Jacobson header compression.

continues

TABLE 5.6, CONTINUED
Remote Access Service Registry Entries

Subkey	Value Entry	Date Type	Key	Description
PPP\IPCP	PriorityBased OnSubNetwork	REG_DWORD	HKEY_LOCAL_ MACHINE\ SYSTEM\ CurrentControl Set\Services\ RasMan\PPP	Specifies for computers that have both a network card and RAS connection that all packets are sent over the RAS connection.
PPP\IPCP	RequestName- ServerAddresses	REG_DWORD	HKEY_LOCAL_ MACHINE\ SYSTEM\ CurrentControl Set\Services\ RasMan\PPP	Prevents IPCP from acquiring Microsoft options extension for WINS and DNS server address negotiation.
PPP\IPCP	RequestVJ- Compression	REG_DWORD	HKEY_LOCAL_ MACHINE\ SYSTEM\ CurrentControl Set\Services\ RasMan\PPP	Prevents IPCP from requesting Van Jacobson header compression.
PPP	IPXCP	REG_EXPAND _SZ	HKEY_LOCAL_ MACHINE\ SYSTEM\ CurrentControl Set\Services\ RasMan\PPP	Sets DLL path of Internetwork Packet Exchange Control Protocol (IPXCP) DLL.
PPP	NBFCP	REG_EXPAND _SZ	HKEY_LOCAL_ MACHINE\ SYSTEM\ CurrentControl Set\Services\ RasMan\PPP	Sets DLL path of NetBEUI Framing Control Protocol (NBFCP) DLL.

Subkey	Value Entry	Date Type	Key	Description
PPP	PAP	REG_EXPAND _SZ	HKEY_LOCAL_ MACHINE\ SYSTEM\ CurrentControl Set\Services\ RasMan\PPP	Sets DLL path of the Password Authentication Protocol (PAP) DLL.
Rdr	RawIo- TimeLimit	REG_DWORD	HKEY_LOCAL_ MACHINE\ SYSTEM\ CurrentControl Set\Services\ Rdr\Parameters	Instructs redirector to send data in 64 kilobyte blocks.
RasArp	Filter- Broadcasts	REG_DWORD	HKEY_LOCAL_ MACHINE\ SYSTEM\ CurrentControl Set\Services\ RasArp\ Parameter	Instructs RAS to transmit broadcast packets and subnet multicasts.
Nbf	InitUIFrames	REG_DWORD	HKEY_LOCAL_ MACHINE\ SYSTEM\ CurrentControl Set\Services\ Nbf\Parameters	Sets number of simultaneous RAS client NetBIOS names that can occur on the network.
NwlnkIpx	DisableDialin- Netbios	REG_DWORD	HKEY_LOCAL_ MACHINE\ SYSTEM\ CurrentControl Set\Services\ NwlnkIpx\ Parameters	Specifies routing of IPX between type 20 packets remote RAS client, a network running the RAS IPX router, and an IPX NetBIOS application running on an RAS server.

Note To get an in-depth description of Windows NT's RAS feature, see *Windows NT Server 4 Professional Reference*, published by New Riders.

The next section shows you where TCP/IP Registry settings are stored. If you are not running TCP/IP on your system, you can skip over the following two sections to the section about troubleshooting specific problems called "Troubleshooting Network Registry Problems."

TCP/IP Registry Entries

TCP/IP is probably the most popular networking protocol in the world due to the popularity of the Internet and intranets. You have the option of installing TCP/IP as your networking protocol, and when you do, Windows NT places a number of value entries in the Registry relating to TCP/IP. The following subkey contains TCP/IP settings:

HKEY_LOCAL_MACHINE\SYSTEM\CurrentControlSet\Services

Under this subkey are a number of other subkeys that contain specific information for your TCP/IP setup:

- ◆ **Windows Sockets\Parameters.** Contains Winsock parameters for a TCP/IP connection.

- ◆ **DHCP\Parameters.** Contains settings for the Dynamic Host Configuration Protocol (DHCP), which assigns IP addresses automatically to a resource.

- ◆ **Ftpsvc\Parameters.** Includes Registry settings for the File Transfer Protocol (FTP) service.

- ◆ **Streams\Parameters.** Includes Registry settings for the Streams protocol for Unix System V.

- ◆ **NetBt\Parameters.** Includes Registry settings for the NetBIOS over TCP/IP service.

- ◆ **Adapter parameters.** Includes TCP/IP Registry settings for the installed network adapter. The settings for an adapter are located under the *adapter_name_no*\Parameters\TCPIP.

- ◆ **WINS parameters.** Includes Windows Internet Naming Service (WINS) parameters. These are described in more detail in the next section, "The Windows Internet Name Server (WINS) Registry Entries."

Table 5.7 lists some of the most common TCP/IP Registry settings.

TABLE 5.7
TCP/IP Registry Value Entries

Value Entry	Data Type	Description
DatabasePath	REG_EXPAND_SZ	Sets the Internet database file path used by the Windows Sockets interface for lmhosts, protocols, hosts, and networks.
DefaultTTL	REG_DWORD	Sets the amount of time an IP packet can exist on the network. This is knows as the Time To Live (TTL) value.
ForwardBufferMemory	REG_DWORD	Sets IP memory allocation in the router packet queue to store packet data.
IpReassemblyTimeout	REG_DWORD	Specifies the amount of time IP continues to receive fragments to reassemble a fragmented packet.
KeepAliveTime	REG_DWORD	Sets the rate at which TCP sends keep alive packets to verify that an idle connection is still connected.
NumForwardPackets	REG_DWORD	Sets allocation of IP packet headers for router packet queue.
TcpKeepCnt	REG_DWORD	Sets the keep alive traffic probe time to determine if a connection is still active.
TcpKeepTries	REG_DWORD	Sets how often TCP probes a connection with keep alive traffic before disconnecting the connection.
TcpMaxConnectAttempts	REG_DWORD	Sets how many times TCP should try to establish a connection before reporting a failed connection.
TcpNumConnections	REG_DWORD	Sets how many simultaneous TCP connections can be established.
TcpSendDownMax	REG_DWORD	Sets the TCP/IP queue size (in bytes).

The following section details the Registry settings for the Windows Internet Name Server (WINS).

The Windows Internet Name Server (WINS) Registry Entries

The Windows Internet Name Server (WINS) is a Microsoft-only standard that is an implementation of the NetBIOS Name Server. WINS is used to simplify setting up names on a TCP/IP network. When users connect to the network and an IP address has changed, WINS maintains a NetBIOS names database for the Windows and TCP/IP programs installed on the Windows network. This way users can continue to use their familiar TCP/IP names even if host names change.

The Registry stores WINS information in the following key:

HKEY_LOCAL_MACHINE\SYSTEM\CurrentControlSet\Services\Wins\Parameters

Table 5.8 lists and describes the WINS entries in the Registry. All of the entries in this table fall under the preceding Registry key.

Tip   For more details on these WINS Registry entries and for a complete list of entries for WINS, see the Microsoft Knowledge Base article Q135922 on the World Wide Web at http://www.microsoft.com/kb/bussys/winnt/q135922.html.

TABLE 5.8
Windows Internet Servers (WINS) Registry Entries

Value Entry	Data Type	Description
BackupDirPath	REG_SZ	Sets backup folder.
BurstHandling	REG_DWORD	Specifies that the WINS server temporarily achieves a steady state on a new database or when several new clients attach to the server.
DbFileNm	REG_EXPAND_SZ	Sets WINS database file path.
DoBackupOnTerm	REG_DWORD	Instructs Windows NT to automatically backup WINS database when WINS service stops.
DoStaticDataInit	REG_DWORD	When set to 0, WINS initializes database with records from the \Datfiles key.

Value Entry	Data Type	Description
InitTimePause	REG_DWORD	Instructs WINS to stay paused until first replication.
LogDetailedEvents	REG_DWORD	Initiates verbose event logging.
LoggingOn	REG_DWORD	Turns on logging to JET.LOG for database changes.
LogFilePath	REG_SZ or REG_EXPAND_SZ	Sets WINS log files path.
MigrateOn	REG_DWORD	Treats multihomed and static unique records as dynamic when conflicting with new registration.
McastIntvl	REG_DWORD	Sets time in seconds for WINS to send out multicasts to other servers.
RefreshInterval	REG_DWORD	Sets the number of times a client registers its name.
VerifyInterval	REG_DWORD	Sets time (in hours) of how long WINS server waits to verify that old names are no longer active.

You can add the \ConsistencyCheck subkey to the HKEY_LOCAL_MACHINE\ SYSTEM\CurrentControlSet\Services\Wins\Parameters subkey to instruct WINS to perform consistency checks on the WINS database. The values you can add to this setting include the ones shown in table 5.9.

TABLE 5.9
WINS Database Consistency Check Registry Values

Value Entry	Data Type	Description
MaxRecsAtATime	REG_DWORD	Sets the number of records to check at one time.
UseRplPnrs	REG_DWORD	Specifies if the owner WINS server (when set to 0) or pull partner (when set to 1) is contacted during a consistency check.
TimeInterval	REG_DWORD	Sets time (in hours) between consistency checks.
SpTime	REG_SZ	Sets exact time (in military time) that the first consistency check is initiated.

Very often, knowing where to locate a setting in the Registry is half the battle. You just learned how and where Windows NT stores Registry settings for your networking components, you are now better prepared to track down problems you might encounter on the network. The following section includes a number of specific tasks you can use to troubleshoot networking problems you might encounter.

Troubleshooting Network Registry Problems

Often you encounter networking problems you can't fix by normal means, such as by changing Control Panel options, by setting user profiles or system policies (see Chapter 6, "Using System Policy Editor to Modify Registry Data"), or by changing application-specific options. These problems range from deleting Transmission Control Protocol/Internet Protocol (TCP/IP) settings, removing old network interface card value entries, and the like. Sometimes you need to open the Registry Editor and modify system entries directly. This section shows some of the ways to use the Registry to troubleshoot or change settings associated with Windows NT networks.

Stop   Before editing or viewing the Registry, be aware that there is no command to undo a setting you've changed or deleted. You should back up your Registry before attempting to make any changes to it (see Chapter 1, "Introducing the Windows NT Registry ").

Also, before attempting to alter network entries in the Registry, make sure you are comfortable using the Registry Editor (REGEDT32.EXE). Chapter 4, "Using the Windows NT Registry Editor," offers ample information about the Registry Editor.

Finally, you need to have administrator rights or user permission for the Registry you want to edit.

Automating the Windows NT Logon

You can use the Registry to modify the Windows NT logon behavior. You might, for instance, want to enable a computer to automatically log on to the network. By default, for security reasons Windows NT requires that you log on to the network each time the system boots. This ensures no unauthorized users gain access to the network. Sometimes, however, you might want a workstation on the network to log on to the network automatically without requiring a user (or you) to physically enter a user name and password. For remote computers secured by other means (such as being locked behind tightly secure doors) or for workstations you are setting up or troubleshooting, enabling the automatic logon feature can be helpful to you. After you diagnose a problem or do not need Windows NT to log on automatically, disable the automatic logon feature on that computer to enforce password-level security.

Stop If you enable the automatic logon feature on a computer, you expose the computer and the network resources that that computer and user can access. For this reason, you should not enable this feature on the server or any computers that have access to sensitive data.

Windows NT does not include a utility to help you enable the auto-logon feature. You must use the Registry Editor and modify the Registry directly to do so. Use the following steps to enable a computer to log on to the network automatically:

1. Open the Registry Editor and locate the following key:

    HKEY_LOCAL_MACHINE\SOFTWARE\Microsoft\Windows NT\
    CurrentVersion\Winlogon

Tip If the AutoAdminLogon value entry is already in the Registry, you can skip step 2.

2. Select Edit, Add Value. Thmmme String Editor dialog box displays. In the Add Value dialog box, enter **AutoAdminLogon** in the Value Name text box (see fig. 5.2). Select REG_SZ from the Data Type drop-down list. Click on OK.

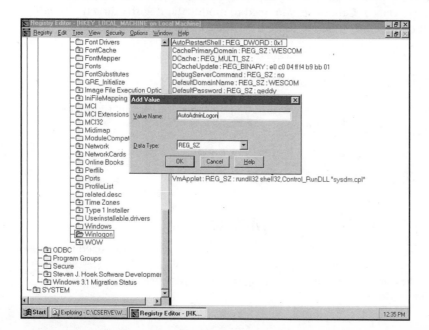

Figure 5.2

You can create a new key called AutoAdminLogon to automate the logon process for remote computers, such as file and printer servers.

3. Enter **1** in the String Editor dialog box. Changing the value from 0 to 1 enables auto-logon. If you want to disable this function, change 1 back to 0. Click on OK.

4. Select Edit, Add Value. In the Add Value dialog box, enter **DefaultPassword** in the Value Name text box. Select REG_SZ from the Data Type drop-down list. Click on OK.

5. Enter the user's password in the String Editor dialog box. The user is the person who normally logs on to the network from the computer you are modifying. Click on OK.

6. Exit Registry Editor and reboot the system.

 Tip If you need to bypass auto-logon at startup, such as if you need to log on as a different user or log on to a different Windows NT domain, press the shift key when Windows NT boots.

Displaying Shutdown Command at Logon

Normally, the Shutdown command is not available on the Welcome screen when you log on to the system. If you have problems with users not knowing how to shut down the system if they do not want to log on, you should include the Shutdown command on the Welcome screen to guide them. When you use system policies, you can enable this feature with a policy setting (see Chapter 6, "Using System Policy Editor to Modify Registry Data"). Otherwise, you need to modify the Registry directly. To add this command to the logon screen using the Registry, use the following steps:

1. Start the Registry Editor and locate the following key:

   HKEY_LOCAL_MACHINE\SOFTWARE\Windows NT\CurrentVersion\Winlogon

2. Double-click on the ShutdownWithoutLogon value entry in the right pane. The String Editor dialog box appears.

3. Change the String value from 0 to **1**. Click on OK.

4. Exit the Registry Editor and reboot the computer.

Creating a Custom Logon Message

Another change you can make to the logon process is to have a customized message display after a user logs on to the network. When users encounter this message, they will need to click on OK to continue logging on to the network. The following steps show you how to do this:

1. Start the Registry Editor and locate the following key:

   HKEY_LOCAL_MACHINE\SOFTWARE\Microsoft\Windows NT\
   CurrentVersion\Winlogon

2. Select Edit, Add Value. In the Add Value dialog box, enter **LegalNoticeCaption**
   in the Value Name text box (see fig. 5.3). Select REG_SZ from the Data Type
   drop-down list. Click on OK.

Figure 5.3

*The caption is the
text that displays
in the title bar of
the notice dialog
box.*

3. Enter the text for the caption of your message in the String Editor dialog box.
   Click on OK. The caption is the title of the message box that displays.

4. Select Edit, Add Value. In the Add Value dialog box, enter **LegalNoticeText** in
   the Value Name text box. Select REG_SZ from the Data Type drop-down list.
   Click on OK.

5. Enter the text for your new caption in the String Editor dialog box. Click on OK.
   An example of a new caption might be a warning to users about unauthorized
   usage of networking services.

6. Exit the Registry Editor and reboot the system.

Deleting Network Adapter Card Registry Settings

Normally, you use the Network application in Control Panel to remove network
adapter cards you no longer use. Or, you might remove the adapter and then reinstall
it if you encounter a setup problem with it. Again, you would use the Network
application to remove and reinstall the card.

Sometimes, however, Windows NT might not remove all of the Registry settings for a
network adapter using this method. If this occurs, use the following steps to manually
remove the NIC using the Registry:

1. Start the Registry Editor and locate the following key:

   HKEY_LOCAL_MACHINE\SOFTWARE\Microsoft\Windows NT\
   CurrentVersion\NetworkCards*card_number*

The *card_number* parameter is a numeric value assigned for your adapter card, such as 1, 2, and so on. Choose the one for the adapter you are removing. You might need to read the Description value entry setting (see fig. 5.4) in each subkey to determine which subkey is assigned to the card you want to remove.

Figure 5.4

You might need to read the Description value entry setting to make sure you select the correct adapter card to delete.

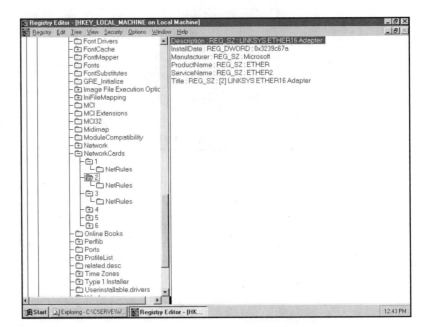

2. Press Del to delete the entire subkey you choose in step 1. Be sure not to delete the \NetworkCards key, only the subkey represented by a numeric value. If there are any subkeys in the \card_number subkey, you might need to delete them before you can delete the \card_number subkey.

3. Exit the Registry Editor and reboot your system.

Correcting Error Received after Deleting a Shared Folder

The Windows NT Event Viewer keeps track of shared folders that you delete before you first remove the share from it. An error message like the following appears in the Event Viewer in these cases::

```
The server service was unable to recreate the share share_name because the
directory drive:\folder_name no longer exists.
```

To remove the preceding error message, use the following steps:

1. Start the Registry Editor and locate the following keying:
   HKEY_LOCAL_MACHINE\SYSTEM\CurrentControlSet\ Services\
   LanmanServer\Shares.

2. Delete the subkey of the share that no longer works.

3. Exit the Registry Editor and reboot the computer.

Installing TCP/IP after SQL Server Has Been Installed

If you previously have installed SQL Server on your machine and are now trying to set up TCP/IP, the Connectivity Utilities option in the Control Panel might be disabled. To install TCP/IP after you install SQL Server, you need to delete the Registry keys installed by the SQL Server Setup program found in the following subtree:

HKEY_LOCAL_MACHINE\SYSTEM\CurrentControlSet\Services\Tcpip

Next, reinstall SQL Server.

Tip To work around this problem, simply install TCP/IP before installing SQL Server in the first place.

Connecting to Apple Printer Shares

If you encounter the following error message when attempting to connect to an Apple printer share, you need to modify the Registry entry:

```
Could not connect to printer. The printer name is invalid.
```

When you install an Apple printer share, sometimes the printer name includes a backslash in it, which the Registry handles as a new subkey instead of a value entry name. You might, for instance, have a Apple LaserWriter 16\600 PS installed. When you view this setting in the Registry, you see that the \600 PS has mistakenly been added as subkey.

To correct the problem, use these steps:

1. Open My Computer and double-click on the Printer folder (or select Start, Settings, Printer). The Printers folder displays.

2. Delete the printer connected as the Apple shared printer.

3. Double-click the Add Printer icon and set up the Apple share printer again, but this time name it without a slash in it.

4. Close the Printers and My Computer folders. You might need to reboot your system for the changes to take effect.

Displaying Serial Numbers for File and Print Services for NetWare Clients

You might encounter situations in which the serial number for File and Print Services (FPNW) is required for a service or user. This information does not display by default, but you can modify the Registry to display the serial number. The following steps show you how:

1. Start the Registry Editor and locate the following key:

   HKEY_LOCAL_MACHINE\SYSTEM\CurrentControlSet\Services\FPNW\ Parameters

2. Select Edit, Add Value. In the Add Value dialog box, enter **SerialNumber** in the Value Name text box. Select REG_DWORD from the Data Type drop-down list. Click on OK.

3. Enter the serial number in the Data field. Click on OK.

4. Exit the Registry Editor and reboot the computer.

Summary

Windows NT's networking features are dynamic and powerful for small- to medium-size LANs. If you are responsible for administering or managing LANs with Windows NT servers and workstations connected, you need to become familiar with the vast configuration keys and entries that are set up in the Registry. This chapter presented you with a number of these settings, as well as where to look for more detailed information. Four of the most popular network services—server, RAS, TCP/IP, and WINS—are described in more detail than other services in case you experience problems when running those services. Finally, you were shown troubleshooting tasks you can use in specific situations to combat network problems. For more trouble-shooting topics for Windows NT, read Chapter 8, "Troubleshooting Specfic Problems Using the Windows NT Registry."

CHAPTER
6

Using System Policy Editor to Modify Registry Data

U p to this point, you've learned the basics of what the Windows NT Registry is, how to view and modify it using the Registry Editor (REGEDT32.EXE), and some of the key networking settings located in the Registry. If you are a little uncomfortable using the Registry Editor to make system changes (and you should be for a little while), you can use another Windows NT tool to modify Registry information. This tool is called the System Policy Editor.

The *System Policy Editor* is used to create system policies for users and computers. System policies control how a user's environment looks, how a local machine runs, which applications run at startup, and other system events. You also can use the System Policy Editor to modify a local or remote computer's Registry. Instead of using the Registry Editor to modify settings in their raw format, you can use the System Policy Editor to change common Registry settings using an easy-to-use utility. There are some limitations to the settings you can make (not all Registry settings are included as system policy options by default), and you cannot modify binary data from the System Policy Editor.

This chapter examines system policies and shows you how to use them to make Registry changes. Specifically, it covers the following topic areas:

◆ Introducing system policies

◆ Installing and using the System Policy Editor

◆ Modifying Registry settings using the System Policy Editor

◆ Creating and configuring system policies

◆ Creating system policy templates

Introducing Windows NT System Policies

System policies (see fig. 6.1) are a tool administrators can use to centrally control user access to network and desktop features, such as sharing data and configuring system settings. System policies are Registry settings that are automatically set when a user logs on to a PC. The system policies can be applied to users, groups of users, or specific computers. Administrators can set, change, and maintain these Registry settings for each of these entities. By combining policies assigned for a certain user, the logged-on machine, and any groups that users might belong to, you can have control over the type of environment and rights a user has. Administrators also can create policy templates to determine the parameters for each policy.

Figure 6.1

Windows NT system policy files enable administrators to control Registry settings for users and computers.

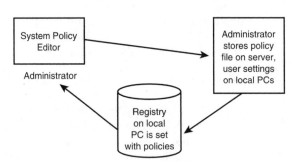

You use the System Policy Editor to create and administer system policies. The System Policy Editor is installed when you run the Windows NT Setup program. The System Policy Editor object can be found in the Start, Programs, Administrative Tools (Commons) folder. You also can find a copy of the System Policy Editor on the Windows NT CD-ROM in the \CLIENTS\SRVTOOLS\WINNT*processor_type* folder with the name POLEDIT.EXE. (The *processor_type* is the type of processor on which you have Windows NT installed, such as I386.)

When you create a system policy, you set Registry values to do the following:

◆ Customize parts of the desktop

◆ Restrict users' actions on a system

◆ Configure and maintain network settings

◆ Determine which Control Panel, Shell, and System options a user can access.

By eliminating specific Control Panel, Shell, and System options, administrators do not have to worry about users changing specific system configurations either by accident or intentionally. This is of real importance when you have users who want to manually install their own applications, alter a networking connection (such as set up a TCP/IP stack for the Internet), or other configuration duty that might jeopardize the integrity of your network and the clients running on it.

Tip
Because the System Policy Editor can alter a user's or computer's Registry values, you should restrict access to the POLEDIT.EXE file. Don't install it on machines that do not need system configuration-type tools. Also, limit the access users have to installing new programs on their computers so they cannot install POLEDIT.EXE from the Windows NT source CD.

Windows NT offers you a predefined set of policies you can choose from to create your system policies. You also have the option of creating your own customized policies to fit your specific needs. You are shown how to create system policy files based on predefined policies as well as how to create custom system policy files in this section.

After you run the System Policy Editor and create the system policy, you place it on the network to be automatically loaded onto the computer when a user logs on. The system policies you create for that user, computer, or group override the Registry settings that are set up for the local computer or user. When the system policy settings override the Registry settings, the actual values set up in the Registry are changed to match those you have in the system policy file. You might, for instance, have a computer on which a user changes the desktop wallpaper to a new one during a session, effectively changing the wallpaper Registry setting. Under normal conditions (that is, when system policies are not used), when the user reboots the computer, say to begin work the next day, the Registry setting for the wallpaper the user set up during the last session is used. If, on the other hand, you have a system policy file that specifies a specific wallpaper setting to be used each time the user logs on (such as an image of the company logo), the Registry setting is changed to the value set in the system policy file.

In the next few sections, you take a deeper look into what comprises system policy files, as well as what specific system policy settings you can change.

Examining System Policy Files

When you configure policies in Windows NT, you are concerned with two types of files, ADM and POL. ADM files are template files that enable you to create system policy files (POL files). POL files are the files that enforce the policies you create.

System policies modify the Registry in a couple of ways. First, when you create a policy under Windows NT, it sets up a NTCONFIG.POL file that overwrites the default Registry settings when a user logs on to the network. Second, logon and network access settings modify the HKEY_LOCAL_MACHINE key. This key affects the Registry settings specific to the computer or the default computer settings. Third, the HKEY_CURRENT_USER key in the Registry is modified, which determines the desktop settings for a specific user.

Tip   System policy settings that affect user settings are defined for a specific user or for the default user.

ADM Files

Before you create a policy file, you need to understand the role of the ADM file. ADM files do not create the policy, but instead allow you to create a policy file. ADM files are policy templates that determine the limits and possible policies you can set defined by POL files. An ADM file, for instance, can include settings that allow the administrator to set system policies on only desktop settings. On the other hand, you can have an ADM file that allows the administrator to set system policies on desktop settings, network settings, system settings, and shell settings.

When you first launch the System Policy Editor (you are shown later in the chapter how to do this), it searches for an ADM file. When the ADM file is located, it defines the types of settings that display in the System Policy Editor for the administrator to choose from. The administrator or user doesn't actually "see" the ADM file, but only responds to the possible policy settings defined by the ADM file. Microsoft includes a few sample templates for you to look at, use, or customize. The COMMON.ADM and WINNT.ADM files are stored in the *%SystemRoot%*\INF folder. You also can use the WINDOW.ADM file stored in the \CLIENTS\SRVTOOLS\WINNT*processor_type* on the Windows NT Setup CD-ROM. Or, you can create your own ADM file, as described in the "Examining Policy Templates" section later in this chapter.

POL Files

The second part of system policies is POL files. These files actually store the configuration information and any limitations you want to set up for a user, machine, or group. POL files implement the system polices based on the options you select on the ADM templates. One way to look at the role of ADM and POL files is to think of how a grocery store (the ADM file) stocks food and what you put in your grocery cart (the POL file). A grocery store has a seemingly endless supply of items from which to stock its shelves. Likewise, an ADM file has a seemingly endless supply of Registry and configuration settings from which to choose. The grocery store, however, only stocks those items it thinks it can sell. An ADM file stores only those settings that the developer or administrator thinks need to be configured through system policies. What you place in your grocery cart is a subset of the available items at the store (you don't purchase everything in the store). Likewise, what you select for the POL files using the System Policy Editor is a subset of the available settings established by the ADM file.

You create a POL file by using the System Policy Editor. Once it is created, you store it in the Netlogon folder in the primary domain controller (PDC) so that when users log on, the policy settings are downloaded to that machine and copied to the user's Registry. You are shown exactly how to create a POL file in the "Creating System Policies" section later in this chapter.

Stop Because system polices overwrite user Registry settings, any POL file you have will take precedence over a user profile set up. Take this into consideration when you decide to create system policies.

Examining System Policy Settings

As you have read, you can create policies for users, groups, and machines. Let's take a look at each of these entities.

Creating Policies for Users

User settings in system policies rely on the fact that the computer you want to use for that user has user profiles enabled. User profiles are configuration settings for each user who logs on to a Windows NT computer or network. User profiles contain settings such as program folders, color settings, printer connections, and user-specific network settings. Under Windows NT, user profiles are automatically created for each new user that logs on to the network.

You can control the following items in a system policy for each user:

- ◆ **Desktop.** Configures system policies to use standard wallpaper and color schemes.

- ◆ **System.** Limits the user to certain applications (including DOS-based programs) and Registry editing utilities. In most installations, you'll want to disable the user's capabilities to make any changes to the Registry.

- ◆ **Windows NT System.** Enables you turn on settings for using environment variables stored in the computer's AUTOEXEC.BAT file. You also can turn on an option that lets all logon scripts completely run before the user's shell starts.

- ◆ **Windows NT Shell.** Enables you to specify custom folders you want to use for the Programs and Startup folders, a custom Network Neighborhood folder, and custom desktop icons. You also can hide the Start menu subfolder using User policy settings.

◆ **Shell.** Enables you to specify how much control users have to customize the desktop and folders, and how they can change the user interface. You also can hide the My Computer icon, Network Neighborhood icon, the taskbar, the Start menu, and more.

◆ **Control Panel.** Enables you to limit the access of certain Display Control Panel items, such as hiding the Screen Saver and Appearance tabs from the Display Properties dialog box.

In the upcoming section, "Using the System Policy Editor," you are shown how each of these settings can be configured. Plus you run through a complete description of each of the settings you can control.

Creating Policies for Computers

Windows NT enables you to set policies for computers to determine how each computer looks and reacts in your environment. You can define the default computer settings, which are used when a new user logs on to a computer for the first time. You also can create customized policies for an individual PC. When you create policies for computers, for instance, users logged on to those PCs cannot modify the hardware and environment settings that you specify in the computer policy. This way you are assured that Windows 95 starts up the same way each time.

Some of the items you can control in the default computer policy are as follows:

◆ **Windows NT Network.** Enables you to set sharing policies, including creating hidden drive shares for either Windows NT Server or Windows NT Workstation.

◆ **Windows NT Printers.** Enables you to set network printing policies, including disabling print spoolers from sharing printer information to other print servers on the network, setting default printing priorities, and enabling a beep to occur when a remote printing job encounters an error.

◆ **Windows NT Remote Access.** Enables you to set remote access services (RAS) settings. These include settings for the number of times someone can have unsuccessful authentication attempts (reduces the chances of a hacker trying to break into your system by using various logon attempts), how much time is allotted for authentication, and how much time must elapse for the next callback from the user. You also can set a time for RAS to automatically disconnect the system from RAS.

◆ **Windows NT Shell.** Enables you to specify custom shared folders, including shared Programs, Start menu, and Startup folders. You also can set custom shared desktop icons.

◆ **Windows NT System.** Includes two major policy settings, Logon and File system. Under the Logon options you can set logon banners, enable shutdown from the Authentication dialog box, instruct Windows NT not to display the last logged user on the Authentication dialog box, and run logon scripts completely before displaying the user's shell. The File system options include settings for instructing Windows NT not to create an 8.3 file name from long file names, allow extended characters in 8.3 file names, and disable the feature that updates the last access time on files that are only being read.

◆ **Windows NT User Profiles.** Includes policies to delete locally cached user profiles when a roaming user logs off, detect slow network connections, set slow network connection timeout (the default is 2000 milliseconds), and set timeouts for dialog boxes to display (the default is 30 seconds).

◆ **Network.** Enables you to set system policy remote update settings.

◆ **System.** Enables you to set Simple Network Management Protocol (SNMP) and Run options, such as permitted SNMP managers, SNMP communities, and applications to run at startup.

Creating Policies for Groups

Windows NT enables you to create logical collections of users or computers called *groups*. You can apply system policies to groups, as you can users and computers. For Windows NT groups, you can select the same types of settings as described in the preceding two sections, but they are applied to an entire group, not just an individual. When you create a system policy for a group, you create it in the same manner as you do for an individual user or computer, but assign the policy to an entire group.

If a policy is located by Windows NT for a user, however, that policy supersedes any group policies you have set up. Also, as a user logs on to a system that includes a number of group policies, the group policies are downloaded to the machine beginning with the lowest priority group and ending with the highest priority group. Each group is processed as it is downloaded. Therefore, the last group policy processed will be the final settings that computer uses when it boots.

To begin creating system policy files, you need to learn how to use the System Policy Editor. The next section shows you how to start and use the System Policy Editor to set policy files as well as modify Registry settings.

Using the System Policy Editor

By default, Windows NT Server installs the System Policy Editor (POLEDIT.EXE) on your system during Setup. The System Policy Editor is placed on the Start menu under Programs, Administrative Tools (Common) folder. You can start it by clicking on it in this folder, or by typing POLEDIT.EXE in the Start menu's Run option.

Tip Windows NT Workstation, however, does not install POLEDIT.EXE by default. If you plan to run System Policy Editor from Windows NT Workstation, you need to copy the POLEDIT.EXE, POLEDIT.CNT, and POLEDIT.HLP files from the \CLIENTS\ SRVTOOLS\WINNT\I386 folder from the Windows NT Server CD-ROM to the Windows NT Workstation system.

Note If you are interested in extending the System Policy Editor programmatically, you can. The ADF format is a text file that can be extended by third-party tool vendors or network managers. The System Policy Editor works via local file I/O and requires that one copy be located on each file server. Consult the Microsoft Win32 SDK for more information.

When you first open the Policy Editor, it searches for an ADM template file. If you want to edit the Registry, simply cancel out of the dialog box looking for the ADM file (see the "ADM Files" section earlier in this chapter). If you want to create a new policy (a POL file), you need to name or browse and locate one of these template files stored in the INF subfolder in the *%SystemRoot%* folder.

Tip You can use the System Policy Editor to directly access and edit the Registry. The advantage this tool has over the Registry Editor is that it is more intuitive and menu-driven than the Registry Editor. You can still make changes that might disable parts of Windows NT you don't intend to, but you have more safeguards in place so you don't corrupt your Registry settings. You also cannot set or change binary data in the System Policy Editor, reducing the likelihood that you will change a binary setting placed in the Registry by an application or device that needs to access that data later.

The downside is that you can't access every setting you might want to modify, therefore requiring you to use the Registry Editor at times.

One use of the System Policy Editor is to change Registry settings, which does not create system policy files. The following sections show how you can use the System Policy Editor to modify the Registry, followed by sections about how to modify user and computer Registry settings. If you want information about how to create system policy files, see the section "Creating System Policies" later in this chapter.

Editing the Registry Using the System Policy Editor

In Chapter 4, "Using the Windows NT Registry Editor," you are shown how to use the Registry Editor to make changes and to view the Registry. You can do this with the System Policy Editor as well. In fact, you might find it quicker to make standard changes to the Registry database using this tool first, then to drill down on other settings you might need to use the Registry Editor.

Tip You can use the System Policy Editor to edit the Registry for a remote computer. To do so, select File, Connect and enter the name of the computer to which you want to connect. Be sure to have the proper administrative privileges for that computer.

To edit the Registry with the System Policy Editor, use these steps:

1. Start the System Policy Editor and select File, Open Registry. This displays two icons in the System Policy Editor—Local User and Local Computer (see fig. 6.2). These correspond to the root keys HKEY_CURRENT_USER and HKEY_LOCAL_MACHINE. The other root keys cannot be edited using the System Policy Editor. Also, remote editing using the System Policy Editor updates the HKEY_CURRENT_USER, while editing remotely with the Registry Editor updates HKEY_USERS.

Tip Before you modify any changes to the Registry, be sure to back it up.

2. Select one of the icons and double-click on it. Select the Local User icon to change settings for the user. These modifications alter the HKEY_CURRENT_USER Registry key. For changes to the computer, select the Local Computer icon. These changes affect the HKEY_LOCAL_MACHINE Registry key.

   The Local User Policies or Local Computer Policies page displays, depending on the item you chose in the preceding paragraph. Figures 6.3 and 6.4 show the different settings you can select for each type of policy, respectively.

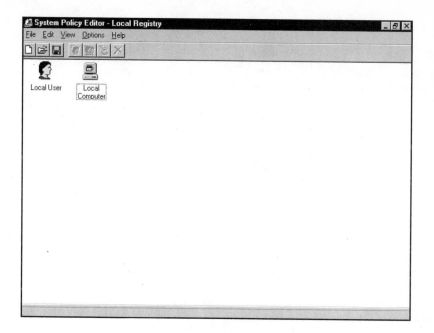

Figure 6.2

When you open the Registry in the System Policy Editor, the Local User and Local Computer icons display.

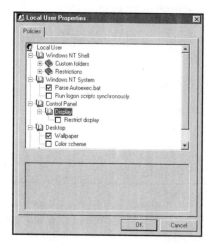

Figure 6.3

You can modify the Local User Properties selections.

Figure 6.4

Or, you can modify the Local Computer Properties settings.

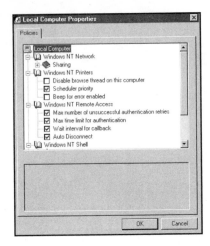

3. To see which settings you can change under a heading, expand the heading by double-clicking on the name of the heading or by double-clicking on the plus sign (+) to the left of the heading name. For some headings, you might need to expand another branch to see more options.

4. When you want to change the setting of an option, click in the checkbox to the left of the option. The way you select an option with the Policy Editor is a little different than normal checkbox options in Windows. Table 6.1 summarizes the three states of actions with Policy Editor options.

5. After you make the necessary changes, click on OK.

6. Shut down and restart the computer to have these changes take effect.

TABLE 6.1
Options States

Checkbox Appearance	Meaning
check	When you include a check mark, the policy is implemented the next time the user logs on. If you are configuring Local User Properties, then the user can log on at a different machine and still have these new options. If it is the Local Computer Properties you are working with, then the next user works on this machine, he will see the changes.

Checkbox Appearance	Meaning
clear	When you clear a box, or if one is already cleared when you start the System Policy Editor, then you know that option will not be implemented the next time the user logs on or the machine is used. When you clear a checkbox, then the previous settings are removed from the Registry.
gray	A grayed box means that this setting has not changed since the user last logged in. If you keep it gray, then Windows NT will not make any modifications to the system configuration. This grayed option is a way for Windows NT to quickly assess the system policy to see if any changes have been made since the last log on.

Tip   You can cycle through each of the three different display options to select the one you need. Just click on the checkbox for the state you want. If an option has not been set either way (checked or unchecked) for a user or machine, then the grayed box will not display until the next time you boot up.

Some of the options you can choose have additional choices or parameters that you must set. If an option has these, you see them at the bottom of the Policies tab, as shown in figure 6.5. In this figure, the Custom Start menu option Shell policy is checked. At the bottom of the tab you have to specify the path where you want Windows NT to get the start menu items from.

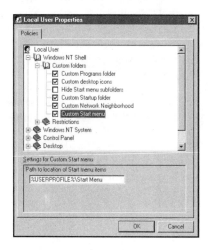

Figure 6.5

You might need to fill in additional information for a policy setting.

Stop The way you select the options in the properties sheet for users or computers is very important. Sometimes you might think clearing an option means that a specific setting is not used, when in reality it might mean that something doesn't happen at all. An example of this is when you set the Run only allowed Windows applications setting (see the "System Policy Options" section later in this chapter). If you click this option and do not specify any applications to run on the specific computer, no programs will be allowed to run.

The following section shows the specific Registry settings you can modify using the System Policy Editor. These settings are also identical to the default system policy settings you can set when the COMMON.ADM template file is loaded.

Modifying Local User System Policy Options

You can use the System Policy Editor to modify Registry settings that affect the user currently logged on. When a user logs on to a Windows NT machine, user settings from the Registry key HKEY_CURRENT_USER are used to control how that user's environment looks. The following sections describe all the options you can choose, how they affect the Registry, and if they have any additional settings you must specify. You can get a quick overview of each of these options in the "Creating Policies for Users" section earlier in this chapter.

Windows NT Shell System Policy Options

When you double-click on the Local User icon in the System Policy Editor, the top choice you can modify is the Windows NT Shell policy options (see fig. 6.6). This option includes items that enable you to use custom folders and icons for a custom-ized desktop. These are described starting with the next subhead, "Custom Folders." Before you create a custom desktop by using system policies, you need to first define custom folders. To do this, use the following steps:

1. Create and place the custom folders in an area where users can access them, such as on the network server. Windows NT uses the path name to find the folder.

2. Create your set of files and shortcuts that you want to appear in each folder. Place these in the custom folders you just created.

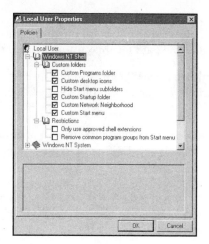

Figure 6.6

The Windows NT Shell system policy options control the use of custom folders and enables you to set restrictions.

Tip   Shortcut properties need to include Universal Naming Convention (UNC) names instead of mapped directory names.

3. In the "Custom Folders" section that follows, where you name the path of the custom folder, enter the full UNC path for the custom folders you just created. Otherwise, Windows NT looks in the default locations for any custom folders you've created.

Custom Folders

This area in the Windows NT Shell policy options list customizes the desktop in six different ways. These are described in the following list:

◆ **Custom Programs folder.** Enables you to customize the contents of the Programs folder on the Start menu. You need to include the UNC path to the custom Programs item you create.

◆ **Custom Desktop icons.** Enables you to customize the user's desktop icons. Again, specify the UNC path to the custom desktop icon folder.

◆ **Hide Start menu subfolders.** Unless you want both your customized Programs folder and the default Programs folder to display on the Start menu, place a check in this box.

◆ **Custom Startup folder.** Enables you to define a custom folder that includes files, applications, or batch files that you want to run automatically at Windows NT startup. You need to enter the path for this custom Startup folder.

◆ **Custom Network Neighborhood.** Enables you to specify specific items, including shortcuts and printers, to appear in the Network Neighborhood folder.

◆ **Custom Start Menu.** Enables you to customize the list of items placed on the Start menu. Again, be sure to include a UNC path to the custom Start menu folder you have created.

Stop

You should not place custom folders in the Network Neighborhood. Doing so might cause you to lose data.

Restrictions

The Restrictions policy options include two settings, as described in the following list:

◆ **Only use approved shell extensions.** Instructs Windows NT to use shell extensions that have been previously approved.

◆ **Remove common program groups from Start Menu.** Enables you to remove any (Common) folders from the Start, Program folder, such as Administrative Tools (Common) and Microsoft Internet Server (Common).

Windows NT System Policy Options

The Windows NT System policy options (see fig. 6.7) enable you turn on settings for controlling how Windows NT using AUTOEXEC.BAT information and logon scripts. These options are described in the following list:

◆ **Parse Autoexec.bat.** Set this option when you want to parse environment variables from the system's AUTOEXEC.BAT file. By default, this option is turned on. Because many legacy hardware devices still use some AUTOEXEC.BAT settings, you might be forced to leave this option turned on. If you have a problem with a device or other setting not working correctly, check out this policy setting to see if it is disabled for that user's machine.

◆ **Run logon scripts synchronously.** Turn on this option if you want Windows NT to run all logon scripts before starting the user's shell. This is a good idea if you want to make sure Windows NT fully logs on a user before any desktop items display on the screen. If this same option is enabled under the Windows NT System options in the Local Computer Properties dialog box, that setting takes precedence.

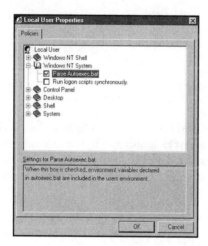

Figure 6.7

The Windows NT System policy options enable you to control how Windows NT parses the AUTOEXEC.BAT file and logon scripts.

Control Panel Policy Options

You read earlier how Windows NT system policies enable you to restrict users from specific areas in Windows NT. The Control Panel option (see fig. 6.8) gives you several options to help you control the way users can change their display settings.

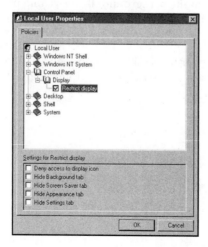

Figure 6.8

The Control Panel system policy options enable you to control how users set their display settings.

The Display option enables you to restrict the Display properties. You can specify to not show the entire Display Control Panel or just limit parts of it. These parts include the following options:

◆ Deny access to display icon

◆ Hide Background tab

◆ Hide Screen Saver tab

◆ Hide Appearance tab

◆ Hide Settings tab

 Tip   If you have the Microsoft Plus! Companion for Windows 95 installed, you do not get an option to restrict access to its display tab. You can, however, uninstall the Plus! items by running the Windows NT uninstall program and deselecting Desktop Themes and Visual Enhancements from your Plus! installation. This will keep users from adding Plus! components to their systems.

Desktop Policy Options

For an environment that needs to look standard across all computers, you can set desktop policies to use the same wallpaper and color schemes. This is handy if you are running a training environment and you need each machine to have the exact same look and feel each time you start up the class. Another place this is useful is when running a kiosk at a sales booth. Each of your machines can have identical wallpaper that shows your company's logo in the background. By restricting users access to this feature, you won't have any surprises during the day as different users use the machine.

The two options you have are under the Desktop system policy item (see fig. 6.9)— Wallpaper and Color scheme. Each is described in the following sections.

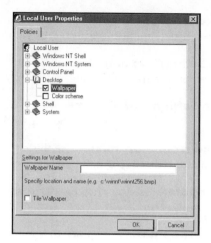

Figure 6.9

The Desktop system policy options enable you to control wallpaper and color scheme options.

Wallpaper

Use this setting to specify a wallpaper to use on all systems. In the Wallpaper name drop-down list, click on the bitmap file of your choice. If you want to include a customized file, such as your company logo, place the BMP file in the *%SystemRoot%* folder before you click on this option.

The Wallpaper option is one that might confuse you when you first start using it. When you check the Wallpaper option, this tells Windows NT to use the specific BMP for the background. If you clear an already checked Wallpaper option, this tells Windows NT not to use any wallpaper. If the Wallpaper option is grayed out, this leaves the choice up to the user.

Click the Tile Wallpaper option to have the bitmap tiled across the user's screen.

Color Scheme

You can set a standard color scheme on the desktop for the users. You need to specify the color scheme, if any, in the Scheme name drop-down list.

Shell System Policy Options

You can control which items Windows NT displays on the desktop and Start menu by using the Shell system policy options (see fig. 6.10). Under the Restrictions item, you have the following choices:

◆ **Remove Run command from Start menu.** Use this choice so users cannot execute programs or install applications using the Run command.

◆ **Remove folders from Settings on Start menu.** Use this choice so the Control Panel and Printers options are not available to users.

◆ **Remove Taskbar from Settings on Start menu.** Use this choice so users cannot modify the Taskbar settings using the Start, Settings, Taskbar option.

◆ **Remove Find command from Start menu.** Use this choice so users cannot use the Find command to do system- and network-wide searches.

◆ **Hide Drives in My Computer.** Use this choice so users cannot see drive names in the My Computer folder.

◆ **Hide Network Neighborhood.** Use this choice to remove the Network Neighborhood icon from the user's desktop. This limits the amount of browsing a user can perform on the network.

◆ **No Entire Network in Network Neighborhood.** Use this option to remove the Entire Network option in the Network Neighborhood folder. This should be used if you do not want to give users the capability to see all servers on the network.

◆ **No workgroup contents in Network Neighborhood.** Use this option when you do not want any workgroup contents displayed in the Network Neighborhood folder.

◆ **Hide all items on desktop.** Use this option when you do not want any icons, shortcuts, or folders displayed on the user's desktop.

◆ **Disable Shut Down Command.** Use this option to remove the Shut Down command on the Start menu. This is handy when you have file and print servers you do not want users to shut down.

◆ **Don't save settings at exit.** Use this option when you do not want users to save system settings they've modified during the current session. This is ideal for computers you might have set up in a classroom environment in which the system should boot up exactly the same each time.

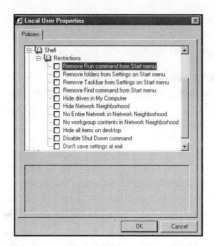

Figure 6.10

The Shell system policy options enable you to control the users' environment.

System Policy Options

The last set of options in the user-specific policy properties is the System settings (see fig. 6.11). The System settings control how the user interacts with the overall Windows NT environment, including restricting access to certain applications and to the DOS prompt.

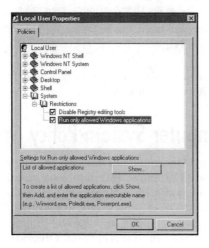

Figure 6.11

The System policy options enable you to control which applications (if any) run under Windows NT.

The Restrictions policies enable you to restrict users from using the Registry Editor and configure only specific Windows applications to run under Windows NT. The following are the choices you can modify:

◆ **Disable Registry editing tools.** It's a good idea to check this option so that users cannot run the Registry Editor to modify the Registry database. As you've seen in this book, the Registry is too technical for many average Windows NT users, but is also very easy to edit or modify by accident.

 Stop

One thing to keep in mind when you click on the Disable Registry editing tools option is that this does not prevent users from using the System Policy Editor to access the Registry. You'll need to make sure users don't have network access to the POLEDIT.EXE file or have a copy of the Windows NT system disks.

◆ **Run only allowed Windows applications.** If you check this option, you need to list all of the applications the user(s) can execute. Make sure you list *all* of the applications, including items like the Explorer, Notepad, and so on. You need to also list the Policy Editor if you plan to edit the user's policy locally.

 Tip

If you forget to add the Policy Editor (POLEDIT.EXE) to the preceding option, you might have a difficult time turning off this option. You can turn this option off using the Registry Editor by accessing the HKEY_CURRENT_USER\Software\Microsoft\ Windows\CurrrentVersion\Policies\Explore. Delete the RestrictRun entry. Shut down and restart Windows NT.

This completes the options you can modify for local users. The next section focuses on the options you can modify for local computers.

Modifying Local Computer System Policy Options

To complete setting up system policies, you need to set up the computer-specific policies. Double-click on the Local Computer or Default Computer icon in the System Policy Editor to display the policies for computers (see fig. 6.12). The settings you access here modify the HKEY_LOCAL_MACHINE Registry key. For a quick overview of the type of options you can modify for local computers, see the section "Creating Policies for Computers," earlier in this chapter. Otherwise, see the following sections for detailed descriptions of each system policy option available for local computers.

Figure 6.12

The System Policy Editor enables you to modify computer-specific Registry and policy options.

Windows NT Network System Policy Options

Figure 6.13 illustrates the sharing option as found in the Windows NT Network item.

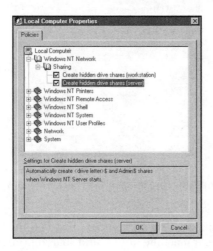

Figure 6.13

The Network system policy option enables you to control the way in which Windows NT sets up shares.

The Sharing option contains the following options under the Windows NT Network item:

- ◆ **Create hidden drive shares (workstation).** Instructs Windows NT to automatically create shares when Windows NT Workstation starts. Windows NT creates <*drives*>$ and Admin$ shares.

- ◆ **Create hidden drive shares (server).** Instructs Windows NT to automatically create shares when Windows NT Server starts. Windows NT creates <*drives*>$ and Admin$ shares.

Windows NT Printers

Figure 6.14 illustrates the Windows NT Printers system policy options.

Figure 6.14

The Printers system policy options enable you to control networking printer options.

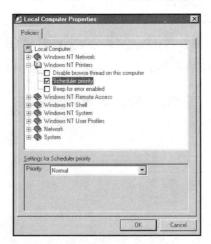

You can control the following network printing options under the Windows NT Printers system policy options:

- ◆ **Disable browse thread on this computer.** Instructs the Windows NT print spooler on the current machine not to send shared printer information to other network print servers. This reduces traffic on the network.

◆ **Scheduler priority.** Select from the Priority drop-down list the priority of the print job. You can choose from Above Normal, Below Normal, and Normal. The default setting is Normal.

◆ **Beep for error enabled.** When an error occurs during a remote print job, you might want to know about it at your local computer. Enable this setting to have Windows NT beep when this happens.

Windows NT Remote Access System Policy Options

Windows NT includes powerful remote access services (RAS) that enable users to access a Windows NT machine from other machines. RAS is an inviting service to use because of the potential it offers users who work from remote office settings, who are traveling, or who work from home. The danger, however, is that RAS can leave the machine exposed to others who are not authorized access to it. Although RAS includes security features to keep out unauthorized users, that doesn't keep people from trying to break into the system (usually termed *hacking*).

The Windows NT Remote Access system policy options are illustrated in figure 6.15.

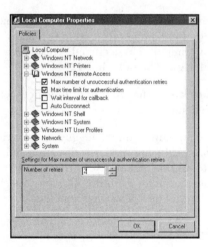

Figure 6.15

The Windows NT Remote Access system policy options enable you to control server-related RAS settings.

The Windows NT Remote Access system policy options should be used whenever you have RAS enabled on a machine. The following list explains each option:

◆ **Max number of unsuccessful retries.** Set this option to limit the number of times a user can attempt to log on to a RAS machine. Often hackers create batch files that repeatedly call a machine to attempt different user names and passwords until an authorized user is found. The default setting, which you specify in the Number of retries field, is 2. You might want to set this to 3 or 5 so that authorized users who are attempting to log on have enough opportunities to connect.

Tip Let authorized users know the maximum number of times they can attempt to log on to the RAS computer. Also, let them know the time they must wait before trying again if you set the Wait interval for callback option (see following options).

Set the number of logon attempts allowed to be the same (within reason) as other systems that users normally log on. This helps the user by not having to remember the different number of logon attempts for the different systems they use. Also, make the wait intervals the same for the different systems as well.

◆ **Max time limit for authentication.** Set this number so that each authentication event has a maximum time limit before sending a message to the user trying to log on that a logon timeout has occurred. This is so users don't tie up the RAS modem trying to log on. The default is 120 seconds.

◆ **Wait interval for callback.** Set the amount of time between each callback to the RAS computer. The default is 2 seconds.

◆ **Auto Disconnect.** Set the amount of time a logged on user can stay connected to the RAS computer before being automatically disconnected. The default is 20 minutes. You might want to set this higher if your users need to spend more time accessing data or other resources from the RAS machine. Twenty minutes isn't very long when downloading or uploading large files via a 14.4 or 28.8 baud modem.

Windows NT Shell System Policy Options

Figure 6.16 illustrates the Windows NT Shell system policy options, which are similar to the custom nonshared options you set in the "Custom Folders" section earlier in this chapter.

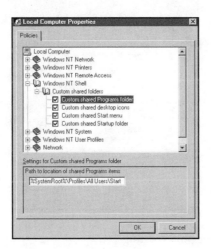

Figure 6.16

The Windows NT Shell system policy options enable you to customize shared folders.

These options enable you to control four different ways to customize shared folders on your system. The Custom shared folders items include the following options:

◆ **Custom shared Programs folder.** Enables you to customize the contents of the shared Programs folder. You need to include the UNC path to the custom Programs item you create.

◆ **Custom shared Desktop icons.** Enables you to customize the user's desktop icons for a shared environment. Again, specify the UNC path to the custom shared desktop icon folder.

◆ **Custom shared Start menu.** Enables you to define a custom shared Start menu folder. Enter the UNC path for this folder.

◆ **Custom shared Startup folder.** Enables you to define a custom shared folder that includes files, applications, or batch files that you want to run automatically at Windows NT startup. You need to enter the UNC path for this custom Startup folder.

Windows NT System Policy Options

Figure 6.17 illustrates the Windows NT System policy options.

Figure 6.17

The Windows NT System policy options enable you to control logon and file system settings.

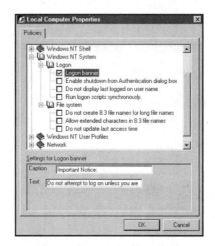

These options include two major policy settings:

◆ Logon

◆ File system

Each of these policy settings is described in greater depth in the following sections.

The Logon Options

Under the Logon options you can set logon banners, enable shutdown from the Authentication dialog box, instruct Windows NT not to display the last logged user on the Authentication dialog box, and run logon scripts completely before displaying the user's shell:

◆ **Logon banner.** The logon banner option enables you specify a banner when a user logs on to the system. It includes a caption and logon text. The default banner is "Important Notice;" the default text is "Do not attempt to log on unless you are an authorized user." Customize these text entries to suit your environment.

◆ **Enable shutdown from Authentication dialog box.** Set this if you want to give the user the authority to click the Shut Down option in the Authentication dialog box. By default, Windows NT Workstation has this option turned on; Windows NT Server has it turned off.

◆ **Do not display last logged on user name.** By default, Windows NT displays the name of the previous person who successfully last logged on to the network at the current workstation. You can turn off this feature to protect user names from unauthorized persons. When you use this option, the user name field is blank during logon.

◆ **Run logon scripts synchronously.** Turn on this option if you want Windows NT to run all logon scripts before starting the user's shell. If this same option is enabled under the Windows NT System options in the Local Computer Properties dialog box, that setting takes precedence.

The File System Options

The File system options includes settings for instructing Windows NT not to create 8.3 file name from long file names, to allow extended characters in 8.3 file names, and to disable the feature that updates the last access time on files that are only being read.

◆ **Do not create 8.3 file names for long file names.** Instructs Windows NT not to truncate long file names to 8.3 format.

◆ **Allow extended characters in 8.3 file name.** Use this option only when you use the same character code page for viewing short file names with extended characters.

◆ **Do not update last access time.** Use this option to improve your file system performance because time stamps do not have to be updated for files only being read.

Windows NT User Profiles

User profiles are created for each new user that logs on to Windows NT. This is standard for both Windows NT Server and Windows NT Workstation. User profile options can be controlled by using the Windows NT User Profiles system policy options (see fig. 6.18).

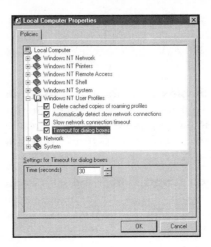

Figure 6.18

The Windows NT User Profiles system policy options enable you to set user profile settings.

The Windows NT User Profiles system policy options are detailed in the following list:

◆ **Delete cached copies of roaming profiles.** With Windows NT, you can have user profiles from roaming users (those users who move from computer to computer during their workday) cached on the local system. Select this option to delete cached copies of these profiles to save local hard disk space.

◆ **Automatically detect slow network connections.** Identifies a slow network connection. If NT detects a slow network connection, it uses the Slow network connection timeout option (see the next option) to enforce timeout for the slow connection.

◆ **Slow network connection timeout.** Specifies a maximum time limit for a slow network connection.

◆ **Timeout for dialog boxes.** Specifies a maximum time limit for displaying of dialog boxes.

Network System Policy Options

Under the Network system policy option item, you have only one option you can set. You can set the Remote update option for system policy updates (see fig. 6.19) for applications using remote procedure calls (RPCs). When you turn on this option, you must select an Update mode (such as Automatic or Manual), provide a path for the updated policy file (if you select the Manual option), whether to display error messages, and whether to activate load balancing on the network.

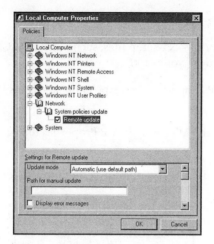

Figure 6.19

The Network system policy options enable you to control various remote settings.

System Policy Options

The System policy options enable or disable SNMP and Run options. The following two sections describe the two options available under the System option.

The SNMP Option

Simple Network Management Protocol enables SNMP consoles and agents to communicate with one another. The SNMP agent is implemented as a Win32-based service and works using Windows Sockets over both TCP/IP and IPX/SPX. The extension agents are implemented as a Win32 DLL.

You need to install the Microsoft SNMP agent from the Windows NT CD-ROM to use it. The policies you can set here are effective only if SNMP is installed on the computer first. Use the following steps to install it:

Tip   TCP/IP must be installed first before installing SNMP.

1. Start the Networks option in Control Panel.

2. Click on the Add button on the Services tab.

3. In the Select Network Services dialog box, select SNMP Service.

4. Click on OK.

5. Enter the path to the Windows NT setup files, such as D:\i386. Click on Continue. The SNMP files copy to your disk.

6. After the Microsoft SNMP Properties dialog box appears, press Enter to continue and configure SNMP.

7. Click on SNMP Server in the Microsoft SNMP Properties dialog box. Click on Properties.

8. Click the Agent tab and enter the agent information, such as location, services, and user information (see fig. 6.20).

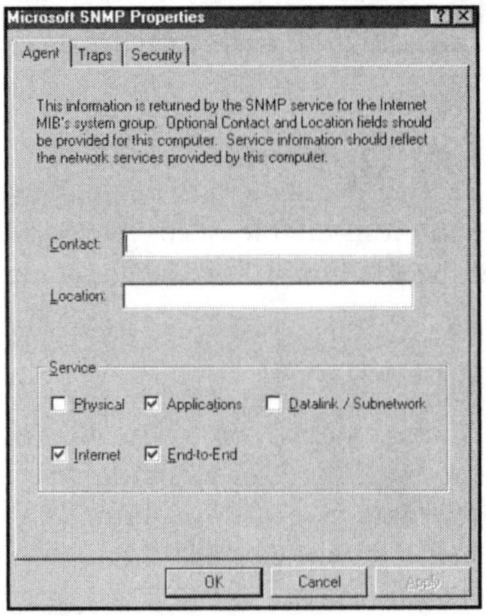

Figure 6.20

Use the Microsoft SNMP Properties dialog box to setup SNMP options.

9. Click the Traps tab and enter trap information, such as trap locations and community names.

10. Click the Security tab and enter security information, such as community and host names.

11. Click on OK to save your settings.

12. You need to restart your computer before the settings take effect.

The SNMP agent settings you can set in the System Policy Editor include the following:

◆ **Communities.** Enables you to specify one or more groups of hosts the selected computer belongs to. Click on the Show button at the bottom of the property sheet to add or remove communities.

◆ **Permitted managers.** Enables you to specify the IP and IPX addresses allowed to obtain information from an SNMP agent. If left unchecked, any SNMP console can query the agent. Again, click the Show button to add or remove managers.

◆ **Traps for Public community.** Enables you to specify IP or IPX addresses of hosts in the public community to which you want the SNMP service to send traps. These are called *trap destinations.* Click on the Show button to add or remove these items.

The Run Option

Use the Run option to set up applications, batch files, and other items you want to run during startup. When you set this option, click the Show button in the Settings for Run section of the Policies tab to display the Show Contents dialog box (see fig. 6.21).

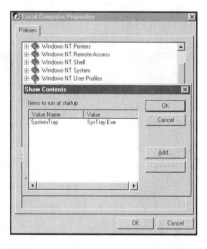

Figure 6.21

You must enter the names of the applications you want to run during startup in the Show Contents dialog box.

Click the Add button and fill in the name of the item to add to the startup procedure and enter the value of the item to add. The value is the path and executable name. The default path is *%SystemRoot%*.

Once you set edit the Registry using the System Policy Editor, select File, Save, and then shut down and restart the system.

Note To set up settings for groups, you use the options for users and computers but assign them to Windows NT group accounts. As group members log on to the network, the settings you establish for users or computers and assign to that group are downloaded and used to configure the workstation.

This concludes the descriptions of each of the Registry options you can modify using the System Policy Editor. The next section shows how to use these same settings to create system policies for users, computers, and groups.

Creating System Policies

In the preceding section, you learned how to use the System Policy Editor to change Registry settings. Setting options for system policies is similar to setting options for the Registry using the System Policy Editor. Instead of opening the Registry using the File menu, however, you select to create a new policy. Use the following steps to do this:

1. In System Policy Editor, select File, New Policy. The Default Computer and Default User icons display (see fig. 6.22).

Figure 6.22

When you create a new policy, the System Policy Editor looks the same as when you edited the Registry using it.

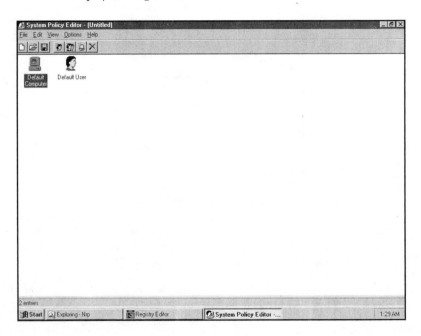

2. Double-click on the icon you want to set policies for, such as Default Computer to set computer options and Default User for user settings.

3. Set each option, as explained in the preceding section. Notice when you create a new policy, all of the policy options are grayed out. When you modified the Registry using the System Policy Editor as shown in the preceding section, some options were selected, grayed out, or blank, depending on the current Registry state.

4. When you finish setting system policy options, select File, Save. The Save As dialog box displays (see fig. 6.23).

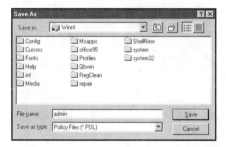

Figure 6.23

Use the Save As dialog box to name your new system policy file.

5. Enter a name in the File name field and select a folder in which to place the new policy file. Windows NT adds POL as the default extension, which must be used to denote policy files. You should place the new file in the *%SystemRoot%* folder.

6. Click on Save.

Note For descriptions of all the system policy options, see the previous sections "Modifying Local User System Policy Options" and "Modifying Local Computer System Policy Options."

Understanding How Windows NT Handles System Policies

You might want to know what the process is when someone logs on to Windows and implements the policy. Figure 6.24 shows an overview of this process. When someone logs on, the logon process follows the UNC path to the user's configuration and then follows the policies to implement the user's environment based on the following steps:

Figure 6.24

This is how a policy is implemented when a user logs on to Windows NT.

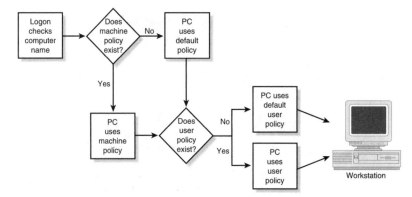

1. Logon checks the computer's name. If a profile for the PC is available, Windows NT uses that profile. If a profile does not exist for that computer, Windows NT uses the default computer profile.

2. The system policy checks the user's name against the group listings. If the user is a member of a group, Windows NT uses that group's policies. This is done by checking the group order that a user belongs to, processing groups from lowest to highest.

3. Windows NT checks the user's name. If a profile for the user logging in is available, Windows NT uses it. If not, Windows NT uses the default user profile.

Examining Policy Templates

Policy templates are the files (ADM files) that determine what policies can be enforced, including the actual options you can set. (The preceding section discussed these options in detail.) ADM files can be written to affect any setting in the Registry. If you have a program that can read the Registry, such as a Windows NT-compliant application, you can set up a system policy to control it for the entire company or workgroup. You also can create a template that can change the default layout of a spreadsheet application so that all users logged on with the same policy can use that layout. This section shows you how to create a policy template.

Creating a Policy Template

Windows NT provides you with a default ADMIN.ADM policy template, but you can create your own as well. You also can use the WINNT.ADM and WINDOWS.ADM files provided with Windows NT. To build a template, you create an ASCII text file that points to specific Registry keys and value entries and that assigns policies to enable or disable those keys and value entries.

 Note You cannot insert binary data into templates because the System Policy Editor does not support binary data.

A template is broken into sections, with each section of the template following a specific hierarchy (see fig. 6.25).

```
Class
    Category
        Policy
            Part
            End Part
        End Policy
    End Category
```

Figure 6.25

An example of a system policy template section hierarchy.

In the hierarchy demonstrated in this figure, CLASS can have two settings. It can be set to MACHINE or USER. MACHINE specifies the computer settings. The following is the CLASS syntax:

```
CLASS Type_of_Category
```

The next level is the CATEGORY settings. These can be either SYSTEM or NET-WORK, as follows:

```
CATEGORY name_of_category
KEYNAME name_of_key
definition statements for the policy...
```

Below the CATEGORY is the POLICY setting, which specifies a policy within a category. Policy names that have spaces, such as Restrict Display Control Panel, must be enclosed within quotations. The syntax for the POLICY setting is the following:

```
POLICY name_of_policy
KEYNAME name_of_key
definition statements for the policy...
```

The next item is the PART. This defines one or more controls that you can set for the values of the policy. Part names that contain spaces must be enclosed in quotes. Policy part types and type-dependent data can contain several key works and values. The syntax for the PARTS item is as follows:

```
PART name type_of_part
type-dependent data...
KEYNAME name_of_key
VALUENAME name_of_value
END PART
```

 Note A list of keywords and part control indicators are included in Chapter 7, "Administering Remote Registries from Windows NT."

A finished ADM template file is shown below. This template file produces a single policy named User Settings under the category named Preferences:

```
CLASS USER
CATEGORY Preferences
KEYNAME Network\Logon
POLICY "User Settings"
PART Part EDITTEXT
VALUENAME UserProfiles
END PART
END POLICY
END CATEGORY
```

Examining a Section of an ADM File

The following is a section copied from the WINDOWS.ADM file provided in the
\CLIENTS\SRV TOOLS\WINNT\I386 folder on the Windows NT Server CD. This
section shows how the ADM template for the Windows NT Shell system policy settings
are set up. To see how these template values display in the System Policy Editor, see
the "Shell System Policy Options" section earlier in this chapter.

```
CATEGORY !!Shell
KEYNAME "Software\Microsoft\Windows\CurrentVersion\Explorer\User Shell Folders"
        CATEGORY !!CustomFolders
                POLICY !!CustomFolders_Programs
                        PART !!CustomFolders_ProgramsPath    EDITTEXT REQUIRED
                        VALUENAME "Programs"
                        END PART
                END POLICY
                POLICY !!CustomFolders_Desktop
                        PART !!CustomFolders_DesktopPath    EDITTEXT REQUIRED
                        VALUENAME "Desktop"
                        END PART
                END POLICY
                POLICY !!HideStartMenuSubfolders
                        KEYNAME Software\Microsoft\Windows\CurrentVersion\
Policies\Explorer
                        VALUENAME NoStartMenuSubFolders
                        PART !!HideStartMenuSubfolders_Tip1 TEXT  END PART
```

```
                        PART !!HideStartMenuSubfolders_Tip2 TEXT   END PART
                END POLICY
                POLICY !!CustomFolders_Startup
                        PART !!CustomFolders_StartupPath EDITTEXT REQUIRED
                        VALUENAME "Startup"
                        END PART
                END POLICY
                POLICY !!CustomFolders_NetHood
                        PART !!CustomFolders_NetHoodPath EDITTEXT REQUIRED
                        VALUENAME "NetHood"
                        END PART
                END POLICY
                POLICY !!CustomFolders_StartMenu
                        PART !!CustomFolders_StartMenuPath EDITTEXT REQUIRED
                        VALUENAME "Start Menu"
                        END PART
                END POLICY
        END CATEGORY
END CATEGORY     ; Shell
```

Notice how this section is broken out as a category called !!Shell. This denotes that the System Policy Editor will display these options under a heading named Shell. Within the main category is a subcategory with the name !!CustomFolders. This denotes that a subfolder heading under Shell will display in the System Policy Editor with the name of Custom folders.

Under the first CATEGORY line is the KEYNAME line. This line shows the Registry subkey that contains the value entries that will be affected by the policy settings in this section of the policy template. In this case the HKEY_CURRENT_USER\Software\ Microsoft\Windows\CurrentVersion\Explorer\User Shell Folders subkey is modified.

Under the Category !!CustomFolders line, is the POLICY !!CustomFolders_Programs line. This line denotes the policy you can set under the Custom Program folders listing.

The PART !!CustomFolders_ProgramsPath denotes that a program path is needed for this policy setting. The EDITTEXT REQUIRED label to the right of the line is a string that denotes that some user input is required. In this case, the user must input the path to the custom program folder.

The VALUENAME "Programs" line specifies the actual Registry value entry that is modified with this policy setting. The Programs value entry is of data type REG_EXPAND_SZ so that it can include several string items under the same value entry, such as the default folder path and any new paths added when the user runs the System Policy Editor.

The END PART and END POLICY lines end the instructions for the Custom Programs folder settings. Following the END POLICY line is the start of a new policy setting (POLICY !!CustomFolders_Desktop), which sets up policy settings for custom desktop icon settings. For each policy setting that is to be displayed under the Custom folders option in the System Policy Editor, a separate POLICY...END POLICY section is included.

Note If you want to view the rest of the WINDOWS.ADM file, open the file in a text editor such as Notepad. You'll be able to see how Registry values and settings are changed using the policies defined therein.

Summary

This chapter examined system policies in Windows NT and showed you how to use them to make Registry changes and create system policy files. System Policies are used to control user's desktops and what users can do on a network. Administrators can use system policies items to control the way users log on and use their computers locally or on the network.

Administering Remote Registries from Windows NT

One of the nicest features of Windows NT is the capability to administer clients on your network remotely. Windows NT extends this capability to enable you to remotely administer Registries on Windows NT workstations. You can administer Windows NT Workstation Registries by using REGEDT32.EXE and opening a remote computer's HKEY_LOCAL_MACHINE and HKEY_CURRENT_USER hives.

You might also be responsible for administering Windows 95 clients on the network. You might, for instance, need to view or edit a remote Windows 95 client's Registry on the network, or make changes to the Windows 95 Registry to affect the way in which a client behaves. With Windows 95 clients, you can create user profiles and system policies that are stored on the server and downloaded each time a user logs on to the network. For workstations that need global settings or changes made to them, storing policies centrally helps reduce the amount of time you spend making changes to each client machine.

In this chapter, you are shown how to modify, view, and change Registry settings for remote clients, including Windows NT Workstation and Windows 95 clients. The majority of the information you need to understand the Windows NT Workstation Registry is covered throughout the rest of the book in general Windows NT Registry discussions. The first part of this chapter focuses on using the Registry Editor to edit a Windows NT Workstation Registry. The rest of this chapter focuses on how to administer remote Windows 95 clients' Registries on your network. To better prepare you for that coverage, the chapter also offers a sound overview of the Windows 95 Registry.

Specifically, in this chapter you learn the following:

◆ How to view and modify a remote Windows NT Workstation Registry

◆ What comprises the Windows 95 Registry

◆ How to use the Windows 95 Registry Editor

◆ How to work with user profiles on the network

◆ How to modify the Registry with the System Policy Editor

◆ How to set up roving users on Windows NT and Novell NetWare

Note   Although many installations run Windows 3.11, Windows for Workgroups, and other versions of Windows 3.x on their network, this chapter focuses on Windows NT Workstation 4 and Windows 95. This is due in large part to how these two operation systems use the Registry to centralize configuration and application settings. For troubleshooting Windows 3.x problems, refer to documentation for Windows 3.x, such as *Inside Windows 3.11*, published by New Riders.

Exploring Remote Windows NT Workstation Registries

Windows NT Workstation has the same Registry that Windows NT Server has. The only difference you might encounter between the two is the type of specific information stored in each. You might, for instance, have user, group, and security account information for the entire network stored in the Windows NT Server, whereas a Windows NT Workstation Registry contains only user and computer-specific information for those users who log on at that workstation.

Another difference you might encounter is how you edit the Windows NT Workstation Registry. Although you can use the Registry Editor (REGEDT32.EXE) to modify a local Windows NT Workstation's Registry, you most likely will use the remote capabilities of the Registry Editor to perform administration duties on your Windows NT Workstation clients. This enables you to remain at your workstation and edit Registry settings on computers attached to the network. For large installations or organizations in which computers might be scattered on several floors in a building, this eliminates the need to go tromping from floor to floor looking for the computer you need to administer. Also, it reduces the number of times you interrupt users from their daily activities to make changes to their system.

To use the Registry Editor to edit remote Windows NT Workstation Registries, use the following steps:

1. Start the Registry Editor (REGEDT32.EXE).

2. Select Registry, Select Computer. The Select Computer dialog box displays (see fig. 7.1).

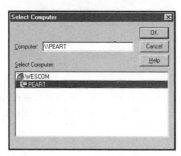

Figure 7.1

The Select Computer dialog box includes the local and remote computers you can select.

3. In the Computer field, enter the name of the computer for which you want to view the Registry. You must use UNC naming conventions, such as *computer_name*. You also can double-click a computer from the Select Computer area.

4. Click on OK. The HKEY_LOCAL_MACHINE and HKEY_USERS hives from the remote computer display in the Registry Editor. These are the only two hives you can modify from a remote computer. In figure 7.2, for example, the two hives from the remote computer PEART are shown (the hives from the local computer are closed to enable you to view the remote hives easier).

Figure 7.2

The Registry Editor displays only the HKEY_LOCAL_MACHINE and HKEY_USERS hives from remote computers.

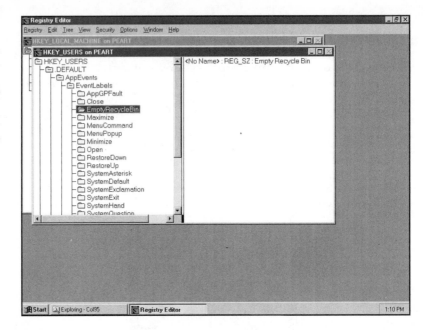

5. View or modify the remote Registry as necessary.

6. After you finish working with the remote Registry, select Registry, Close. This closes the remote Registry. The next time the user on the remote computer reboots his or her system, the Registry settings will take affect.

Tip When you modify a remote Registry, you cannot use the Auto Refresh command on the Options menu. This is because it is assumed that the remote computer is in use as you edit the Registry. If you select Options, Auto Refresh, the command acts like it is working, but it is not. Further, when the Auto Refresh command is selected, the Refresh All and Refresh Active commands are dimmed on the View menu.

Examining the Windows 95 Registry

Many Windows NT network administrators are responsible for managing and maintaining more than one type of operating system on their network. In a perfect network world, you would have only one type of client attached to your network. In the practical world, however, you might have a handful of different types of clients on your network, including Windows 95. Because Windows 95 clients are becoming more popular on network installations and because Windows 95's Registry is incompatible with Windows NT's, you need to understand how Windows 95 uses the Registry and how it is designed.

 Note   The Windows 95 Registry is in some ways similar to the Windows NT Registry. Both Registries are designed as central configuration databases for user and system configurations. They both contain keys, value entries, and value data. And they both can be viewed and modified using the Registry Editor. The two Registries, however, are not compatible with each other. The first time you might encounter this is if you try to upgrade your Windows 95 system to Windows NT. After you upgrade to Windows NT, you need to reinstall all your applications to work with Windows NT. This is because the application-specific settings stored in the Windows 95 Registry are not automatically transferred to the Windows NT Registry.

As you read through the following discussions about the Windows 95 Registry, you can get an idea of how the Windows 95 Registry is structured and how it differs from the Windows NT Registry. To get an in-depth understanding of the Windows 95 Registry, read *Windows 95 Registry Troubleshooting*, published by New Riders.

One of the big differences between the Windows NT and Windows 95 Registries is how Windows 95 stores the Registry files. Windows 95 uses only two files— SYSTEM.DAT and USER.DAT—to store user and system configuration information. For most end users, knowing which file contains what is not important. Administrators, however, should know that the USER.DAT file contains information specific to the individual, such as customized desktop settings and the like. The SYSTEM.DAT file, on the other hand, includes those settings specific to the machine, such as default desktop settings, hardware profiles, and network information.

Both SYSTEM.DAT and USER.DAT are hidden files that are stored in your Windows 95 folder. When Windows 95 installs, it creates these two files and creates a back-up file for each. These backups, which are also hidden files in your Windows 95 folder, are named SYSTEM.DA0 and USER.DA0. These two backups are on your system in the event your SYSTEM.DAT and USER.DAT files become corrupted. Each time you boot your PC, Windows automatically updates these back-up files by copying your current Registry files to the DA0 files. In theory, this enables you to always have a "last best boot" configuration on your machine.

Stop The DAO files are not always fail-safe to system problems. In the event of a corrupt SYSTEM.DAT or USER.DAT or both, you can use the DAO files to copy both of the DAT files. There have, however, been cases where the DAO files are corrupt as well. This is good reason to create several different backups of your DAT files, storing some of these backups on floppy disks or tape backups in case of emergencies.

As you just read, SYSTEM.DAT file and USER.DAT files differ: one is for holding system settings, and one is for holding user-specific information. But why not have one file with different headings, somewhat like INI files, listing user and system settings instead of two distinct files?

The answer to this gets to the foundation of why Windows 95 uses a Registry in the first place. By having two files, Windows 95 can now separate the user from the computer (see fig. 7.3), enabling a more dynamic computing environment for the user and system administrator. By having the USER.DAT file located on a network server, the individual user can move from machine to machine and still have his or her customized settings. When a user logs on to a computer, the user information is accessed, usually via a profile, from the server.

Figure 7.3

In this schematic view, you can see how the Registry separates the user from the computer.

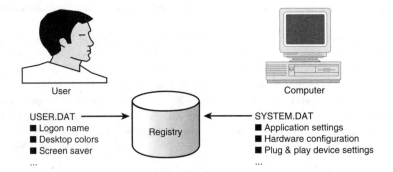

Another way this is useful is for users who work in mobile office settings and must change their systems to adapt to a specific environment. A salesperson, for instance, might carry a laptop computer to a client's site where no network or printing services are available, but a phone line is available that enables access to a remote PC. The user can log on to Windows using a new name, such as "MOBILE," which configures Windows to start up without searching for a network connection, but it enables the remote access configuration that the user has established for the MOBILE user.

In both of these cases, the hardware stays consistent. The trackball or mouse settings remain unchanged; display configurations are unchanged; hard drive, floppy drive, and CD-ROM drive settings are the same; and applications stay virtually untouched (except for any settings that the user changes in the application, such as toolbar options and the like). All these settings are contained in the SYSTEM.DAT file and remain the same for most situations.

User settings contained in USER.DAT include the following:

◆ Desktop icons and placement

◆ Control panel settings such as sounds, keyboard, and Desktop Themes

◆ Application settings

◆ Post office files

The Registry includes information about the on-screen location of desktop files for each user. It keeps one list of the files or links of files on the desktop. The Registry, however, does not include information about the owner of the file or file link, which can cause problems if a person deletes a file that he does not currently own.

This can happen as a result of the lack of file-level security in Windows 95. A simple scenario of this would be as follows. Suppose, for example, you have a file on your desktop named EXAMPLE1.LNK and another user has the same file name on his desktop. The difference between the files is the actual content stored in them. The information for these files is stored in USER.DAT for each user. If you then move to that other person's computer and log on using your name, thereby accessing your USER.DAT file on the server, then your individual settings appear on-screen. These settings are the desktop color and so forth. The file EXAMPLE1.LNK also appears because the user of that machine created it. By mistake, you might edit, delete, or move this file thinking it is your EXAMPLE1.LNK file. In reality, it is not. Windows 95 cannot tell the two files' contents apart, leaving management of files strictly up to the individual user.

Note   Windows 95 does not support the Windows NT File System (NTFS), which enables you to set permissions on each file. If you want to use NTFS, you must install Windows NT Workstation on your client desktops.

For this type of situation, you should consider creating user profiles that restrict certain folders for certain users. Set up folders that only specific people can use on a machine, much like you do with your network server resources.

SYSTEM.DAT includes the computer-specific information, including all the hardware information on your computer. This is the same information stored in the Device Manager in Control Panel (see fig. 7.4).

Figure 7.4

The Device Manager in Windows 95 displays configuration information for your hardware and devices.

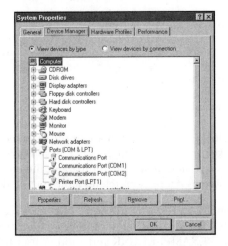

Another way the Windows NT and Windows 95 Registries differ is the way the Windows 95 Registry stores hardware information. A fundamental role of the Windows 95 Registry is to hold hardware-specific information for the hardware detection phase during system setup and startup. It is also the central database for Plug and Play system components, which Windows NT does not currently support (future versions of Windows NT probably will support Plug and Play). When you install a piece of hardware, the Windows 95 Registry automatically acquires information about it. This information is used to help you automatically configure the hardware device.

Windows 95 uses a *hardware enumeration process* that checks the hardware device and identifies it during the bootup process. During bootup, the device's name and type (such as CD-ROM or network adapter) are identified. As you boot up your PC after you install a new device, the system checks the Registry to find out what resources have been used and what resources are available on your machine. These resources include I/O addresses, DMA channels, and IRQs and are checked to make sure you don't encounter a hardware conflict with the new device.

The Registry is designed to eliminate many of the burdens placed on system integrators and users during hardware installations. The method used in Windows 3.x is to place system and application information inside INI files. SYSTEM.INI, for instance, holds all your system information, including device drivers and hardware configuration information. Individual hardware components further complicate hardware installation by including dip switches and jumpers to set, as well as by requiring you to configure various batch files to invoke hardware device drivers. The result for many users is that a hardware conflict keeps the device from working or cause another device to quit working. In extreme, but not uncommon, cases entire systems quit working or data loss occurs during these hardware upgrades.

Note

What happens to INI files in Windows 95? If you upgrade from Windows 3.x to Windows 95, you still have INI files on your system. Similar to Windows NT, Windows 95 does not require INI files (future versions of Windows and Windows NT might not even recognize them), it does use them for compatibility with Win16 applications. Win16 applications use INI files for user- and application-specific information. The Registry also uses them for system configuration information in order for the applications to run. Windows 95 needs to retain this type of information for your older applications to run correctly.

Besides other INI files specific to your system, Windows 95 retains the SYSTEM.INI and WIN.INI files during the Windows 95 installation stage. When you boot Windows 95, it looks at the [386Enh] section of the SYSTEM.INI file for virtual driver information and locations. For a complete description of the INI settings mapped to Windows 95, see *Windows 95 Registry Troubleshooting*, published by New Riders.

Examining the Windows 95 Registry Editor

Because the Windows NT Registry is different from the Windows 95 one, you use a different Registry Editor to edit, view, and modify Registry keys and values. This section includes an explanation of how to use the Windows 95 Registry Editor, REGEDIT.EXE. To make changes to a Windows 95 Registry on the network, you must be logged on to the network from a Windows 95 computer or edit the Registry from the local workstation. Because the Windows NT and Windows 95 Registries are incompatible, you cannot edit a remote Windows 95 Registry from a Windows NT system. If you are like many system administrators, then you would like to make as many remote changes as possible from your desktop. If you administer a mixed Windows 95 and Windows NT client environment, then you either need two machines—one running Windows 95 and the other NT—or you should have both Windows 95 and Windows NT installed on the same machine and reboot to the one you want.

Stop As with the Windows NT Registry Editor, the Windows 95 Registry Editor is quite simple to use. What isn't simple is ensuring that the edits and modifications you make to your working Registry database are the correct ones for your machine. For this reason, make a backup copy of the SYSTEM.DAT and USER.DAT files on the system you plan to edit. This way you can always return to the original Registry settings if you make an error modifying the Windows 95 Registry.

Note As you read through this section, some of the information is similar to information located in other parts of the book that focus on Windows NT. Although the Windows 95 and Windows NT Registries are similar and the Windows 95 Registry Editor is similar to the Registry Editor found in Windows NT, you should read this discussion closely since the details of each are different.

Running the Registry Editor

Before you run the Registry Editor, you need to find it on your system. If you installed Windows 95 from a CD-ROM, the file REGEDIT.EXE is installed in your Windows 95 folder. REGEDIT.EXE might also be installed in your Windows NT *%SystemRoot%*. Locate REGEDIT.EXE on your system and double-click on it to start. You also can enter the path of your Windows 95 folder and \REGEDIT.EXE on the Open line of the Run dialog box from the Start menu.

Start the Registry Editor now so that you can begin to uncover its features and capabilities. Your screen will look similar to the one shown in figure 7.5. As you can see, the Windows 95 Registry Editor looks slightly different from the Windows NT Registry Editor. Primarily, in the Windows 95 Registry Editor, all of the subtrees display in one window, instead of separate windows for each subtree as is the case with Windows NT.

Figure 7.5

The Windows 95 Registry Editor is used to change Windows 95 Registry settings.

When the Registry Editor starts, it displays the entire Registry database, which comprises SYSTEM.DAT and USER.DAT files in your Windows 95 folder. For the most part, you do not have to know the difference between these two files when you work in the Registry Editor. The Registry Editor automatically updates each file appropriately when you make changes in the Registry Editor.

Examining the Registry Editor Interface

As a quick reference to using the Registry Editor, this section shows and describes each feature of the Registry Editor. Later sections describe how to use each of these features to modify or navigate your Windows 95 Registry.

The Registry Editor has four main areas (see fig. 7.6), as follows:

◆ **Menu bar.** Displays the four menus: Registry, Edit, View, and Help.

◆ **Left pane.** Displays the Registry hierarchy, organized in keys, subkeys, and values.

◆ **Right pane.** Shows the current settings of a selected entry, known as values.

◆ **Status bar.** Displays the path of the selected item. You should use the status bar to show you the subkey or key to which a value belongs.

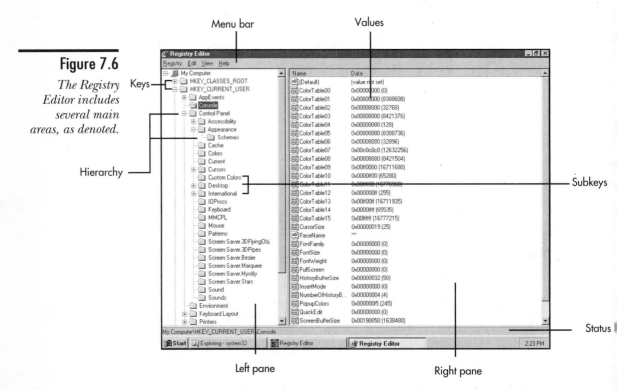

Figure 7.6

The Registry Editor includes several main areas, as denoted.

A quick review of each menu item will help you understand how to navigate and use the Registry Editor.

In the Registry menu, the Import Registry File option enables you to import files into the Registry, including ASCII files and REG files. See the section called "Importing Registry Information" later in this chapter for more information about this feature.

The Export Registry File command enables you to save your Registry or part of the Registry to a different file type, such as an ASCII file.

Note You are shown in the section "Searching By Using a Text Editor" how to use the Export Registry File command to save part of the Registry and use WordPad to search for entries.

You can use the Print command in the Registry menu to make a hard copy print out of your entire Registry (this might consume several pages). You also can select to print out a portion of the Registry, which is the best alternative.

The Connect Network Registry option enables you to specify the name of the computer where a remote Registry resides (see fig. 7.7). Use the browse button to find the computer name if you are not sure where it is.

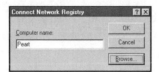

Figure 7.7

Insert the name of the remote computer to edit a remote Registry file.

Note To enable remote Registry editing, you must install the Remote Registry Service in Windows 95. To do this, open Control Panel and double-click on the Network icon. Click the Add button and click the Server option from the Select Network Component Type dialog box. Click the Have Disk button and enter the path **ADMIN\NETTOOLS\REMOTEREG** folder to your Windows 95 CD-ROM. Click on OK. In the Select Network Service dialog box, click the Microsoft Remote Registry option and click on OK. When you run the Remote Registry Service, the WINREG.DLL file is used to route access to remote Registries from across the network.

To disconnect from a remote Registry, use the Disconnect Network Registry command. This option is dimmed if you are not currently connected to a remote Registry.

The Edit menu contains six options that enable you to find and modify specific Registry entries: Modify, New, Delete, Rename, Find, and Find Next. To change the setting of a value in the Registry, use the Modify option. This option is available only when you have selected a value name in the right-hand pane of the Registry Editor. You are shown how to make modifications to entries in the section called "Editing Registry Settings" later in this chapter.

The New option enables you to add a new key or new string, binary, or Dword values. These options are available when you click on the New option and view the resulting fly-out menu. These same options are available when you right-click on a data field of a Registry value in the right-hand pane of the Registry Editor. Again, these items are covered in more detail later when editing registry settings is discussed.

The Delete and Rename options in the Edit menu are self-explanatory—they let you delete or rename a value. You can delete a value also by clicking on it and pressing the Del key. Likewise, to rename a value quickly, right-click on the name select Rename and type in the new name. This is similar to renaming a file in the Windows Explorer.

Stop As with the Windows NT Registry Editor, the Windows 95 Registry Editor does not include an Undo feature. So be extra careful when you want to delete a value. Be sure you really want to delete it for good. Windows does display a dialog box asking if you are sure you want to delete the item, but once you press Yes, there's no turning back.

The Find and Find Next commands are used to locate specific entries or data (such as strings or words) in the Registry. These commands are discussed in detail in the next section.

The View menu (see fig. 7.8) controls the way the Registry looks. If you should want the status bar turned off at the bottom of the Registry Editor window, you can do so by using the Status Bar option in the View menu. The status bar is the quickest way to see where you are in the Registry, though, and it is best to keep it turned on.

You can adjust the size of each Registry Editor pane by sliding the middle divider to the left and to the right. Sometimes you'll want to see all the subkeys in the left hand pane, and you might need to move the divider over to the right a little. An example of this is shown in figure 7.9. In this example, the hierarchy of the selected key is several subkeys (sometimes called subtrees in Windows 95) long, making it difficult to see all of it once.

The Split option in the View menu moves the mouse pointer to the divider so all you have to do is move the mouse left or right, find a new position for the divider, and left-click.

Tip You can quickly resize the Registry Editor panes with only your mouse. Just move the mouse pointer over the pane divider until the pointer changes to a double-arrow, hold down the left mouse button, and slide the mouse left or right. Release the mouse button when done.

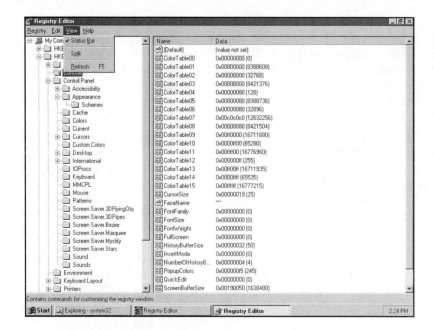

Figure 7.8

The View menu enables you to modify how the Registry Editor looks.

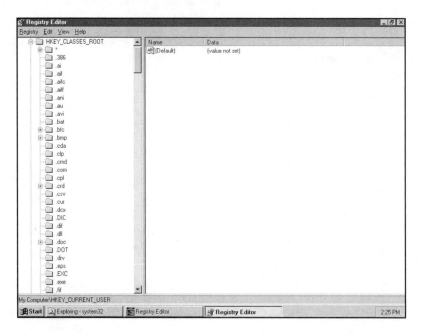

Figure 7.9

This is an example of viewing a long Registry subtree.

Another option on the View menu is the Refresh command. After you make changes to the Registry, some of the changes are not immediately displayed in the Registry Editor. You'll need to refresh the Registry Editor using the Refresh command or by pressing F5. This refreshes the Registry Editor interface, but the change usually doesn't take effect until the next time you reboot your system. Some changes, such as adding system events via the Registry, take effect as soon as you refresh the Registry.

Viewing Value Entries in the Registry Editor

The Registry Editor displays Registry keys, subkeys, and value entries in two panes. The keys and subkeys are in the left pane, and the values are in the right pane. Keys and subkeys are denoted with folders, either open or closed depending on if there are subkeys within a key. These are the same folder icons that you can see in the Windows 95 or Windows NT Explorer and My Computer.

When you first open the Registry Editor, only the top-most keys are shown, branching off the My Computer icon. Each of these root keys can display its subkeys when you click on the plus sign next to the key. This expands the key to the next level of subkeys (see fig. 7.10), much like expanding folders and subfolders in Windows Explorer.

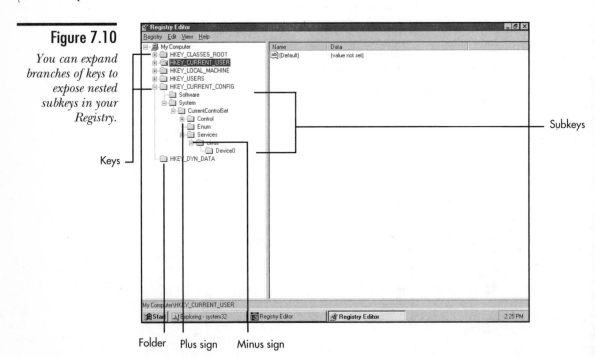

Figure 7.10

You can expand branches of keys to expose nested subkeys in your Registry.

Keys

Subkeys

Folder   Plus sign   Minus sign

You can expand or collapse subkeys the same as you can in the Windows NT Registry Editor. When you get to the bottom of the nesting, a minus sign appears to the left of the subkey indicating that you cannot display any more items and can only move back up the hierarchy. If a subkey does not have a plus sign or minus sign next to it, you know that it does not contain subkeys.

In the right-hand pane of the Registry Editor are the value entries, as denoted in figure 7.11. Each value entry contains three different parts: data type, name, and the value itself.

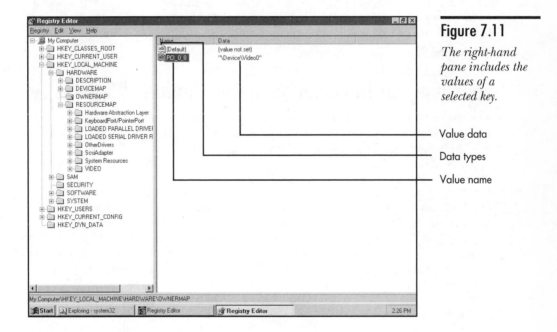

Figure 7.11

The right-hand pane includes the values of a selected key.

The data type of the value is shown as an icon, rather than listed as in the Windows NT Registry Editor. The data type icons are used so that you can quickly distinguish between binary type and text type. These icons are described in table 7.1

TABLE 7.1
Windows 95 Registry Editor Data Types

Data Types	Description
![binary icon]	Denotes that the value type is in binary format.
![text icon]	Denotes text and characters that you can read, such as "On The&MicrosoftNetwork".

Each value can have a name or can use empty quotation marks ("") to denote a value without a name. Many of the values provided by Microsoft use the name (Default), as you'll see when you start using the Registry Editor a great deal. Value names appear under the Names column in the right pane. These names help you understand the function of the value and are usually provided by application designers and hardware providers.

In the Data column in the Registry Editor is where you'll find the actual text or binary entry for the selected key. This is the data that controls how the key behaves and is the data that you edit, modify, or create to change or enhance the way a Windows 95 feature works. The value entry is limited to a size of only 64 KB (unlike the 1 MB size limit in Windows NT), which in most cases is sufficient unless you include a large binary data type.

Searching for Information in the Windows 95 Registry

As with the Windows NT Registry Editor, the quickest approach to search for a value using the Windows 95 Registry Editor is to use the Find option. This enables you to quickly move through the Registry until you find exactly what you need. Another way to search through a long Registry is to export that piece of the Registry to an ASCII file and use a text editor to search for the entry.

On the Edit menu is the Find command. When you select it, the Find dialog box appears (see fig. 7.12), in which you can describe the key, value, or data you are searching on. You can search for keys, values, data in values, or any combination of these items. (With Windows NT, you can search only for keys.) The values you search for can be text or number values, returning very precise searching results for you.

Figure 7.12

Enter the search criteria in the Find what text box to begin your search.

To use the Find command, enter the value in the Find what text box in the Find dialog box. You can choose to narrow your searches using the following Look at options:

◆ **Keys.** Finds matches to your searches that are Registry keys only. Finds both root keys and subkeys.

◆ **Values.** Finds only values of keys. This is the information displayed in the right pane under the Name column.

◆ **Data.** Narrows your search to find only those matches that correspond to data in the entries.

You can use all three search options (which is the default) or only those you want. To speed up your searches and to narrow your search results, try to use one or two of the Look at options.

Another option to use in the Find dialog box is the Match whole string only option. After you fill out the Find dialog box, click on the Find Next button to start the search.

When the Registry Editor finds a match, it highlights the item. This helps you locate where the item resides, that is, in which key or subkey is it nested. If the match is on a key or subkey (see fig. 7.13), you'll have little problem determining the full path of the item.

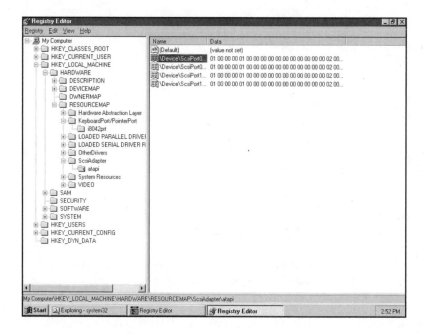

Figure 7.13

When the Registry Editor finds a match for your word or number, it highlights the item.

For data or values found, nested subkeys associated with that item are opened in the left pane for you to view. Also, the value name is highlighted. The shortcoming to this is that it is difficult to tell which key the data belongs to. You have to look closely at the subkeys in the right pane to see which folder is open.

Tip   One trick you might want to use when you search for a value or value name is to look at the bottom of the screen after the search is done. Usually (but this isn't always the case) the subkey that is associated with the entry is near the bottom of the screen.

Figure 7.14 shows an example of an item found that you cannot readily tell to which key or subkey it belongs. To find this out, you can scroll up the left hand pane to view the folder hierarchy.

Figure 7.14

Sometimes it's difficult to determine the parent folder of the found value.

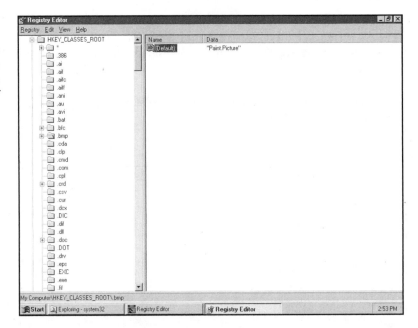

The best way to view the full path of the value is to look at the status bar. The status bar shows the entire path of the value, including all the subkeys, keys, and computer (which in most cases will be My Computer).

Now that you've found an item, is it the correct one? You'll have to determine that when you find it. You can now modify the item (see the section called "Editing Registry Settings" later in this chapter), end the search, or simply ignore the search result and continue the search. Press F3 or select Edit, Find next to go to the next occurrence of the matched item.

Searching by Using a Text Editor

First, export a portion of the Registry. The best way is to export a branch of the Registry, such as the HKEY_CLASSES_ROOT, by clicking on it in the left pane and selecting Registry, Export Registry File. When the Export Registry File dialog box displays (see fig. 7.15), you'll need to input a name for the file in the File name text box. Windows automatically knows that it is a Registration file and gives it a REG extension but does not give it a default file name. You can store the file in any folder on your system, but you might want to store it in an archive folder other than your Windows 95 folder.

Figure 7.15

Fill in a file name in the Export Registry File dialog box.

Tip

A common practice of network administrators who manage several Windows 95 clients is to use the Registry Editor to make configuration changes for one client, export the Registry for that machine, and import it on the other Windows 95 clients. This enables them to reuse settings from one machine to another, decreasing the amount of time devoted to setup and troubleshooting. Of course, for this to work, all client workstations need to have the same hardware devices and applications installed.

Notice in the Export range area that you have the option of exporting the entire Registry database (using the All option) or just a portion of it (using the Selected branch option). Unless you want to make a backup of your Registry or share its entire contents with someone else (see the section "Sharing Registry Information" later in this chapter), choose the Selected branch option. This is especially true if you need to work in only a portion of the Registry.

Click on the Save button and the file is saved to disk. Don't wait for a prompt or message telling you that it has been saved. You don't get one in this case.

Now open the file in a text editor. Your display will look something like the one in figure 7.16. This shows the HKEY_CURRENT_CONFIG key from the author's machine. Select Search, Find and enter the text or numbers you want to locate in the Find what text box.

Figure 7.16

WordPad's search utility can be used to find a specific Registry setting.

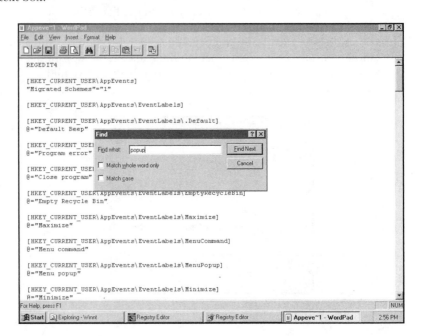

Editing Registry Settings

Modifying a Registry value or key in the Windows 95 Registry Editor differs somewhat from the same task using the Windows NT Registry Editor. Remember, keys or values can quickly be deleted or changed without much effort. Before going any further, make a backup of your Registry. You can, for instance, copy SYSTEM.DAT and USER.DAT to a backup floppy. The key is to make sure that if you make a mistake editing a value or key, you can always return to a working copy of the Registry.

Tip

If you plan to modify the Registry Editor often, invest in the *Windows 95 Resource Kit* from Microsoft Press to get a couple of utilities that help you make backups of the Registry. CFGBACK.EXE is a file on the Resource Kit floppy disks that backs up the Registry and can make up to nine copies of it. This ensures that you have an ample number of replacements in case you run into problems. (You also can find CFGBACK.EXE on your Windows 95 source CD in the \OTHER\MISC\ CFGBACK\CFGBACK.EXE.)

The backed-up Registry files are stored in your Windows 95 folder in a file with an RBK extension.

To edit a value, use the following general steps:

1. If it is not already open, start the Registry Editor.

2. Locate the value or key that you want to modify or delete (see the previous section on searching if you need help doing this).

3. If you want to modify a value of a key, double-click the value entry in the right pane of the Registry Editor window. You'll need to double-click on the name of the value, not the data itself.

As shown in figure 7.17, the Edit String dialog box displays. This shows the name of the value, which in this example is (Default), and the value data. Because this example shows a text string being edited, the entire data field is highlighted, letting you know that you can edit it directly.

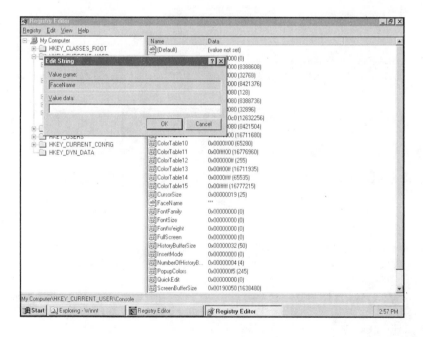

Figure 7.17

The Edit String dialog box enables you to modify the string setting for a Registry value entry.

The other type of value data you can edit is in binary format. To do this, select a value that has the binary format icon to the left of it (see fig. 7.18). Double-click on the value name. This displays the Edit Binary Value dialog box (see fig. 7.19). In this box, you can change the value name by highlighting it and typing in a new name. You also can input a new binary string by highlighting the information in the value data and replacing it with your new binary string.

Figure 7.18

The binary format icon denotes binary data type value entries.

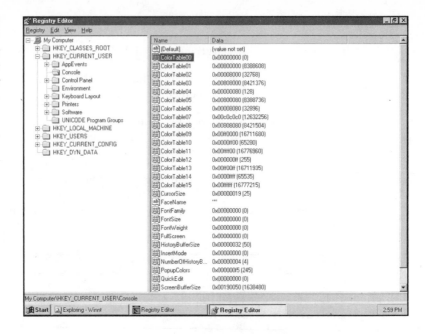

Figure 7.19

The Edit Binary Value dialog box enables you to modify binary data type value entries.

Adding a Key to the Registry

The Registry Editor can be used to add a key to your Registry. You might need to do this, for example, to install a device driver that does not have an installation program.

Use the following steps to add a key to the Registry:

1. Select the key or subkey under which you want the new key to appear.

2. From the Edit menu, choose New, Key.

Tip   You can also use the right-click context menu to access the New, Key option.

3. In the new key folder (see fig. 7.20), insert a new name for the key. Notice how this action is similar to the way you add names to folders in the Windows Explorer.

Figure 7.20

You can easily add a name to a new key in the Registry.

4. Press Enter after you input the name.

Like the Windows NT Registry, the Windows 95 Registry key names cannot contain backslashes (\) and must be unique to that hierarchy. Other subkeys at the same level cannot have the same name. After you add a key to the Registry, you'll more than likely want to assign a new value entry to it.

You can use the following steps to add a value entry to a new Registry key, or to an existing key:

1. Select the subkey to which to add the value entry.

2. Select Edit, New, and select the type of data format you want to input: String Value, Binary Value, or DWORD Value.

3. In the New value field, enter a name for the value.

You now can modify the value as you did earlier in the chapter in the section called "Editing Registry Settings."

Deleting Registry Values and Keys

You can delete a key or value entry using one of several methods, as described in the following list:

♦ Select the item to delete and then press the Del key on your keyboard.

♦ Select the item to delete and then choose Edit, Delete from the Registry Editor menu.

♦ Right-click on the item to delete and select Delete from the context menu.

Regardless of which method you choose, Windows prompts you to confirm the file deletion. Click on Yes to delete the selected item. You can click on No if you are not sure that you've selected the correct key or value to delete.

 Stop   One way to retrieve a key that you deleted is to restart the computer in Safe Mode and return to your previous last best boot into Windows 95.

Before you start thinking that Microsoft was going to let you shoot yourself in both feet, be aware of this. You cannot delete or rename the six main root keys in the Registry. These are the keys listed as follows:

♦ HKEY_CLASSES_ROOT

♦ HKEY_CURRENT_USER

♦ HKEY_LOCAL_MACHINE

♦ HKEY_USERS

♦ HKEY_CURRENT_CONFIG

♦ HKEY_DYN_DATA

These root keys are protected from changes.

Printing Registry Information

To print from the Registry Editor, use the following steps:

1. Select a branch that you want to print. You can select any branch to print, including the root key all the way down to the lowest level branch or subkey.

2. Choose Registry, Print to display the Print dialog box (see fig. 7.21).

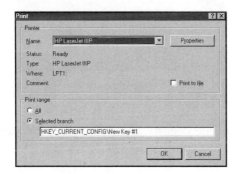

Figure 7.21

You can control whether to print the entire Registry or just a branch from the Print dialog box.

3. In the Print dialog box, select the print range of the print job. By default, the Registry prints the selected branch only.

4. Click on OK.

Sharing Registry Information

You use the Import and Export option in the Registry Editor to store and retrieve Registry information. This is a good way to back up Registry keys and subkeys before making changes to the Registry. It also is a convenient way to send information from a Registry on one machine to another. And, as you've already seen, you can export part of the Registry to search it using a text editor.

Registry information is imported and exported to and from REG files. REG files are editable text files. Do REG files sound familiar? They should. You might remember them from Windows 3.x when you had to manually register an OLE 2.0 setting for an application on your system. Those files contained all of the registration information for a specific application.

Those files are still supported for the most part in Windows 95. But now REG files contain more than just OLE information. They can contain the entire Registry if you export it to a REG file.

Importing Registry Information

You can quickly import Registry information by double-clicking on the REG file in Windows Explorer. This imports the information and returns a message similar to the one shown in figure 7.22.

Figure 7.22

Importing Registry information from a REG file in Explorer.

You get the same results by using the Registry, Import Registry file command in the Registry Editor. This displays the Import Registry File dialog box, from which you can specify the REG file you want to import. After you click Open, the same message that appears in figure 7.22 appears.

Note One thing to keep in mind when you import a Registry file is that it might not work perfectly with your system. If you export part of your Registry to edit it in a text editor, then import it, your computer might not work correctly. Also remember that the Windows NT and Windows 95 Registries are not compatible, so don't try mixing them with each other.

Exporting Registry Information

If you read the earlier section about searching the Registry, you have already seen how to export a branch of the Registry. If you didn't read that section, see the following steps:

1. Select the branch that you want to export and choose Registry, Export Registry File.

2. Input a file name in the File name text box. By default, the file is saved as an REG file.

3. Choose to save only the selected branch or the entire Registry. It is a good idea to save the entire Registry every so often if you are one who likes to tinker with the Registry a lot. This gives you additional insurance in case of accidental deletion or corruption of the Registry during those late night editing sessions.

4. Click on Save.

You can view the saved file to make sure it is OK by using an ASCII text editor. Exported Registry files contain plain ASCII text, without any control characters embedded within them.

When you view a Registry file in a text editor, such as with WordPad, you can always tell it is a Windows 95 Registry file by examining the first line of the file. The label REGEDIT4 identifies the version of the Registry Editor (which is version 4 in Windows 95) that created the file.

 Stop   Do not attempt to import a Registry file created in Windows 95 into an earlier version of Windows or into Windows NT. You might cause irreparable damage to your system. By looking at this first line of the REG file, you can tell whether or not you should import it. In many cases, the REG files distributed with applications do not contain this leading information, so it is usually safe to import the file into any version of Windows. This does not, however, guarantee that the application runs correctly.

In the REG file, the second line is left blank as a delimiter, and the third line lists the Registry root key, such as HKEY_CURRENT_CONFIG. The backslashes (remember that you cannot add backslashes when you create a new key) in the listing instruct the Registry Editor to create a new key level.

The next line includes the key value, which you saw in the right pane in the Registry Editor. Default entries are denoted by an @ symbol at the start of a line. Also, string values are shown with quotation marks around them, which is consistent with the way the Registry Editor displays them. Finally, DWORD values have a dword: delimiter, while binary values have a hex: delimiter.

The following are some sample lines exported from the HKEY_CURRENT_USER\ Control Panel\Accessibility subkey:

```
REGEDIT4

[HKEY_CURRENT_USER\Control Panel\Accessibility]
"Keyboard Preference"="0"
"Blind Access"="0"
"Warning Sounds"=dword:00000001
"Sound on Activation"=dword:00000001

[HKEY_CURRENT_USER\Control Panel\Accessibility\Stickykeys]
"On"="0"
"OnOffFeedback"="1"
"AudibleFeedback"="1"
```

```
"TriState"="1"
"TwoKeysOff"="1"
"HotKeyActive"="0"
"Available"="1"
"ConfirmHotKey"="1"
"ShowStatusIndicator"="1"
```

Running REGEDIT in Real-Mode

Suppose, for example, that you've encountered a problem and you can't boot into Windows properly. In fact, if you're like most mortals this has already happened to you, probably right after you installed Windows 95 or after you spent hours tweaking a hardware device.

If this happens to you, you can edit the Registry from the DOS prompt. Although it is not recommended to do this, you certainly can give it a try if you feel up to the challenge. You should, however, try every other means to recover from the problem, such as booting in Safe Mode or using the Start Up disk you created at installation time.

In most cases, you'll need to run REGEDIT at the DOS prompt for the following reasons:

◆ The Registry is corrupted and needs to be replaced with a backup copy.

◆ The Registry needs to be edited before it will work properly.

When you run REGEDIT at the DOS prompt, you need to provide it with parameters to specify the location of DAT files, where to create the Registry, and where to export the Registry.

The following is the syntax for using REGEDIT to import a file into the Registry:

REGEDIT /L:*PathOfSystem.Dat* /R:*PathOfUser.Dat* ***NameOfImportFile(s)***

In the preceding syntax, *PathOfSystem.Dat* denotes the path for the SYSTEM.DAT Registry file. This usually resides in the Windows 95 folder on your system. Likewise, *PathOfUser.Dat* denotes the path for the USER.DAT file. Again, this is usually in your Windows 95 folder.

The argument *NameOfImportFile(s)* is the file name for the Registry file you want to import. This can be a Registry file that you previously exported or backed up on your system, when you took the time to prepare for a situation like this.

You also can use the following two arguments instead of the *NameOfImportFile(s)* option. /C *NameOfFileToCreate* is used when you want to specify a file name from which to create the Registry. /E *NameOfFileToExportTo* is used when you want to specify a file name to export the Registry to. When you use this latter switch, you also can use the regpath option, which specifies the starting Registry key from which to export. By default, this option exports the entire Registry.

Stop   Do not import a Registry branch back into the Registry using the /C option. If you do, your Registry will have only one branch—namely the one from which you created the Registry file. Make sure you use a file that includes an entire Registry if you need to use the /C option.

Setting Windows 95 User Profiles for Remote Users

User profiles contain user-specific information stored in the USER.DAT Registry file. User profiles also contain special Windows 95 directories. User profiles are used to help maintain a user's system preferences, network settings, and application settings.

Unlike Windows NT, which creates a user profile automatically for every user that logs on to the system, Windows 95 requires you to manually turn on user profiles. You might want to store user profiles on individual Windows 95 workstations if users generally work at the same workstation every day. Or, you might want to store user profiles on the Windows NT server (in the user's home directory) so users can roam from machine to machine and download his or her user profile from the server regardless of the computer to which he or she logs on. Many of the settings in the HKEY_CURRENT_USER key in the Registry are included in user profiles. By default, the user profile is stored in the user's WINDOWS\PROFILES\ subfolder or on the network server.

With Windows 95, you can set up user profiles that save configuration settings to use on other machines. Each Windows 95 user has a number of customizable features available to him or her. Wallpaper files, screen savers, desktop preferences, and application settings are just a few features users can customize. The reasons for customizing the environment are as diverse as the number of users in a workgroup. Everyone, including the top-level MIS director, customizes Windows 95 to work and look best for him or her. One of the problems with setting user-specific preferences has always been that as users moved from one machine to another, the settings did not follow them.

Inside a User Profile

Each user profile includes several parts. These parts include the USER.DAT and USER.DA0 files, a Desktop folder, a Recent folder, a NetHood folder, and a Start menu folder under the Start menu folder. An example of this hierarchy is shown in figure 7.23.

Figure 7.23

You can view a user profile in the Explorer.

The following list describes each of these elements in more detail:

◆ **USER.DAT and USER.DA0.** Part of the Registry database that stores user settings. USER.DA0 is a backup of USER.DAT.

◆ **Desktop folder.** Stores shortcuts to the items on the desktop for the logged on user.

◆ **Recent folder.** Stores shortcuts to the last items from the most recently used folder, as shown in the Work folder (see fig. 7.24).

◆ **NetHood folder.** Contains shortcuts to resources displaying in the Network Neighborhood folder.

◆ **Start Menu folder.** Includes shortcuts and items from the Start menu. You can right-click on the Start menu and click on Open, or use the Settings, Taskbar option to remove or add items to the Start menu. For some users, for instance, you might want to remove the Control Panel and Run items from the Start menu. This eliminates easy access to these items without setting up system policies (as you will learn about later).

◆ **Start Menu\Programs folder.** Stores shortcuts to programs in the Start menu's Programs folder. All submenus off the Programs folder are also included.

◆ **Start Menu\Programs\Startup folder.** Contains programs you've placed in the Startup folder. You'll find it handy to customize user profiles to include specific applications, documents, or files that start up automatically depending on the user who logs on.

Stop Do not place folders in the Network Neighborhood. You might experience some problems accessing or using them once they are placed there.

Figure 7.24

This shows an expanded contents view of a user profile named WORK.

The first time a profile is created is after the user or system administrator enables the User Profiles feature in the Password Properties sheet in the Control Panel. You also can create custom system policies during the Windows 95 installation process to eliminate the necessity to create individual user profiles after setup.

One way to fully understand how user profiles work is to understand Windows 95 shortcuts. Shortcuts are the primary way that user profiles store configuration information about a user. Shortcuts are OLE links between an icon and a program, document, file, or other type of object in Windows 95. Your desktop probably has a few shortcuts now, perhaps for the applications you use most, or to the Windows Explorer, or to a resource such as a printer. Shortcuts are denoted by small arrows on the icons and are named in the file system with a LNK suffix.

To enable user profiles, use the following steps:

1. Double-click on the Passwords icon in the Control Panel and click the User Profiles tab (see fig. 7.25).

Figure 7.25

Click the User Profiles tab to enable user profiles.

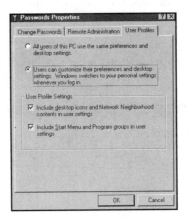

2. Click the Users can customize their preferences... option. This activates the User Profile settings options on the bottom half of the User Profiles tab.

3. Click the options under the User Profile settings to tell Windows 95 what to include in each profile. These options are described as follows:

   ◆ **Include desktop icons.** This option displays shortcuts to files the user has established. Any user-defined links established in Network Neighborhood are also included. Users need to be reminded that the desktop icons are shortcuts only; the actual file is maintained on the original machine. This is important for users if they log on one machine while the actual file is stored across the network on another computer. Users might think the file is stored locally.

   ◆ **Include Start menu.** This option enables the user profiles to include the contents of the Start menu and the Program groups in the Profiles folder.

4. Click on OK to save the settings you select.

5. Shut down and restart Windows 95 for the settings to take effect.

Upon bootup you'll be asked to log on using a user name and password. If you haven't established a password for this user, you'll need to insert and confirm a new one.

Using User Profiles

Say you want to create a user profile for yourself on a local machine. You might want to do this if you want to dictate the way in which Windows 95 looks for different circumstances.

Logging on with a user name of WORK, for instance, might have your primary work applications loaded in the Start menu to start up during bootup. In this situation, you might have your word processor, e-mail application, and scheduling application start up and display on your desktop, ready for you to begin work. On the other hand, if you don't want to boot straight into work applications but into entertainment applications, you can set up a user name like GAMES to start your favorite game or entertainment software.

When you log on to Windows 95 under one of the user names, such as WORK, set up the environments as you want. Put shortcuts to applications you want automatically to start in the Startup folder. For those applications you want displayed on the desktop (instead of minimized on the taskbar, for instance), open the property sheet for that shortcut (right-click on the icon and select Properties). Next, click on the shortcut tab and adjust the Run option to display a Normal or Maximized window.

Tip   To quickly add an application's shortcut to the Startup folder, drag and drop the icon on top of the Start button on the taskbar. This automatically adds it to the Startup folder.

After you enable the User Profiles option and set up a profile, if you install a new application, only the user logged on at the time will include an entry for that new application. This entry can be found in the Programs menu. For other users, you'll need to add a shortcut to that application manually in the Programs menu.

Now, look at setting user profiles on a network.

Setting User Profiles on Networks

As you've just seen, using user profiles on local machines can come in handy at times. The real power of user profiles doesn't show itself until you set them up on a network server. Instead of storing the profile on a local hard disk, the profile is stored on a server, enabling users to roam from machine to machine and still access the profile. Figure 7.26 shows how this looks schematically.

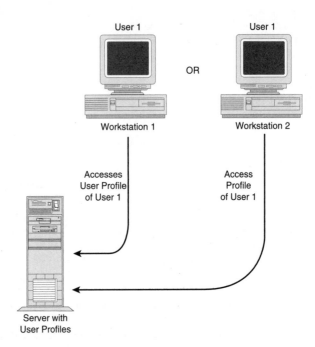

Figure 7.26

You can use user profiles on a network.

An important factor when setting up networked user profiles is the name of the directory in which Windows 95 is installed. This directory name must be the same on each computer that the user will log on to. Say, for instance, you have several PCs attached to a server, which stores user profiles for all users. In this setup, a user named User1, for example, will set up her configuration on PC1. PC1 has Windows 95 stored in the C:\WINDOWS directory. Now say User1 wants to use PC2. PC2 must have Windows 95 installed in the C:\WINDOWS directory for User1's user profile to function correctly. If other PCs store Windows 95 in other directories, such as C:\WIN95 or C:\WINDOWS, some of the user profile settings will not work properly.

Stop   Windows 95 also has to be placed on the same drive letter, such as C:\, on all machines that share user profiles.

Long file name support must be in place so that user profiles function across different LANs. When long file names are not used, USER.DAT is the only user profile component that is shared. Other components, including the Start menu and Network Neighborhood folders, cannot be accessed by users.

To enable user profiles on a network, you need to make sure that the computers are running a 32-bit, protected-mode network client, such as Client for Microsoft Networks. When using Microsoft networks, such as a Windows NT network, each user must have a home directory on the network server in which to store user profiles.

Tip When you run a NetWare network or a system running Windows NT and NetWare servers, the user profiles are stored in the ever present SYS\MAIL*user_id* directory. The *user_id* parameter refers to the 8-digit bindery object ID.

After you satisfy the preceding requirements, a copy of the USER.DAT file is stored on the network server. At logon time, the USER.DAT file located on the server is compared to any USER.DAT files stored on the local workstation. A copy of USER.DAT always exists on the local machine. When USER.DAT is placed in the user's logon directory, and when the user logs on, the file is copied to the user's local machine. If one already exists there (which will be the case in most situations) Windows 95 compares the two files and uses the most recently revised file.

 Note SYSTEM.DAT remains on the local workstation even when you invoke user profiles. SYSTEM.DAT contains all workstation-specific information.

When users log off, Windows 95 saves any changes made by the user to the local USER.DAT file and updates the server-based USER.DAT file. This ensures that the next time the user logs on, whether it is at the same workstation or another one, he or she will have the most recent configuration settings downloaded to the local PC.

 Note Can users roam between Windows 95 and Windows NT workstations? No. User profiles do not transfer between NT and Windows 95 at this time because Windows 95 and Windows NT use different Registries. Microsoft might provide this functionality in future versions of Windows NT and Windows 95.

User Profiles that Do Not Change

One of the more powerful features of user profiles for administrators is the mandatory user profile setting. Mandatory user profiles are profiles you establish for users that they can not change. Each time a user logs on to the network, the file USER.MAN is used instead of USER.DAT. USER.MAN is a file you create from a USER.DAT that contains any settings you want applied every time for that user or group of users.

Like regular user profiles, mandatory profiles can be created to work on Windows NT or NetWare networks. Users who log on and use mandatory profiles cannot save changes to the USER.MAN file. Only the administrator has rights to modify or delete this file. If a user makes configuration changes to his machine while logged on, these changes are simply forgotten when the user logs off the server.

To create a mandatory profile, enable user profiles in Windows 95. Next, customize the desktop to be like you want it for all users who will be assigned the mandatory profile. Next, for each user, copy this new USER.DAT file (it is still a DAT file at this point) into the user's home directory on the Windows NT server. If you are running a NetWare network, copy it into the user's home directory within the Mail directory on the NetWare server. As you'll see later, for regular user profiles, the USER.DAT file is copied automatically into these server directories. To finish setting up mandatory profiles, rename the USER.DAT file to USER.MAN in each of the users' home or Mail directories. Reboot the Windows 95 computer and log on for the mandatory profile to be activated.

Setting Up Roving Users on Windows NT and NetWare

Many installations use a mixture of Novell NetWare and Windows NT servers on their networks. This is especially true for companies who are setting up "test networks" to evaluate Windows NT. For this reason, this section discusses how to set up roving Windows 95 users on a NetWare network. If you do not have a NetWare server on your network, you can skip this section to the "Using System Policies To Modify Registry Settings on Remote Windows 95 Clients" section.

You need to perform specific configuration steps to set up roving users on your network. Both Windows NT and NetWare can handle these roving users. Use the following steps for setting up Windows NT after you have enabled user profiles on all the attached Windows 95 computers (see earlier section called "Inside a User Profile").

1. Activate the Network icon in Control Panel.

2. In the Primary Network Logon list (see fig. 7.27), make sure Client for Microsoft Networks is selected. This is on the Configuration tab.

Figure 7.27

Make sure you have the correct client network selected.

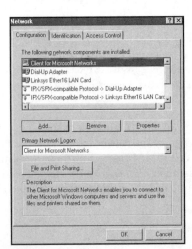

3. On the Windows NT server, ensure the roving user is set up and has an assigned home directory. The path for this is \\server_name\home_directory.

4. Synchronize the clocks on all computers on the network, including Windows NT and Windows 95 machines. You can use the NET TIME command to help you set the times.

Tip

The NET TIME command can be executed from the Start, Run command line and is run in DOS. NET TIME displays the time or synchronizes your PC's clock with the shared clocks on other machines, such as NT, NetWare, Windows for Workgroups, and Windows 95. The syntax for this command is as follows:

```
NET TIME \\computer_name ¦ /WORKGROUP:workgroup_name /SET /YES
```

Specify the computer name to check on or to synchronize using the computer_name parameter. WORKGROUP tells Windows 95 to use a time server in another workgroup. The workgroup_name parameter defines that other workgroup. Use the SET switch to synchronize the clocks, and YES to have NET TIME automatically perform the command without prompting you for information or confirmation.

Windows 95 automatically stores the user profiles on the Windows NT Server network in the appropriate home directories when the user logs off the server.

For NetWare networks, you need to use these steps:

1. Make sure user profiles are enabled and that the Client for NetWare Networks option is selected in the Network Configuration properties sheet.

2. On the NetWare server, set up each user with a Mail directory. The syntax for this is \\server\sys\mail\user_id. You can determine a user's ID by running the SYSCON utility.

3. Synchronize the clocks on all computers.

Windows 95 automatically stores the user profiles on the NetWare server in their appropriate Mail directories when the user logs off the server.

If you don't want a specific user to roam from machine to machine but still use networked user profiles, you can disable the roving feature for that user. Locate the HKEY_LOCAL_MACHINE\Network\Logon key and add a DWORD entry called UseHomeDirectory to it. You can do this by opening the Registry Editor, finding the above key, and selecting Edit, New, DWORD Value. Type in UseHomeDirectory as the new value (see fig. 7.28). Shut down and restart Windows 95. When the user logs on, he or she is restricted to the machine that the user profile was created on.

Figure 7.28

You can disable roving user profiles.

Using System Policies To Modify Registry Settings on Remote Windows 95 Clients

In Chapter 6, "Using System Policy Editor To Modify Registry Data," you get an overview of how the Windows NT system uses system policies. In general, this is the same for Windows 95. Except for some specific changes in the options available in the System Policy Editor, once you learn how to set up policies for a Windows NT Server or Windows NT Workstation computer, you can do the same for Windows 95. Also, you can edit some Registry values using the Windows 95 System Policy Editor, the same as you can with the Windows NT System Policy Editor. This section discusses the differences in policy files, where they are stored for Windows 95, and the specific policy options from which you can select.

The System Policy Editor is provided on the Windows 95 CD-ROM in the \ADMIN\APPTOOLS\POLEDIT directory. After you create the system policy, you place it on the network and it is automatically loaded onto the computer when a user logs on.

Examining Policy Files

As with Windows NT, Windows 95 creates two system policy files, ADM and POL. ADM files are template files that establish the scope of administrative polices. POL files are the files that enforce the policies you create.

In Windows 95, system policies modify the Registry in a couple of ways. First, when you create a policy, it sets up a CONFIG.POL file that overwrites the default USER.DAT and SYSTEM.DAT Registry settings when a user logs on to the network. Second, logon and network access settings modify the HKEY_LOCAL_MACHINE key. This key affects the SYSTEM.DAT file that is specific to the computer or the default computer settings. Third, the HKEY_CURRENT_USER key in the Registry is modified. This key determines the desktop settings and contains the USER.DAT settings.

 Note   See Chapter 6, "Using System Policy Editor To Modify Registry Data," for more information about ADM and POL files.

When you use Windows 95, it's a good idea to store the POL files on a network server to enable you to quickly and easily update and maintain them. Also, you should think about where you want to keep the POL file stored—either in the default location or on a central network location. The default location is easy because you don't have to make any Registry changes for Windows 95 to locate the POL file upon bootup. The latter location, such as storing the POL file on a network directory, is handy so an administrator can update a policy once and not have to change all the POL files for every user. The problem with this scenario is that you need to provide a pointer to the new location of the POL file. You can do this by adding an entry in the default location and changing the Registry so that it looks in the correct location. You can do this by editing the HKEY_LOCAL_MACHINE\Network\Logon subkey.

Using the System Policy Editor

Before you use the System Policy Editor, you need to perform a few administrative tasks. You must install the ADMIN.ADM, POLEDIT.EXE, and POLEDIT.INF files from the Windows 95 CD-ROM. All of these files are found in the ADMIN\APPTOOLS\POLEDIT subdirectory. You also might want to copy the POLEDIT.HLP and POLEDIT.CNT files for the online help. When you install these files (use the Add/Remove Programs icon in Control Panel), the ADMIN.ADM file is placed in the INF subdirectory in your Windows 95 directory. This file provides the system policy templates for you to use in the System Policy Editor.

After you install the preceding system policy files, you can install the GROUPPOL.INF files to enable you to create group system polices. When you do this, the GROUPPOL.DLL is placed in the \WINDOWS\SYSTEM subdirectory. For each client you have on your network you must have this file installed in that directory. Group policies can be created only for Windows NT and NetWare networks that already have existing groups set up. You cannot, for instance, use the System Policy Editor to create a new group for either of these networks.

When you install the System Policy Editor, Windows 95 places it on the Start menu under Programs, Accessories, System Tools folders. You can start it by clicking on it in this folder or typing POLEDIT.EXE on the Start menu's Run option.

Using the System Policy To Edit the Windows 95 Registry

As with the Windows NT System Policy Editor, you can use the Windows 95 System Policy Editor to make changes to the Windows 95 Registry. To edit the Registry, use these steps:

1. Start the System Policy Editor and select File, Open Registry. This displays two icons in the System Policy Editor, Local User and Local Computer.

2. Select one of the icons and double-click on it. Select the Local User icon to change settings for the user. For changes to the computer, select the Local Computer icon.

   The Local User Policies or Local Computer Policies page displays, depending on the item you chose in step 2. Figures 7.29 and 7.30 show the different settings you can select for each type of policy.

Figure 7.29

You can select from Local User Properties selections.

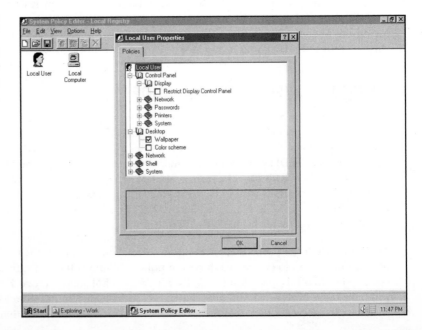

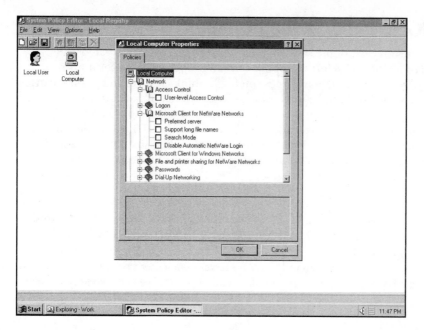

Figure 7.30

Or, select from Local Computer Properties settings.

3. Expand the options (see fig. 7.31) you want to change the state of by double-clicking on the name of the option or clicking on the plus sign (+) to the left of the name. For some options, you might need to expand another branch to see more options.

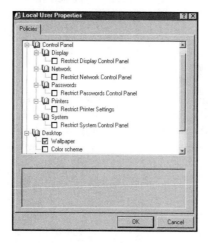

Figure 7.31

You should expand options to make specific choices.

4. After you make the necessary changes, click on OK.

5. Shut down and restart the computer to have these changes take effect.

Windows 95 Policy Setting Options

This section details each of the system policy setting options you can choose in Windows 95. The way you select the options in the properties sheet for users or computers is very important. Sometimes you might think clearing an option means that a specific setting will not be used, when in reality it might mean that something doesn't happen at all. One example of this setting is the Client for Microsoft Networks Domain. If you check it, you are setting the Windows NT Logon domain. If you uncheck it, then you delete the domain setting from the Registry. On the other hand, if the box is grayed, the user can configure the domain in the Network option in Control Panel.

 Tip Because it is so easy to check or uncheck a setting, you might want to think about reviewing a user's policy first when you encounter a networking program. By doing this, you can alleviate a number of hours of troubleshooting if you've deleted a domain setting or a preferred NetWare server from a user's policy. A quick glance at the HKEY_LOCAL_MACHINE\NETWORK\LOGON key in the Registry will also help you isolate this problem.

The following sections describe all the options you can choose, how they affect the Registry, and if they have any additional settings you must specify. Some of these options are the same as Windows NT options you read about in Chapter 6, "Using System Policy Editor To Modify Registry Data." The Windows 95 System Policy Editor, however, includes different options and different lists of options from which to choose, with some exceptions. If you don't understand a setting in the Windows 95 System Policy Editor, be sure to reference this chapter instead of Chapter 6, which only covers the options available in the Windows NT System Policy Editor.

Control Panel Policy Options

You read earlier about how Windows 95 system policies enable you to restrict users from specific areas in Windows 95. The Control Panel options (see fig. 7.32) gives you several options to help control the way users can change their display, networks, and other options.

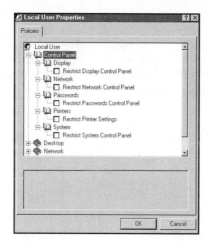

Figure 7.32

The Control Panel system policy options control display, networks, and other features.

Display

The Display option enables you to restrict the Display properties. You can specify to not show the entire Display Control Panel or just limit parts of it. These parts include the following options:

◆ Hide Background page

◆ Hide Screen Save page

◆ Hide Appearance page

◆ Hide Settings page

Tip   If you have the Microsoft Plus! Companion for Windows 95 installed, you do not get an option to restrict access to its display tab. You can, however, uninstall the Plus! items by running the Windows 95 uninstall program and deselecting Desktop Themes and Visual Enhancements from your Plus! installation. This will keep users from adding Plus! components to their systems.

Network

Another option in the Control Panel policies section is the Network section. Later you'll see how to control other aspects of the network, namely in the Network policies section and the Local Computer policies. This option, however, enables you to restrict access to the Network properties sheet. The tabs you can restrict individually include the following:

◆ Disable Network Control Panel

◆ Hide Identification Page

◆ Hide Access Control Page

You might want to choose all these settings to limit the amount of potential damage users can do to their network connections.

Passwords

Another setting you might want to restrict access to is passwords. This policy option limits the amount of changes the user can make to passwords. You can elect to hide the Passwords icon that normally appears in the Control Panel. You also can limit the tabs that display in the Passwords properties sheet, including the Change Passwords, Remote Administration, and User Profiles tab.

Printers

Windows 95 makes it so easy to set up and configure local or network printers that some administrators would rather keep the feature away from some users. You can elect to control the way users have access to individual printer properties by choosing from the different Printers policies. These include the following:

◆ Hide the General and Detail pages (see fig. 7.33)

◆ Disable Deletion of Printers

◆ Disable Addition of Printers

You might want to disable all printer configuration tools (the Printers icon in Control Panel) and elect to not allow users to add or delete printers. Unless users frequently add printers to the network, you should restrict users from deleting printers from the system so they cannot remove a local printer that others might need to access across the LAN.

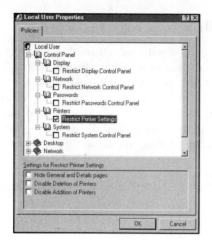

Figure 7.33

The Printers Policies page enables you to control printer settings.

System

Here again is evidence that Windows 95 might be too easy to configure in some cases. The System policy options include ways for you to limit who can make system-level changes. You can restrict users' access to system management tools, such as the Device Manager, Hardware Profile tab, File System utility, and virtual memory button. By disabling these settings, users will not be able to make changes to these settings on their local machines.

In some cases, however, you might elect to let some users maintain control over settings such as File System buttons. Users who need flexibility in the way their system caches files, such as graphics professionals, might want to keep this control locally configured.

The choices you have under the System policy option include these:

◆ Hide Device Manager page

◆ Hide Hardware Profiles page

◆ Hide File System button

◆ Hide Virtual Memory button

Tip   If you check the Hide File System button in the System settings, users will not be able to use the Troubleshooting tab on the File System Properties sheet.

Desktop Policy Options

For an environment that needs to look standard across all computers, you can set desktop policies to use the same wallpaper or color schemes. This is handy if you are running a training environment and you need each machine to have the exact same look and feel each time you start it up. Another place where this is useful is when running a kiosk at a sales booth. Each of your machines can have identical wallpaper that shows your company's logo in the background. By restricting users access to this feature, you won't have any surprises during the day as different people use the machine.

The two options you have are Wallpaper and Color Schemes. Each are described in the following sections.

Wallpaper

Use this setting to specify a wallpaper to use on all systems. In the Wallpaper name drop-down list, click on the bitmap file of your choice. If you want to include a customized file, such as your company logo, place the BMP file in the \WINDOWS folder before you click on this option.

The Wallpaper option is one that might confuse you when you first start using it. When you check the Wallpaper option this tells Windows 95 to use the specific BMP for the background. If you clear an already checked Wallpaper option, this tells Windows 95 not to use any wallpaper. If the Wallpaper option is grayed out, this leaves the choice up to the user.

Click the Tile wallpaper option to have the bitmap tiled across the user's screen.

Color Scheme

You can set a standard color scheme on the desktop for the users. You need to specify the color scheme, if any, in the Scheme name drop-down list.

Network Policy Options

The Network policy options include the capability to disable file and print sharing controls for a user. The Disable File Sharing Controls removes the Sharing properties from folders in the Windows 95 Explorer. The Disable Print Sharing Controls removes the Sharing properties from the Printer properties.

Shell Policy Options

The Shell policy options includes items that enable you to use custom folders and icons for a customized desktop. Before you create a custom desktop by using system policies, you need to first define custom folders. To do this, use the following steps:

1. Create and place the custom folders in an area where users can access them, such as on the network server. Windows 95 uses the path name to find the folder.

2. Create your set of files and shortcuts that you want to appear in each folder. Place these in the custom folders you just created.

 Tip   Shortcut properties need to include UNC names instead of mapped directory names.

3. In the following section where you name the path of the custom folder, enter the full UNC path for the custom folders you just created. Otherwise, Windows 95 will look in the default locations for any custom folders you've created.

Custom Folders

This area in the Shell policy options list lets you control six different ways to customize the desktop. These are described in the following list:

◆ **Custom Programs Folder.** Enables you to customize the contents of the Programs folder on the Start menu. You need to include the path to the custom programs item you create.

◆ **Custom Desktop Icons.** Enables you to customize the user's desktop icons. Again, specify the path to the custom desktop icon folder.

◆ **Hide Start Menu subfolders.** Unless you want both your customized Programs folder and the default Programs folder to display on the Start menu, place a check in this box.

◆ **Custom Startup Folder.** Enables you to define a custom folder that includes files, applications, or batch files that you want to run automatically at Windows 95 startup. You need to enter the path for this custom Startup folder.

◆ **Custom Network Neighborhood.** Enables you to specify specific items, including shortcuts and printers, to appear in the Network Neighborhood folder.

◆ **Custom Start Menu.** Enables you to customize the list of items placed on the Start menu. Again, be sure to include a path to the custom Start menu folder you have created.

Stop You should not place custom folders in the Network Neighborhood. Doing so may cause you to lose data.

Restrictions

The Restrictions policy options includes a number of settings that hide or remove common Windows 95 features.

- ◆ Remove Run command

- ◆ Remove folders from Settings on Start Menu

- ◆ Remove Taskbar from Settings on Start Menu

- ◆ Remove Find Command

- ◆ Hide Drives in My Computer

- ◆ Hide Network Neighborhood

- ◆ No Entire Network in Network Neighborhood

- ◆ No workgroup contents in Network Neighborhood

- ◆ Hide all items on Desktop

- ◆ Disable Shut Down Command

- ◆ Don't save settings at exit

All of the preceding options are pretty self-explanatory except for the Hide Drives In My Computer. This option prevents users from accessing the My Computer folder. By limiting access to My Computer, you can keep users from accessing the Control Panel, Printers, and Dial-Up Networking folders. These folders all contain options that enable users to change settings and reconfigure their computers. You might want to limit this capability on your users' machines.

System Policy Options

The last set of options in the user-specific policy properties is the System settings. The System settings control how the user interacts with the overall Windows 95 environment, including restricting access to certain applications and to the DOS prompt.

The Restrictions policies enable you to restrict users from using the Registry Editor, to configure only specific applications to run, or to limit their usage of DOS.

◆ **Disable Registry editing tools.** It is a good idea to check this option so that users cannot run the Registry Editor to modify the Registry database. As you've seen in this book, the Registry is too technical for many average Windows 95 users but is also very easy to edit or modify by accident.

◆ **Only run allowed Windows applications.** If you check this option, you need to list all of the applications the user(s) can execute. Make sure you list ALL of the applications, including items like the Explorer, Notepad, and so on. You need to also list the Policy Editor if you plan to edit the user's policy locally.

Tip
If you forget to add the Policy Editor (POLEDIT.EXE) to the preceding option, you might have a difficult time turning off this option. You can turn this option off using the Registry Editor by accessing HKEY_CURRENT_USER\Software\Microsoft\ Windows\CurrrentVersion\Policies\Explore. Delete the RestrictRun entry. Shut down and restart Windows 95.

If you still can't change this value for the user, run the Windows 95 startup disk and activate the real-mode Registry Editor in DOS to disable user profiles. Chapter 6 shows you how to use the real-mode Registry Editor.

◆ **Disable MS-DOS prompt.** Although for many users the DOS prompt is still a useful tool, many users do not need access to it. Restrict its use by checking this option. Then you won't run the risk of users accessing the system "through the backdoor" with DOS.

◆ **Disable single-mode MS-DOS applications.** Probably one of the most useful settings to check. This prevents users from launching DOS-mode applications in Windows 95. When this occurs, Windows 95 shuts down and then runs the DOS application. When the user exits the application, the system reboots to Windows 95 automatically. This causes the network connection to be lost and then forces the user to re-log on. An example of these types of programs are many of the DOS-based games available on the market. It is also a good idea to check this option if you want to use a specific computer as a peer server, and you can't afford it to be taken off the LAN to run a DOS-based application exclusively.

Stop
One thing to keep in mind when you click on the Disable Registry editing tools option is that this does not prevent users from using the System Policy Editor to access the Registry. You need to make sure users do not have network access to the POLEDIT.EXE file or have a copy of the Windows 95 system disks.

Setting Local Computer Policies

To complete setting up system policies, you need to set up the computer-specific policies. Double-click on the Local Computer or Default Computer icon in the System Policy Editor to display the policies for computers (see fig. 7.34). Only two major headings display under here, Network and System. When you save these settings, they get placed in the SYSTEM.DAT Registry file.

Figure 7.34

The computer-specific policy options enable you to set network and system settings.

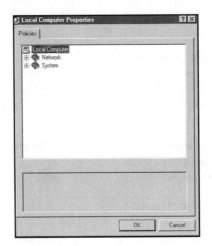

The following sections describe the various options available under the Network settings.

Access Control

Under this policy is the User-level Access Control option. This option enables you to specify user-level security on the local machine. When you do this, it determines whether a NetWare or Windows NT server is used for pass-through security that provides bindery-based user and group assignments for accessing directories and printers on the local workstation.

To do this, enter the server and type of authentication for a Windows NT or NetWare server. You can input the Authenticator Type manually, or select from NetWare 3.x or 4.x, a Windows NT Domain, or Windows NT Server or Workstation.

Logon

The Logon policy includes two options from which to choose. This policy enables you to specify a logon banner and whether you want the network server to validate each user who logs on before Windows 95 starts. The logon banner includes a caption and logon text. The default banner is "Important Notice;" the default text is "Do not attempt to log on unless you are an authorized user." Customize these text entries to suit your environment.

Microsoft Client for NetWare Networks

These policy settings deal with the 32-bit network client for NetWare. The options you can choose are as follows:

◆ **Preferred server.** Enables you to choose to have a preferred server for users logging on. You need to input the name of the server in the Server Name Field. This indicates the first server that the user logs on to when they boot up Windows 95.

◆ **Support long file names.** Here you can choose whether NetWare recognizes long file names. By default, this choice is not selected. You can select the All NetWare servers that support LFNs (long file names) option, or the NetWare 3.12 and above choice.

◆ **Search Mode.** Sets the NetWare search mode from 0 to 7.

◆ **Disable Automatic NetWare Login.** Configures the system to not connect to a NetWare server using the user's name and password from the password list file. The default is to have Windows 95 automatically log on to a NetWare server with this list. Users will need to enter a logon name and password when attempting to attach to a NetWare network.

Microsoft Client for Windows Networks

If you are running Windows 95 on a Windows NT network, you can set some specific options as well.

◆ **Log On To Windows NT.** Indicates that the selected computer can belong to a Windows NT domain. You need to enter the domain name in the Domain name field. You also can choose to have Windows 95 display a message when the domain controller validates the user logon by checking the Display domain logon confirmation option.

The other option, Disable caching of domain password, is useful when you want Windows 95 to not cache the password during logon. Activating this setting is largely dependent on your work environment. For large installations where security of resources is very important, make sure this option is checked. For smaller networks where security is not a major concern, such as in a small office or home environment, you might find it less irritating to leave this option unchecked.

Note Password caching is a way to enable users on Windows 95 to not re-enter a password each time a resource is accessed. By default, passwords are saved (or cached) when a user logs on into a password file list. Windows 95 associates those passwords with the Windows 95 password, making it appear as if the passwords for Windows 95 are the same for all the password-protected resources, such as disks or printers. When you disable password caching, users must enter a password each time they access a password-protected resource.

◆ **Workgroup.** Indicates that this computer belongs to a workgroup. Enter the name of the workgroup in the bottom area of the tab.

◆ **Alternate Workgroup.** Enables you to specify an alternate workgroup for peer services if the primary workgroup (see previous option) runs File and Printer Sharing for NetWare and does not include File and Printer Sharing for Microsoft Networks. Input the name of a workgroup that supports File and Printer Sharing for Microsoft Networks.

File and Printer Sharing for NetWare Networks

By default, the SAP Advertising option is disabled for File and Printer Sharing for NetWare Networks. SAP (Service Advertising Protocol) Advertising is used by NetWare 2.15 servers and above to announce their presence on the network. You should click on the Disable SAP Advertising option in this policy if you need to enforce the configuration of the File and Printer Sharing service.

A couple of things to keep in mind when you are setting this option is that you do not need SAP Advertising if you want to use the Windows 95 Net Watcher tool to administer file systems running File and Printer Sharing for NetWare Networks. Also, you do not need SAP Advertising if you are performing remote Registry functions. SAP Advertising should be enabled only on computers that need to share resources such as CD-ROM drives with NETX and VLM clients.

Tip You do not need SAP Advertising if you only intend to share resources between Windows 95 computers on a NetWare network.

Passwords

You can use system policies to increase the level of security for your system by requiring that users follow specific password guidelines. A couple of these password settings are handled by previous policies, but in the Passwords policies you can set the following:

◆ **Hide share passwords with asterisks.** Displays asterisks (****) in the password text fields when users enter their passwords. This setting is for share-level security only and is checked by default. You should leave it set this way for most situations.

◆ **Disable password caching.** Prevents Windows 95 from saving the share-level passwords for resources, applications, and NetWare passwords. By default, this option is not selected, but you might want to check it for a tighter level of security.

◆ **Require alphanumeric Windows passwords.** Requires that users logging on to Windows 95 use passwords that include both numbers and letters, such as R2D2C3PO.

◆ **Minimum Windows password length.** Requires that Windows 95 pass-words be a specific length, such six characters long.

Dial-Up Networking

Dial-Up Networking in Windows 95 enables users to dial into a remote Windows 95 computer using a modem. Although this is a handy utility, it also can be a system administrator's nightmare. Security is limited to only a password, meaning that a user's system, and potentially the entire network, could be at risk of intrusion. You can disable the dial-in feature by selecting the Disable dial-in option in the Dial-Up Networking policy.

Note The Windows 95 installation CD does not include the Dial-Up Networking Server utility. You must purchase the Microsoft Plus! Companion for Windows 95 to get this feature.

Sharing

The Sharing policy allows you to enable or disable file and print sharing over a network. If users are experiencing difficulties sharing files and printers, and policies are invoked, check out this setting to make sure they are clear or grayed out (without a check mark). On the other hand, if you want to specify certain computers or groups that cannot share these resources, check one or both of these options.

SNMP

Simple Network Management Protocol enables SNMP consoles and agents to communicate with one another. The SNMP agent in Windows 95 conforms to the SNMP version 1 specification and enables you to monitor remote connections to computers running Windows 95. The SNMP agent is implemented as a Win32-based service and works using Windows Sockets over both TCP/IP and IPX/SPX. The extension agents are implemented as Win32 DLL.

You need to install the Microsoft SNMP agent from the Windows 95 CD-ROM to use it. The policies you can set here are effective only if SNMP is installed on the computer first. You can find the SNMP agent in the ADMIN\NETTOOLS\SNMP directory. Use the following steps to install it:

1. Activate the Networks option in Control Panel.

2. Click on the Add button.

3. In the Select Network Component Type dialog box, click on Service and click on the Add button. This displays the Select Network Services dialog box (see fig. 7.35).

Figure 7.35

Use the Select Network Services dialog box to install the SNMP agent in Windows 95.

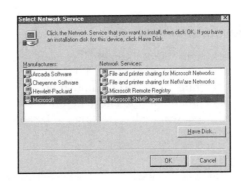

4. Click on the Have Disk button.

5. Click on the Browse button, specify the path *cd_drive*:**\ADMIN\NETTOOLS\SNMP\SNMP.INF**, and click on OK. The *cd_drive* parameter should be replaced by your CD_ROM drive letter.

6. In the Select Network Service dialog box, make sure the Microsoft SNMP agent option is selected.

7. Click on OK to copy the files onto your system. Click on OK again.

   You might be prompted for the location of additional files. You need to specify the Windows 95 source file location, such as D:\WIN95 on the CD-ROM.

8. After the files copy, you need to shut down and restart Windows 95 for the changes to take effect.

The SNMP agent settings you can set in the Policy Editor include the following:

◆ **Communities.** Enables you to specify one or more groups of hosts the selected computer belongs to. You'll need to click on the Show button at the bottom of the property sheet to add or remove communities.

◆ **Permitted managers.** Enables you to specify the IP and IPX addresses allowed to obtain information from an SNMP agent. If left unchecked, any SNMP console can query the agent. Again, click the Show button to add or remove managers.

◆ **Traps for 'Public' community.** Enables you to specify IP or IPX addresses of hosts in the public community to which you want the SNMP service to send traps. These are called *trap destinations*. Click on the Show button to add or remove these items.

◆ **Internet MIB (RFC 1156).** Enables you to specify the contact name and location if you are using Internet MIB. MIBs are objects that represent various types of information about a device used by SNMP to manage devices. MIB stands for management information base. RFC stands for Request for Comments, one of the steps used in the development of standards.

Note To configure Windows 95 SNMP agent to send traps to a community that is not a public community, you must edit the HKEY_LOCAL_MACHINE\System\ CurrentControlSet\Services\ SNMP\Parameters\TrapConfigurations subkey in the Registry. Create a new value and name it what you want for the new community. Create new string values for each console to which you want the SNMP agent to send traps. The names should start at 1 and advance by one, such as 1, 2, and so on.

The value data for each string needs to be the IP or IPX address of the SNMP console to which the traps are sent. This value might be something like 198.70.147.184.

Update

The Update policy enables you to specify how system policies are updated. This policy has only one option, the Remote Update setting, but includes the following items you can set:

◆ **Update Mode.** You can specify how you want the system policy downloaded. You can choose Automatic or Manual. If you select Automatic, Windows 95 looks in the default path for the system policy, which is the user's home directory on the server. When you specify Manual, you need to fill in the name of the path for the policy file. You do this in the Path for manual update. Be sure to specify the name of the file in UNC form.

◆ **Display error messages.** When a user logs on and the system policy is not available, an error message displays if you check this option. Otherwise, the default settings are used for that user. You might want to set this option if you are performing troubleshooting tasks to determine if a computer is reading the proper system policy. Otherwise, you might want to keep it off or users might be confused by the message during system logon.

◆ **Load-balance.** Enables Windows 95 to search a Windows NT network for policy files stored on the server.

System Policies

After you set up the Network system policies, you need to set up the system options for the system policies on the computer. These options are for the network path for setup and user profiles. The options you can set are described in the following list:

◆ **Enable User Profiles.** Specifies that this computer allows user profiles to be used.

◆ **Network path for Windows Setup.** Specifies the location of the Windows 95 Setup program on the network. You must enter the UNC path for this directory.

◆ **Network path for Windows Tour.** Specifies the location of the Windows 95 Tour files on the network. You must enter the path of the file, with the name of the file being TOUR.EXE.

◆ **Run.** Specifies applications you want to run when a user logs on. You must specify these applications by clicking on the Show button.

◆ **Run Once.** Specifies applications, files, or batch files you want Windows 95 to run once when the user logs on for the first time. You must specify these applications by clicking on the Show button. The Run Once Registry key is updated with this application name each time you log on to Windows. After it runs, the name is automatically removed from the Registry. If you only want an application to run once and then be deleted from the Registry for good, you need to make sure you clear this item after it runs that first time.

◆ **Run Services.** You can specify services to run at system startup, such as SNMP services. Again, specify these services by clicking on the Show button. You must include the name of the item and the value of the item to be added.

Once you set all the system policy options for your user and computer, click on OK and shut down and restart the system.

How Windows 95 Handles System Policies

You might want to know what the process is when someone logs on to Windows and implements the policy. Figure 7.36 shows an overview of this process. When someone logs on, the logon process follows the UNC path to the user's configuration and then follows the policies to implement the user's environment based on the following steps:

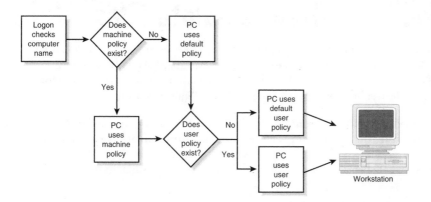

Figure 7.36

A general view of how a policy is implemented when a user logs on to Windows 95.

1. Logon checks the computer's name. If a profile for the PC is available, Windows 95 uses that profile. If a profile does not exist for that computer, Windows 95 uses the default computer profile.

2. The system policy checks the user's name against the group listings. If the user is a member of a group, Windows 95 uses that group's policies. Groups are checked from lowest to highest groups until all the groups in the policy file are processed.

3. Windows 95 checks the user's name. If a profile for the user logging on is available, Windows 95 uses it. If not, Windows 95 uses the default user profile.

Examining System Policy Templates

Policy templates are the files that determine what policies can be enforced, including the actual options you can set. The preceding section discussed these options in detail. ADM files can be written to affect any setting in the Registry. If you have a program that can read the Registry, such as a Windows 95-compliant application, you can set up a system policy to control it for the entire company or workgroup. You can also create a template that can change the default layout of a spreadsheet application so that all users logged on with the same policy can use that layout.

Chapter 6, "Using System Policy Editor To Modify Registry Data," shows you how to create policy templates. Use the same instructions as provided in that chapter to help you create policy templates for Windows 95 machines. The following is a comprehensive list of template settings you can use to create your own files. The examples shown here use the Windows 95 Registry.

Creating Your Own Template Files

System policy templates (ADM files) enable you to define settings that are specific to your users' Registry settings. You'll want to create customized ADM files when the System Policy Editor does not include specific settings that you want to include for users configuration, such as e-mail package settings, database settings, and the like.

You also can create several different policy templates that can be used for different scenarios depending on the need of the user or administration task. When a user logs on and invokes a policy you've defined, the settings you've put in the ADM files are transferred to the Registry to set the configuration of the user's machine.

Looking at Template Files

Before you start creating a template file, you'll need to understand the syntax and type of information that a template file contains. The following is the generic syntax of a template file:

```
CLASS Type_of_Category
     CATEGORY name_of_category
          KEYNAME name_of_key
               definition statements for the policy...
     END CATEGORY
     POLICY name_of_policy
          KEYNAME name_of_key
               definition statements for the policy...
     END POLICY
     PART name type_of_part
          type-dependent data...
     KEYNAME name_of_key
     VALUENAME name_of_value
       END PART
```

As you can see, there are four main sections: Class, Category, Policy, and Part. You also can nest sections with other sections, such as subcategories within a category.

An example from the ADMIN.ADM file is shown below (only the first few lines from the file are shown). This file is provided by Microsoft, is stored in the INF folder in your Windows 95 folder, and is the default template when you set policies.

```
CLASS MACHINE

CATEGORY !!Network
KEYNAME Software\Microsoft\Windows\CurrentVersion\Policies\Network

    CATEGORY !!AccessControl
        POLICY !!AccessControl_User
        KEYNAME System\CurrentControlSet\Services\VxD\FILESEC
        VALUENAME Start
        VALUEON NUMERIC 0 VALUEOFF DELETE
        ACTIONLISTON
            KEYNAME System\CurrentControlSet\Services\VxD\FILESEC
            VALUENAME StaticVxD VALUE filesec.vxd
        END ACTIONLISTON
```

Now this listing will be broken down a little to help you understand what it does. The first line CLASS MACHINE lists the Registry key that can be edited, in this case MACHINE. This policy will be editing the HKEY_LOCAL_MACHINE Registry key (you can name only MACHINE or USER for this key word). The next line, CATEGORY !!Network, is a string value that defines a category in the System Policy Editor when you view it (see fig. 7.37).

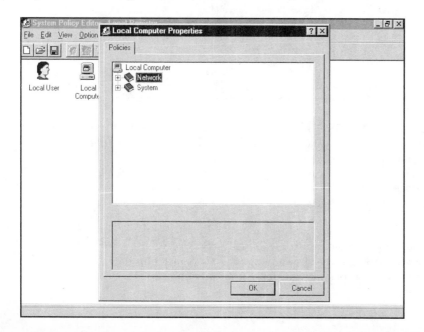

Figure 7.37

The System Policy Editor shows the policy categories named in the ADM file.

Notice how the top two levels of the policy are Network and System. To define the System category, you would include the following line (which is part of ADMIN.ADM later in the code):

```
CATEGORY !!System
```

The next line in the ADMIN.ADM file `KEYNAME Software\Microsoft\Windows\` `CurrentVersion\Policies\Network` includes the full Registry key path. In this particular case, you would be editing the Registry subkey shown in the Registry Editor in figure 7.38. This figure is shown only as a graphical way to let you see how the policy template adjusts the Registry.

Figure 7.38

The ADMIN.ADM file will first edit this subkey in the Registry.

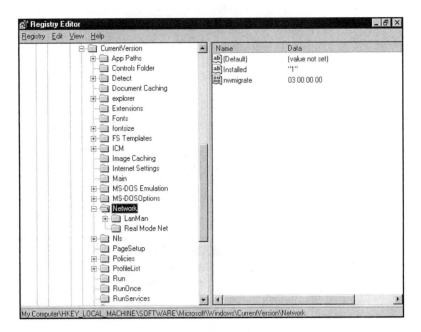

Continuing with the ADMIN.ADM file, the next two lines include information for a subcategory under Network called Access Control and a policy. The policy defined is the User-level Access Control setting shown in figure 7.39.

```
CATEGORY !!AccessControl
      POLICY !!AccessControl_User
```

The rest of the code shown adds values to specific Registry subkeys, in this case the FILESEC subkey in the System\CurrentControlSet\Services\VxD\FILESEC key. The way this looks in the Registry is shown in figure 7.40. Notice how the key word ACTIONLISTON sets a specific value for a key word entry.

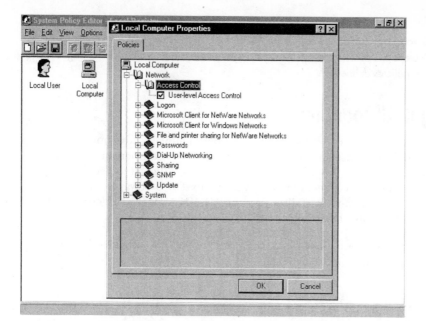

Figure 7.39

The ADMIN.ADM sets the User-Level Access Control setting in the System Policy Editor.

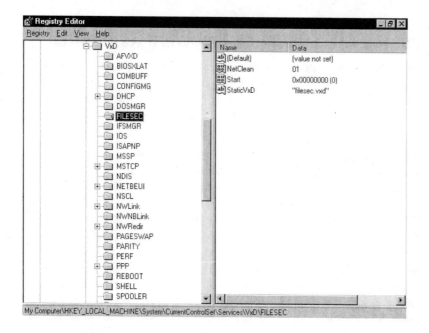

Figure 7.40

You can use the ACTIONLISTON key word to set a specific value in the Registry.

Note If you want to view the rest of the ADMIN.ADM file, open it in a text editor such as Notepad. You'll be able to see how Registry values and settings are changed using the policies defined.

Putting It All Together

You've seen a breakdown of a small chunk of a policy template. You should be able to create your own for your specific needs. To write an ADM file, open a text editor like WordPad or Notepad and input the template listings. You'll need to decide what types of policies you want to include in each template. The best way I've found to do this is to study the System Policy Editor with the ADMIN.ADM file loaded to see the types of policies available by default.

You'll also want to examine the type of data stored in the following two Registry branches. These are the two branches that the policy key words can point to in a template:

HKEY_LOCAL_MACHINE

HKEY_CURRENT_USER

Examining the ADM Template Key Word Reference

This section describes the available key words you can use in your policy templates. Also shown are the controls you use to design items like combo boxes in policy templates.

CLASS

CLASS sets the Registry key your template will modify. When you use the USER key word, you will edit the HKEY_CURRENT_USER branch. When you use the MA-CHINE key word, you will edit the HKEY_LOCAL_MACHINE branch. You cannot name any of the other three main branches in the Registry. The syntax is CLASS User or CLASS Machine. These names also correspond to the icon you see when you first open the System Policy Editor.

Note You can include a couple of different modifiers that are not key words, including string values and comments. When you use a string value, you can define a section of strings such as *var_name* =*string* value. Comments can be placed inside the template file by adding a semicolon (;) in front of the comment line. Everything after (that is, to the right of) the semicolon is handled as a comment. The following is an example:

```
CLASS USER ; denotes USER as the CLASS
```

CATEGORY

The CATEGORY key word is the name of a category in the System Policy Editor, such as Control Panel, Shell, System, or a custom name you create. When the name has spaces in it, you need to enclose it with quotation marks.

> The !! characters can be used to indicate a string value, such as !!Shell. Also, there are no ending delimiters.

Tip

The syntax for the CATEGORY key word is CATEGORY `name_of_category`.

END CATEGORY

The END CATEGORY key word is like a "wrapper" that encloses a category and its contents. It is used to indicate the end of the category and policies within the category you create. Contained within the CATEGORY and END CATEGORY key words are the POLICY, CATEGORY (for subcategory), and PART statements for a particular policy.

So, you might have a category named SYSTEM that contains several policies, such as Enable User Profiles, Run, Run Once, and so on. After these policies are named, use the END CATEGORY to tell the System Policy Editor that you have no more polices for the specified category.

The syntax is simply END CATEGORY. If you want to denote which category is ended here, use a semicolon to mark a comment and insert the category named by the CATEGORY key word. This will look like the following:

```
END CATEGORY      ;Shell
```

PART

Enclosed in the category sections are parts and policies. The PART key word is used to specify one or more controls to set the values of a policy. Controls can be part types, such as check boxes, text boxes, and the like, and type-dependent information, such as check box values, numeric values, and so on. The syntax is PART `name_of_part`.

The part controls and their values are described in the next sections.

CHECKBOX Part Control Indicator

This part control instructs the System Policy Editor to display a check box. When a user clicks in the check box, the value becomes a nonzero value. When the user clears the check box, the value entry is deleted from the Registry.

The values you can assign to CHECKBOX are described in the following list:

◆ **ACTIONLIST.** Denotes actions or events that are to take place when a response is entered by the user. You must enclose the ACTIONLIST modifier with an END ACTIONLIST key word.

◆ **ACTIONLISTON.** When the check box is on (which is usually when it is checked), this value specifies events that are to take place. You might, for instance, include an ACTIONLISTON of values to change for specific DLL files that are placed in the Registry if the user inputs a certain password. You must enclose the ACTIONLISTON modifier with an END ACTIONLISTON key word.

◆ **ACTIONLISTOFF.** When the check box is off, this value specifies events to take place. You must enclose the ACTIONLISTOFF modifier with an END ACTIONLISTOFF key word.

◆ **DEFCHECKED.** Sets the default value of the CHECKBOX control to be checked, or true.

◆ **VALUEON.** Specifies a Registry action to be taken when the ON value is selected. This overrides the default action of the ON value for a checkbox control.

◆ **VALUEOFF.** Specifies a Registry action to be taken when the OFF value is selected. This overrides the default action of the OFF value for a checkbox control.

COMBOBOX Part Control Indicator

This control specifies that a combo box is displayed in the System Policy Editor. Combo boxes are a combination of text fields in which users input values and a drop-down list box that contains values already defined.

The values you can assign to COMBOBOX are described in the following list:

◆ **DEFAULT** *value.* Denotes the default string that is entered in the combo box when the user first invokes it. You can leave this out of the syntax to have the field initially empty. The *value* parameter includes the actual string you want to display.

◆ **MAXLEN** *value.* For settings that can only be a certain length, use this setting. The *value* parameter is a numeric value between 1 and 255.

◆ **REQUIRED.** Enables you to specify when a user must input or select an item from the combo box for a part to be enabled.

◆ **SUGGESTIONS.** Lets you specify a list of suggestions in the combo box. When you include suggestions, you separate the values with spaces, and any value with a space already in it (such as Windows NT) are enclosed in quotation marks. You must enclose the list of suggestions with an END SUGGESTION modifier. The following is an example:

```
SUGGESTIONS
Red "Light Blue" Green Blue
END SUGGESTIONS
```

Stop

A few things to watch out for when you input the SUGGESTIONS list:

◆ Do not place commas between the suggestions.

◆ Do not forget to use the trailing "s" in SUGGESTIONS.

◆ Do not forget the quotations marks around suggestions with spaces, or that suggestion will be broken up in the final drop-down list.

DROPDOWNLIST Part Control Indicator

The DROPDOWN list control creates a drop-down list that includes entries that you define. The user has the option of selecting one value from the list, which then gets entered in the Registry. Sometimes you might want to create a list box in which, depending on the entry selected, different sets of parts or policies appear, from which the user can select more Registry modifications.

The values you can assign to DROPDOWNLIST are described in the following list:

◆ **ITEMLIST.** Defines the list of items you want placed in the drop-down list in the System Policy Editor. To define an item, use the following general syntax:

```
NAME item_name VALUE item_value
ACTIONLIST items_action
```

In the preceding syntax, the item_name is the name you want to appear in the list, such as All NetWare servers that support LFN. The *item_value* parameter is the value entry that is sent to the Registry when the item is selected. The default data type for the item_value parameter is a string value. If you want to include numeric value, include NUMERIC after VALUE in the syntax (such as VALUE NUMERIC *item_value*).

Tip   You can include the value DELETE in the ITEMLIST, such as VALUE DELETE, to delete the selected item from the Registry.

The ACTIONLIST command is an optional set of actions that are carried out when a specific item is selected from the drop-down list.

You must enclose the ITEMLIST with an END ITEMLIST modifier.

◆ **REQUIRED.** Enables you to specify when a user must select an item from the drop-down list for a part to be enabled.

EDITTEXT Part Control Indicator

This control creates a text field in which the user inputs alphanumeric data. This is common when you prompt users to input paths or text values, such as the text for a logon banner.

The values you can assign to EDITTEXT are described in the following list:

◆ **DEFAULT** *value.* Denotes the default string that is entered in the text field when the user first invokes it. You can leave this out of the syntax to have the field initially empty. The *value* parameter includes the actual string you want to display.

◆ **MAXLEN** *value.* For settings that can only be a certain length, use this setting. The *value* parameter is a numeric value between 1 and 255.

◆ **REQUIRED.** Enables you to specify when a user must input an item in the text box for a part to be enabled.

LISTBOX Part Control Indicator

The LISTBOX control creates a list box that shows Add and Remove buttons. You can use this value to modify several values under one Registry key at one time.

The values you can assign to LISTBOX are described in the following list:

◆ **ADDITIVE.** By default, LISTBOX values will override the values in the Registry. When you use the ADDITIVE modifier, you specify that the values in the list box are added to the Registry and do not override existing settings.

◆ **EXPLICITVALUE.** Requires that the user specify value name and value data. When used, the list box that displays has two columns, one for the value name and one for the value data.

◆ **VALUENAME.** Defines a name for the list box. For an entry in the list box, an identical value name and value data are created.

◆ **VALUEPREFIX *prefix_name*.** Defines a prefix to be used with a changing value to create the full value name. When you define a *prefix_name* and you add entries to the list box, the *prefix_name* is increased by one. The *prefix_name* "File" would change to File1, File2, File3, and so on as you add entries.

 Stop You cannot use the EXPLICITVALUE modifier when you use the VALUEPRFIX modifier.

NUMERIC Part Control Indicator

You can create a text field in which users input numeric values using the NUMERIC part control indicator. As an option, you can specify to include a spin control that increments the value as users input data.

The values you can assign to NUMERIC are described in the following list:

◆ **DEFAULT *value*.** Denotes the default value that is entered in the numeric field when the user first invokes it. You can leave this out of the syntax to have the field initially empty. The *value* parameter includes the actual value you want to display.

◆ **MAX *value*.** For settings that can only be a certain length, use this setting. The default is 9999.

◆ **MIN *value*.** For settings that must be a certain length, use this setting. The default is 0.

◆ **REQUIRED.** Enables you to specify when a user must input a value in the numeric box for a part to be enabled.

◆ **SPIN *value*.** Enables you to specify a spin control increment value. If you use SPIN1 (the default), the spin control is added. If you use SPIN0, the spin control is removed.

◆ **TXTCONVERT.** Inserts values into the Registry as strings instead of binary values.

TEXT Part Control Indicator

This creates a simple label that does not affect the Registry at all. The Text control does not contain type-specific values, as do the other part controls.

POLICY

The POLICY key name specifies the policy within a category. The syntax for the POLICY key name is as follows:

```
POLICY name_of_policy
      KEYNAME name_of_key
      part definitions
END POLICY
```

The following example lists a policy named Workgroup that has a check box included:

```
POLICY Workgroup
      PART !!Names_Workgoups CHECKBOX
      END PART
END POLICY
```

END POLICY

The END POLICY key name marks the end of a policy statement and encloses all the parts within the POLICY.

VALUEON

The VALUEON key word is used to indicate the setting to assign to a value when a user checks the policy.

VALUEOFF

This key word is used to indicate the setting to assign to a value when the user does not check the policy.

KEYNAME

The KEYNAME key word is an optional modifier and denotes the full path of the Registry key. You do not need to include the first part of the key including HKEY_CURRENT_USER and HKEY_LOCAL_MACHINE. These are established when you set the CLASS key word.

When you set the KEYNAME key word, all the categories, policies, and parts that fall below it use that Registry key assigned. You can, however, define a new key by inserting another KEYNAME key word where you want it.

VALUE

The VALUE key word is an optional modifier. It denotes the Registry value to set to a named VALUENAME key word.

VALUENAME

The VALUENAME key word is an optional modifier and denotes the Registry value entry name. An example of this is as follows:

```
VALUENAME "Control Speed" "80"
```

This setting sets the Control Speed entry in the Registry to 80. The Control Speed entry is for the mouse keys.

Summary

This chapter examined how to view and modify remote Registries for clients that run on Windows NT networks. You saw how to modify a remote Windows NT Workstation Registry. You also learned how the Windows 95 Registry differs from the Windows NT Registry and how to use the Windows 95 Registry Editor to view and modify the Windows 95 Registry. Finally, you learned how to modify user profiles and system policies to make Registry changes and control remote Registry files.

C H A P T E R

8

Troubleshooting Specific Problems Using the Windows NT Registry

S o far, you've learned how to use the Registry to find specific entries and values. You've also learned how to use some of the other tools Windows NT provides to let you configure and troubleshoot your Windows NT system, including the System Policy Editor.

There comes a point, however, when you have to go straight to the source and edit some Registry settings directly. This might be due to bugs in the software, hidden features that only the application programmer is aware of, or a new way of using an old feature. You'll find in this chapter a hefty selection of specific problems users have encountered in Window NT while performing all kinds of OS tasks. You'll find solutions to these problems as well. This chapter has been organized in such a way that it addresses and solves problems in the following areas:

◆ Startup and shutdown tasks

◆ System and file system tasks

◆ Networking tasks

◆ Internet tasks

Correcting and Customizing Windows NT Startup and Shutdown

The following sections feature some of the ways you can troubleshoot and customize the way in which Windows NT boots up and shuts down.

Tip As mentioned in Chapter 1, "Introducing the Windows NT Registry," you should always make a backup copy of your Registry before attempting to edit it. You should also get in the habit of routinely backing up the Registry during computer- or network-wide backup sessions. This ensures that if you have a Registry error or damaged Registry hive, you can rebuild the Registry using the backed up files.

Note Chapter 5, "Examining Network Settings in the Windows NT Registry," also includes some logon customization tasks you can perform with the Registry.

Switching System Configurations at Startup

The Windows NT Registry contains a set of control sets that contain system information relating to startup, system recovery, device driver loading instructions, services, and hardware profiles. The control sets are stored in the following Registry subkey:

HKEY_LOCAL_MACHINE\SYSTEM\

Within this subkey are usually four control sets:

\Clone

\ControlSet001

\ControlSet002

\CurrentControlSet

When you boot Windows NT, the control set that is usually used is \ControlSet001. The \ControlSet002 usually contains the information for what is known as the Last Known Good configuration, which controls how your last best bootup is configured. (See Chapter 1, "Introducing the Windows NT Registry" for more information about control sets.) This is the control set Windows NT uses if the first control set it tries does not successfully boot Windows NT. In many cases, this process is invisible to you, unless you've made a number of system changes that, upon your next bootup, do not get registered to the \ControlSet002 setting. Each time you have a successful startup, the settings for the control set used for that bootup are saved to the \ControlSet002 subkey.

 Note Windows NT automatically creates a backup of your system configuration files in case there are bad sectors in the System hive of the Registry. The SYSTEM.ALT file contains a copy of the System hive and is stored in the %*SystemRoot*%\SYSTEM32\CONFIG folder on your system. In most cases, Windows NT automatically switches to this file if the system has trouble booting.

The \CurrentControlSet subkey is a pointer to one of the other control sets. This subkey usually contains the most up-to-date information about your system and should be used if you must edit entries in a control set directly. The \Clone subkey is a duplicate of the \CurrentControlSet and is created when you boot the system using the kernel initialization process. Usually this subkey is grayed out.

If you want to manually select the Last Known Good option, use the following steps:

1. Start your computer and select to boot Windows NT 4 from the OS Boot Manager screen.

2. Press spacebar as soon as you perform step 1.

3. Press L to select the option to use the Last Known Good Configuration from the Hardware Profile/Configuration Recovery Menu.

4. Press Enter.

Tip   You can exit the Hardware Profile/Configuration Recovery Menu by pressing F3.

Restoring Configuration Files

If you must resort to restoring a user's or system's configuration files, you can use two methods. You can use the emergency repair disk (ERD) that Windows NT creates during system setup to restore the system files. This method is the easiest of the two, but it also is the most unreliable unless you continually update your version of the ERD whenever you make system changes. If the ERD is not updated, it contains only those system settings configured during setup. Consequently, any changes you've made to the system since that time are not included. If, for instance, you've set up security changes, added users or groups, or installed new software or hardware, these changes will not be saved to the ERD.

The next option is only possible if you have previously made a backup of the Registry hives as detailed at the end of Chapter 1, "Introducing Windows NT Registry." You then can use those backup files and save them to the \%*SystemRoot*%\ SYSTEM32\ CONFIG folder from a different session of Windows NT or another operating system. If Windows NT is running on a FAT file system, you can use DOS, Windows 3.x, or Windows 95 to copy these files. If, however, you have NTFS (NT File System) in-stalled, you must use another session of Windows NT to copy the files.

Disabling the Displaying of the Last Logged On User

When you log on to Windows NT, you can see the last person who logged on that computer in the Username field of the Windows NT Logon dialog box. For most users, this feature eliminates the need to retype their user name each time they log on. For some environments, however, this feature might pose a security risk because it reveals a valid user name. A hacker can attempt to break into the system using the user name and trying different passwords. If your server or workstations are exposed to possible logon violations by unauthorized users, you might want to disable this feature so the Username field is blank, requiring all users to fill in the Username and Password fields at logon time.

To disable the displaying of the last logged on user, use these steps:

1. Start the Registry Editor and locate the following key:

   HKEY_LOCAL_MACHINE\SOFTWARE\Microsoft\Windows NT\ Current Version\WinLogon

2. Double-click on the DontDisplayLastUserName entry.

3. Change the String value to **1** in the String Editor (see fig. 8.1). Click on OK.

4. Exit the Registry Editor and reboot the computer.

Figure 8.1

Change the Dont DisplayLastUser Name entry to 1 to instruct Windows NT not to display the name of the last person who logged on.

Customizing Startup Verification

If you run an environment in which you need a verification program to run before a computer can be successfully logged on to the network, you can set up the verification program using the BootVerificationProgram Registry values. You can use these values, for instance, to verify that a remote computer successfully logs on to the network. You might also use these values to set a verification program to run for computers to rely on the last known good boot configuration. To control the boot verification for a remote computer, you use the BootVerification Registry values.

The following explains how to change a system startup to use the last known good boot configuration:

1. Start the Registry Editor and locate the following key:

   HKEY_LOCAL_MACHINE\SYSTEM\CurrentControlSet\Services\
   Name_of_Service

   The *Name_of_Service* key is the name of the service you want to modify.

2. Double-click on the ErrorControl: REG_DWORD: entry.

3. In the Dword Editor, change the Data value to 2, which specifies that the LastKnownGood setting should be invoked.

4. Exit the Registry Editor and reboot the computer.

Tip   If the system doesn't boot as you intended, shut down and restart the computer again. This time manually select the LastKnownGood option from the Hardware Profile/Configuration Recovery Menu. Now all the settings from your previous session are removed and replaced with the current values.

To specify that a custom verification program (that the administrator creates) should be used at bootup, use the following steps:

1. Start the Registry Editor and locate the following key:

   HKEY_LOCAL_MACHINE\SYSTEM\CurrentControlSet\Control\
   BootVerificationProgram

2. Select Edit, Add Value. In the Add Value dialog box, enter **ImagePath** in the Value Name text box. Select REG_SZ or REG_EXPAND_SZ from the Data Type drop-down list. Click on OK.

3. In the String Editor, enter the path to your verification program in the String field. Click on OK.

4. Locate the following key:

   HKEY_LOCAL_MACHINE\SOFTWARE\Windows NT\
   CurrentVersion\WinLogon

5. Double-click on the ReportBookOK: REG_SZ: value.

6. Set the String value to 1 in the String Editor. Click on OK.

7. Exit the Registry Editor and reboot the computer.

If you want to verify the system startup for remote computers using the BOOTVRFY.EXE program, you must enter the BootVerification service in the Registry. This service is used to instruct the local computer to save the current boot configuration as the last known good boot configuration. By default, this service is not installed in Windows NT. To enable this service, use the following steps:

1. Start the Registry Editor and locate the following key:

   HKEY_LOCAL_MACHINE\SYSTEM\CurrentContolSet\Services

2. Select Edit, Key. In the Key Name field, enter **BootVerification** and click on OK.

3. Select the BootVerification subkey and select Edit, Add Value. In the Add Value dialog box, enter **Start** in the Value Name text box. Select from REG_DWORD the Data Type drop-down list. Click on OK.

4. Enter **0x00000003** in the Data field of the DWORD Editor. Click on OK.

5. Use the same process as shown in steps 3 and 4 and add the value entries listed in table 8.1.

6. Exit the Registry Editor and reboot the computer.

TABLE 8.1
Verify Remote System Startup Values

Value Name	Data Type	Data
Type	REG_DWORD	0x00000020
ErrorControl	REG_DWORD	0x00000001
ImagePath	REG_EXPAND_SZ	bootvrfy.exe
ObjectName	REG_SZ	LocalSystem

Turning On Shutdown and Power Off Options

If your system BIOS has a feature to enable Windows NT to support software shut-down, you can modify the Registry to enable this feature. Many laptop computers have this type of feature. When this feature is enabled, the command Shutdown and Power Off is added to the Shutdown Computer Power Off dialog box.

Use the following steps to enable this feature:

1. Start the Registry Editor and locate the following key:

    HKEY_LOCAL_MACHINE\SOFTWARE\Microsoft\Windows NT\ CurrentVersion\WinLogon

2. Double-click the PowerdownAfterShutdown entry.

3. Change the String value to **1** in the String Editor. Click on OK.

4. Exit the Registry Editor and reboot the computer.

Changing System and File System Registry Entries

Although Windows NT includes several tools to help you manage your system and files, you might need to use the Registry Editor to view or manage some of these settings. In this section, you read about common troubleshooting tasks for modifying system and file settings in the Registry. You might, for instance, have problems using long file names on your network. You can disable this feature in Windows NT, as shown in the "Disabling Short File Name Support on NTFS Partitions" section.

Preventing Auto Parsing of AUTOEXEC.BAT Settings

When Windows NT installs, it automatically parses environment settings in the system's AUTOEXEC.BAT file to the Registry. This enables applications, hardware device settings (if any or in the AUTOEXEC.BAT), and the PATH statement to be available under Windows NT. In many cases, this option is fine. In some cases, however, such as if you have legacy settings on computers you don't want to parse, you can disable parsing in the Registry. If you want to ensure that no settings in the AUTOEXEC.BAT are placed in the Registry, use the following steps:

1. Start the Registry Editor and locate the following key:

   HKEY_CURRENT_USER\SOFTWARE\Microsoft\Windows NT\Current Version\WinLogon

2. Select Edit, Add Value. In the Add Value dialog box, enter **ParseAutoexec** in the Value Name text box (see fig. 8.2). Select REG_SZ from the Data Type drop-down list. Click on OK.

Figure 8.2

Add the ParseAutoexec value entry to control the way Windows NT parses AUTOEXEC.BAT instructions.

3. Enter **0** in the String field of the String Editor. Click on OK.

4. Exit the Registry Editor and reboot the computer.

5. Upon bootup, look in the following subkey to check the environment settings to see if any settings from AUTOEXEC.BAT are added:

   HKEY_LOCAL_MACHINE\SYSTEM\CurrentControlSet\Control\ SessionManager\Environment

Tip For some software, hardware, and services running under Windows NT, you might need Windows NT to parse the PATH statement to set environment settings. Without this setting, some of your applications might not work properly.

Disabling Short File Name Support on NTFS Partitions

When you create a file using a Windows NT application and save it as a long file name (instead of the 8.3 characters of DOS), the file name is truncated when read by older applications and MS-DOS. NTFS supports short file names for DOS clients and applications that can read only short file names. By default this support is turned on.

If you encounter problems with files being truncated and not being readable by applications or resources, consider disabling short file name support. To disable short file name support on NTFS partitions, use the following steps:

1. Start the Registry Editor and locate the following key:

    HKEY_LOCAL_MACHINE\SYSTEM\CurrentControlSet\Control\FileSystem

2. Double-click on the NtfsDisable8Dot3NameCreation entry.

3. In the DWORD Editor, set the Data value to **1**. Click on OK.

4. Exit the Registry Editor and reboot the computer.

Disabling Long File Name Support On FAT Partitions

On File Allocation Table (FAT) file systems, the long file name support is enabled by default in Windows NT. Unfortunately, some disk diagnostic tools have difficulty handling long file names. You can turn off this feature in Windows NT using the Registry Editor. The following steps show you how. The changes shown here affect the entire partition on which Windows NT resides; you cannot change this support per Windows NT installation if more than one instance is on a partition.

1. Start the Registry Editor and locate the following key:

    HKEY_LOCAL_MACHINE\SYSTEM\CurrentControlSet\Control\FileSystem

2   Double-click on the Win31FileSystem entry (see fig. 8.3).

3. In the DWORD Editor, change the Data value to **1**. Click on OK.

Tip Set the Win31FileSystem entry back to **0** if you want to use long file names under Windows NT.

3. Exit the Registry Editor and reboot the computer.

Figure 8.3

The Win31FileSystem entry controls if short file names are used on FAT file systems.

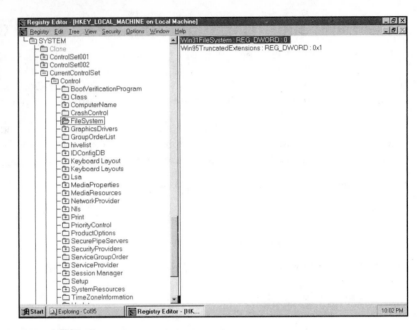

Increasing Paged Pool Memory

If you get an error like the following, you might need to increase the amount of paged pool memory in Windows NT:

```
Not enough server storage is available to process this command.
```

Earlier versions of Windows NT set the paged pool size to a maximum value regardless of the physical memory you might have on your system. Use the following steps to correct this problem in the Registry:

1. Start the Registry Editor and locate the following key:

    HKEY_LOCAL_MACHINE\SYSTEM\CurrentControlSet\Control\
    Session Manager\Memory Management

2. Double-click on the PagedPoolSize value entry.

3. Change the value to 0.

4. Exit the Registry Editor and reboot the computer.

Viewing Devices Using Unlisted Serial Ports

You can use the Registry Editor to view a device that is using an unlisted serial port. You might have problems knowing what a port setting is if it is unlisted. This type of information is helpful when you are connecting devices to the serial ports. Use the following steps (no changes are actually performed in these steps; they only show how to obtain information about your serial port settings):

1. Start the Registry Editor and locate the following key:

   HKEY_LOCAL_MACHINE\HARDWARE\DESCRIPTION\System\ MultifunctionAdapter*serial_port*#\SerialController

   Each serial port is represented by numeric keys, starting with 0 as COM1, 1 as COM2, and so on. A mouse device using a COM port is displayed under the PointerPeripheral subkey.

2. View the settings under each of the subkeys for your COM ports to determine which devices use which serial port.

3. Double-click on the ConfigurationData value entry for a COM port. This displays the Resources dialog box (see fig. 8.4), in which you can see configuration information about a device. This is the same information you see when you run the Windows NT Diagnostic Program (WINMSD.EXE). Click on OK.

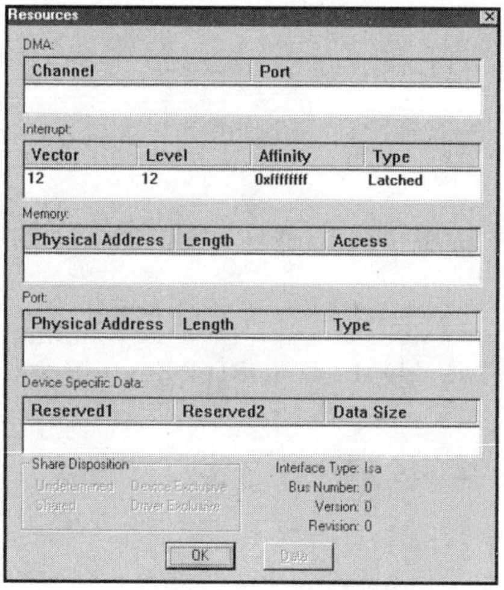

Figure 8.4

The Resources dialog box displays similar information that the Windows NT Diagnostics Program displays.

4. Close this Registry key without making any changes.

Tip To delete a serial port from your system using the Registry, locate the serial port value entry (such as Serial0: REG_SZ: COM1) in the following subkey and delete the value entry:

HKEY_LOCAL_MACHINE\HARDWARE\DEVICEMAP\SERIALCOMM

Next, locate the specified COM ports Serial key (such as in the following subkey (*nn* is the COM port number) and delete the value entry:

HKEY_LOCAL_MACHINE\SYSTEM\CurrentControlSet\Services\Serial\Parameters\Serial*nn*

Changing Driver Loading Controls

Usually, Windows NT controls how your system loads and uses error control for devices or services. You use the Control Panel options or Administrative Tools (Common) utilities to make most of the configuration and startup settings for a device or service. You can, in extreme cases, use the Registry Editor to change how a driver or service behaves if you think the load sequence is affecting the way in which a service or driver runs. You can, for instance, control when a driver is loaded, when a service loads, the order in which a driver or service is loaded, and parameters of the service or driver. The Registry also can be modified to control how error control of a driver or service is implemented in the event of startup problems.

The following shows you how to change when a driver loads or when a service starts under Windows NT:

1. Start the Registry Editor and locate the following key:

   HKEY_LOCAL_MACHINE\SYSTEM\CurrentControlSet\Services\
   Name_of_Driver

   The *Name_of_Driver* subkey (such as \ati for an Ati graphics adapter) is the driver or service you want to modify.

2. Double-click the ErrorControl value entry and use the following settings to help you set how the driver loads. Fill in the DWORD Editor with one of the values in this list.

   ◆ **Ignore.** To instruct Windows NT to ignore any error controls, use the value 0x0.

   ◆ **Normal.** To instruct Windows NT to continue startup when the driver fails but to issue a warning message, use the value 0x1.

◆ **Severe.** To instruct Windows NT to use the last known good boot if a driver fails, use the value 0x2. If the last known good boot is already being used, this setting causes Windows NT to continue with startup.

◆ **Critical.** To instruct Windows NT to quit (or fail) the startup if a driver fails, use the value 0x3.

3. Click on OK to save the entry from the DWORD Editor to the Registry.

4. Double-click on the Group value to change the group dependency for the driver or service. Enter the group name in the String field of the String Editor. Click on OK.

5. Double-click the Start value to change when the selected driver or service is loaded. In the DWORD Editor, use one of the following values to fill in the Data field:

◆ **Disabled.** To instruct Windows NT to not start the driver or service for any reason, use the value 0x4.

◆ **Load on demand.** To instruct Windows NT to make the driver or service available but only to be started by the user, use the value 0x3.

◆ **Auto load.** To instruct Windows NT to load or start the driver or service at startup, use the value 0x2.

◆ **System.** To instruct Windows NT to load the driver or service at kernel initialization, use the value 0x1.

◆ **Boot.** To instruct Windows NT to load the driver or server at boot using the Boot Loader, use the value 0x0.

6. Click on OK to save the entry from the DWORD Editor to the Registry.

7. Exit the Registry Editor and reboot the computer.

 Note The Type value in the driver of service keys specifies the type of service or driver the item is. The following list summarizes the valid values (you usually don't have to modify these settings):

◆ 0x1 is for a kernel device driver (such as a hard drive device driver).

◆ 0x2 is for a file system driver.

◆ 0x4 is a set of arguments for an adapter.

◆ 0x10 is a Win32 application that runs in a process by itself and is started by the Service Controller.

◆ 0x20 is a Win32 service that shares processes with other Win32 services.

Eliminating Conflicts with PCI Resources on Intel Machines

If your Intel-based computer hangs or does not operate after you install a PCI device, your Registry might need to be modified. The reason is because the Hardware Abstraction Layer (HAL) assigns a memory address or I/O port address to the new PCI device that has already been assigned to another device. This causes a conflict with your devices.

To overcome this problem, use the preceding section's instructions to change the driver load order in the Registry for the PCI adapter. Although this option is recommended by Microsoft, it might not work if the load order is predefined.

You also can obtain a HAL distributed by Microsoft to fix the problem. Currently, the HALs released include HAL.DLL, HALMPS.DLL, and HALAPIC.DLL.

Making Internet- and Network-Related Registry Changes

In Chapter 5, "Examining Network Settings in the Windows NT Registry," you learn about many of the Registry values and settings you can make in Windows NT to affect networking performance or services. You also saw some ways to make changes to the Registry for specific network troubleshooting issues. The following sections include several more of these same types of Registry troubleshooting tasks, as well as tasks relating to Windows NT and the Internet.

Uninstalling Java Support in Microsoft Internet Explorer 3.0

Although the Java programming language has become extremely popular over the past two years, you might experience some problems running Java programs or applets on workstations or servers. One way to eliminate these problems is to remove the Java support from your World Wide Web browsers. If you were one of the millions or so users who installed a beta version of the Microsoft Internet Explorer 3.0 Web browser, however, you might have trouble removing the Java support feature in the release version of Internet Explorer 3.0. Normally, to remove this option you use the Install/Uninstall tab when you run the Add/Remove Programs application from Control Panel. If you get the error message

```
Can't run 16-bit Windows program.

This application is not supported by Microsoft Windows NT.
```

use the following steps to correct the problem:

1. Start the Registry Editor and locate the following key:

   HKEY_LOCAL_MACHINE\SOFTWARE\Microsoft\Windows\
   CurrentVersion\Uninstall\Java VM

 Tip Notice the preceding subkey uses the \Windows subkey, not \Windows NT, which many of the solutions presented in this chapter use.

2. Delete the Java VM subkey.

3. Exit the Registry Editor and reboot the computer.

Re-creating a Post Office for Windows NT Mail

Once you set up a Microsoft Mail post office using the Workgroups Mail option in Windows NT, you cannot change the post office name. In some cases, however, you might want to change the post office name to one that other servers in a wide area network can read, or you might change it for other reasons. For these cases, you need to remove the old post office from your system and setup a new one (make sure you back up all your messages in the post office before deleting the old post office). You can use the Add/Remove Programs application in Control Panel and remove the Windows Messaging choice on the Windows NT tab. If that doesn't work, you can use the following steps:

1. Start the Registry Editor and locate the following key:

   HKEY_CURRENT_USER\Software\Microsoft\Mail\Microsoft Mail

2. Double-click on the Login value.

3. In the String Editor, delete the entry in the String field, leaving it blank. Click on OK.

4. Double-click on the ServerPath value.

5. In the String Editor, delete the entry in the String field, leaving it blank. Click on OK.

6. Exit the Registry Editor and reboot the computer. When you start Microsoft Mail, the initialization screen displays, with which you can set up a new post office.

Enabling a RAS Server to See a RAS Client

The Windows 95 RAS client application might experience an error when attempting to access a Windows NT RAS server. If this occurs, the following error message displays:

```
No Domain server was able to validate your password. You may not be able to
gain access to some network resources.
```

This error occurs only when the RAS client connects through an IPX PPP connection. To correct this problem, follow these steps in Windows NT:

1. Start the Registry Editor and locate the following key:

   HKEY_LOCAL_MACHINE\SYSTEM\CurrentControlSet\Services\NwlnkIpx\ Parameters

2. Double-click on the DisableDialinNetbios value entry.

3. In the DWORD Editor, change the value in the Data field to **0** to disable the DisableDialinNetbios option. Click on OK.

4. Exit the Registry Editor and reboot the computer.

Enabling RemoteListen on RAS

The RemoteListen parameter of Windows NT enables RAS clients to be accessed as if they are part of the local area network. This is handy if you want certain remote clients to appear as local clients. The RemoteListen parameter is set on the RAS server to support IPC, mail slots, RPC, named pipes, and NBF/NetBEUI features.

To enable RemoteListen, use these steps:

1. Start the Registry Editor and locate the following key:

   HKEY_LOCAL_MACHINE\SYSTEM\CurrentControlSet\Services\RemoteAccess\ Parameters\NetBIOSGateway

2. Select Edit, Add Value. In the Add Value dialog box, enter **RemoteListen** in the Value Name text box. Select REG_DWORD from the Data Type drop-down list. Click on OK. If this value is already entered (see fig. 8.5), double-click the RemoteListen value to modify its value entry.

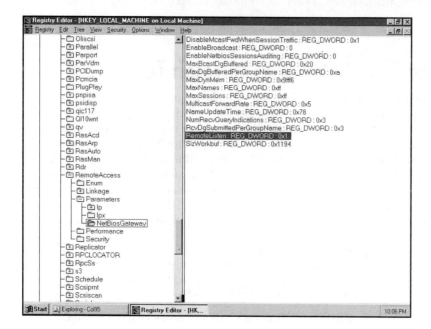

Figure 8.5

On some systems, the RemoteListen value entry will already be in the Registry.

3. In the DWORD Editor, enter **2** in the Data field. Click on OK.

4. Exit the Registry Editor and reboot the computer.

Hiding a Server from a Network Browser

Sometimes a server needs to be available on the network for services, but not available for clients to browse. If you have problems or anticipate problems with a server being browsed that should not be, consider hiding it from clients. This way the server name does not appear in a client's Explorer or Network Neighborhood. You can hide a server from the browser on a local area network by modifying the following Registry entry:

1. Start the Registry Editor and locate the following key:

   HKEY_LOCAL_MACHINE\SYSTEM\CurrentControlSet\Services\
   LanmanServe\Parameters

2. Select Edit, Add Value. In the Add Value dialog box, enter **Hidden** in the Value Name text box. Select REG_DWORD from the Data Type drop-down list. Click on OK.

3. In the Data field, enter 1. This enables hiding of the server. Click on OK.

4. Exit the Registry Editor and reboot the computer.

Detecting Dead Gateway in Microsoft TCP/IP

Although Microsoft TCP/IP for Windows NT includes a mechanism to detect when a gateway is functioning, it does not automatically detect when the gateway becomes active on the network. A gateway that is not functioning, however, is not easy to detect. These type of gateways are called *dead gateways*. The dead gateway feature works when you have more than one default gateway addressed in the Advanced Options of the TCP/IP Configuration dialog box. You can display this dialog box by launching the Network application in Control Panel, selecting the Protocols tab, and double-clicking on the TCP/IP Protocols option. Next click on the Advanced button. When the default gateway does not respond to TCP requests, IP uses the backup gateway.

You can enable the dead gateway feature by using the following Registry value:

1. Start the Registry Editor and locate the following key:

   HKEY_LOCAL_MACHINE\SYSTEM\CurrentControlSet\Services\Tcpip\Parameters

2. Select Edit, Add Value. In the Add Value dialog box, enter **EnableDeadGWDetect** in the Value Name text box. Select REG_DWORD from the Data Type drop-down list. Click on OK.

3. In the DWORD Editor, enter **1** in the Data field, to enable detection. Use 0 to turn off detection. Click on OK.

4. Exit the Registry Editor and reboot the computer.

Correcting Ethernet Segment Communication Problem in FDDI Rings

A conflict arises when Windows NT Server and Windows NT Workstation computers use TCP/IP and FDDI network adapters resulting in an Ethernet segment problems in FDDI rings. What happens is that both adapters want to use the same maximum transmission units size (MTU) of the FDDI, but the Ethernet segment does not transmit packets larger than 1500 bits.

Use the following steps to correct Ethernet segment communication problems in FDDI rings:

1. Start the Registry Editor and locate the following key:

   HKEY_LOCAL_MACHINE\SYSTEM\CurentControlSet\Services\ *NIC_Name_and_*#\Paramters\Tcpip

   The *NIC_Name_and_*# variable is the name of the network interface card installed.

2. Select Edit, Add Value. In the Add Value dialog box, enter **MTU** in the Value Name text box. Select REG_DWORD from the Data Type drop-down list. Click on OK.

3. In the DWORD Editor, enter the MTU size for the Ethernet segment, or 1500. Click on OK.

4. Exit the Registry Editor and reboot the computer.

Increasing LMHOSTS Entries for TCP/IP for Windows NT

Windows NT uses the LMHOSTS file to map IP addresses to NetBIOS names of remote servers for TCP/IP communication. By default, Windows NT reads the first 100 entries in the LMHOSTS file (denoted by #PRE notation). If you anticipate having more than 100 entries in your LMHOSTS file, you can increase the number Windows NT reads by modifying the Registry using the following steps:

1. Start the Registry Editor and locate the following key:

   HKEY_LOCAL_MACHINE\SYSTEM\CurrentControlSet\Services\NBT\ Parameters

2. Select Edit, Add Value. In the Add Value dialog box, enter **MaxPreLoads** in the Value Name text box. Select REG_DWORD from the Data Type drop-down list. Click on OK.

3. In the DWORD Editor, enter the maximum LMHOSTS, such as 500. Windows NT usually timeouts after 1000 entries.

4. Exit the Registry Editor and reboot the computer.

Repairing WINS Database Corruption

Under normal conditions, Windows NT automatically creates a backup of the WINS database (which you can set in the Database Backup Path field in the WINS Server Configuration dialog box) and uses it if the primary WINS database becomes corrupted. If, however, both the primary and backup databases become corrupted, you can correct the corruption using the Starting Version Count (or ID) within the WINS preferences to increase the Highest Version ID of the Local Database value. The Starting Version Count is the highest version ID number for the WINS database. You can make this value higher than the current Highest Version ID value.

 Tip After you set the Starting Version Count value, you cannot lower it. If you want to lower it, you must delete the WINS database and reinstall WINS.

Use the following steps to modify the Staring Version Count:

1. Start the Registry Editor and locate the following key:

   HKEY_LOCAL_MACHINE\SYSTEM\CurrentControlSet\Services\WINS\ Parameters

2. Double-click on either the VersCounterStartVal_LowWord or VersCounterStartVal_HighWord.

3. Increase the value as needed in the DWORD Editor. Click on OK. For example, increasing a Starting Version ID of FF78 to FF79 is done by modifying the VersCounterStartVal_LowWord value and changing it to 0x0000FF79.

4. Exit the Registry Editor and reboot the computer.

 Tip To see more examples of setting this value, read the Microsoft Knowledge Base article *Repairing a Corrupted WINS Database with Starting Version Count* at http://www.microsoft.com/kb/busys/winnt/ Q135405.htm.

Limiting Packets Used by NBF

If you often experience send and receive packet errors on your Windows NT network running NBF (NetBEUI), you can increase the values of these parameters to alleviate these errors. NBF uses send packets for connection-oriented data. Receive packets are used to handle incoming frames. The SendPacketPoolSize and RecievePacketPoolSize parameters in the Registry control the number of send and receive packets it allocates.

To modify these parameters, use the following steps:

1. Start the Registry Editor and locate the following key:

   HKEY_LOCAL_MACHINE\SYSTEM\Services\NBF\Parameters

2. Change the SendPacketPoolSize to a value over 100 (the default is 100). Change the ReceivePacketPoolSize to a value over 30 (the default is 30).

3. Exit the Registry Editor and reboot the computer.

Increase Domain Synchronization over WAN

The ReplicationGoverner parameter enables Windows NT to increase its performance of replication across slow network links. If you experience poor performance results during the replication process, you can modify the Registry to increase Windows NT performance during replications. The primary domain controller (PDC) uses this setting to control the size of the data transferred and the rate at which it sends the data (frequency). The ReplicationGoverner also is used by the backup domain controller (BDC) to increase the domain synchronization performance over wide area networks (WANs).

 Note   Each BDC must have this entry manually entered. Also, the PDC must be a computer running Windows NT 3.5 or above.

To add the ReplicationGoverner value entry to the Registry, use these steps:

1. Start the Registry Editor and locate the following key:

   HKEY_LOCAL_MACHINE\SYSTEM\CurrentControlSet\Services\Netlogon\Parameters

2. Select Edit, Add Value. In the Add Value dialog box, enter **ReplicationGovernor** in the Value Name text box. Select REG_DWORD from the Data Type drop-down list (see fig. 8.6). Click on OK.

   In the DWORD Editor, enter a value between 0 and 100 in the Data field. The value you enter is the percentage for the amount and frequency of data transferred on each call to the primary domain controller. The default setting is 100, which uses a 128 KB buffer. You can cut this buffer size (thereby reducing the size of the data sent)in half by entering a value of 50. This in turn reduces the frequency of synchronization over a slow WAN by 50 percent as well. By using a small number, you might never complete a synchronization. Also, do not enter a 0 or else the user account database never synchronizes.

Figure 8.6

Use the ReplicationGovernor value to control domain synchronization on a WAN.

Starting the Directory Replicator

Sometimes the Directory Replicator fails to start under Windows NT and an error of 1057 or 1069 appears in the Event Viewer. The main causes for this are that the password entered is not valid or the account was never granted Logon as a service permission. To start the directory replicator, try shutting down the client and logging the client back on again. Other causes for this problem include an error in the Directory Replicator service configuration, an error in the Registry, or information from a domain user account that is not synchronized. The following steps show you how to start the directory replicator if it fails to start:

Note Before you modify the Registry, ensure the user is set up with an account using the User Manager for Domains. Also, enable the Password never expires option and grant the account Logon as a Service rights. In the Server Manager, select the computer and select Computer, Services. From the Services dialog box, select Directory Replicator and click the Startup button. Click the Automatic option and specify the user name in the This Account field. Enter the user's password and click on OK, then Close.

If the Directory Replicator service still does not work, use the following steps to manually edit the Registry. For more information on setting up domain users, see *Windows NT Server 4 Professional Reference*, published by New Riders.

1. Start the Registry Editor and locate the following key:

   HKEY_LOCAL_MACHINE\SYSTEM\CurrentControlSet\Services\Replicator

2. View the ObjectName value entry. It should be set to the domain name for the user account you set up (see previous Note). If it is not, double-click on it and change the value in the String Editor to the correct setting. Click on OK.

3. Exit the Registry Editor and reboot the computer.

4. Try using the Directory Replicator service. If you still encounter problems, ensure that the user account and user account databases are configured properly and are synchronized on all of the domain servers.

Enabling Multiple Internet Domain Names and Addresses over RAS

By default, Windows NT RAS does not enable you to use multiple IP addresses and Internet domains. This can be a problem if a preconfigured IP address is taken already, or if the domain is busy or down. You can enable a Windows NT computer to use multiple IP address and multiple Internet domains to dial into the Internet using RAS. Use the following steps to do this:

1. Configure Windows NT so your first IP address is used by the RAS connection.

2. Configure Windows NT so your second IP address is used by the network adapter.

3. Start the Registry Editor and locate the following key:

   HKEY_LOCAL_MACHINE\SYSTEM\CurrentControlSet\Service\RasArp\ Parameters

4. Select Edit, Add Value. In the Add Value dialog box, enter **DisableOtherSrcPackets** in the Value Name text box. Select REG_DWORD from the Data Type drop-down list (see fig. 8.7). Click on OK.

Figure 8.7

Add the Disable-OtherSrcPackets entry to enable Windows NT to use multiple IPs for multiple network adapters.

5. In the DWORD Editor, enter **0** in the Data field. Click on OK.

6. Exit the Registry Editor and reboot the computer.

Removing TCP/IP Settings from the Registry

If you've ever deleted TCP/IP settings using the Network application in Control Panel, some of the settings still linger in the Registry. To reinstall TCP/IP, you need to have all of these settings removed or you receive the error The Registry Subkey Already Exists.

The following shows you the Registry subkeys you need to delete using the Registry Editor. Depending on the services you have installed, you may not have all these subkeys.

```
HKEY_LOCAL_MACHINE\SOFTWARE\Microsoft\DhcpMibAgent

HKEY_LOCAL_MACHINE\SOFTWARE\Microsoft\DhcpServer

HKEY_LOCAL_MACHINE\SYSTEM\CCS\Services\DhcpServer

HKEY_LOCAL_MACHINE\SOFTWARE\Microsoft\Wins

HKEY_LOCAL_MACHINE\SOFTWARE\Microsoft\WinsMibAgent

HKEY_LOCAL_MACHINE\SYSTEM\CCS\Services\Wins

HKEY_LOCAL_MACHINE\SOFTWARE\Microsoft\SimpTcp

HKEY_LOCAL_MACHINE\SYSTEM\CCS\Services\SimpTcp

HKEY_LOCAL_MACHINE\SOFTWARE\Microsoft\FTPSVC

HKEY_LOCAL_MACHINE\SYSTEM\CCS\Services\FTPSVC

HKEY_LOCAL_MACHINE\SOFTWARE\Microsoft\LPDSVE

HKEY_LOCAL_MACHINE\SOFTWARE\Microsoft\TcpPring

HKEY_LOCAL_MACHINE\SYSTEM\CCS\Services\LPDSVC

HKEY_LOCAL_MACHINE\SOFTWARE\Microsoft\RFC1156Agent

HKEY_LOCAL_MACHINE\SOFTWARE\Microsoft\SNMP

HKEY_LOCAL_MACHINE\SYSTEM\CCS\Services\SNMP

HKEY_LOCAL_MACHINE\SOFTWARE\Microsoft\NetBT

HKEY_LOCAL_MACHINE\SOFTWARE\Microsoft\Tcpip

HKEY_LOCAL_MACHINE\SOFTWARE\Microsoft\TcpipCU

HKEY_LOCAL_MACHINE\SYSTEM\CCS\Services\DHCP

HKEY_LOCAL_MACHINE\SYSTEM\CCS\Services\Services\Lmhosts

HKEY_LOCAL_MACHINE\SYSTEM\CCS\Services\NetBt

HKEY_LOCAL_MACHINE\SYSTEM\CCS\Services\NetDrivern\Parameters\Tcpip
```

In the preceding subkey, NetDriver*n* denotes the number of the network adapter.

Summary

This chapter focused on providing practical configuration and troubleshooting tasks you can perform by using the Registry Editor to affect the Registry directly. The chapter presented tasks in separate sections, including startup and shutdown problems, system and file system tasks, Internet problems, and networking tasks.

When you configure Windows NT, most of your configuration settings are done using Control Panel applications, application options, and the Administrative Tools (Common) folders utilities. When you need to make something work that these programs can't fix, use the Registry Editor to fix it. Many times when you cannot fix a setting, you need to contact the vendor (for hardware needs) or consult the Microsoft Knowledge Base at http://www.microsoft.com/kb to see if a solution to your problem is available. Often there is, you just need to know where to look.

APPENDIX A

Windows NT Registry Values

This appendix outlines a collection of value entries for the Windows NT Registry. These entries are categorized within specified keys or subkeys in the Registry. The main categories include the following:

- ◆ Registry Entries for Software

- ◆ Registry Entries for Winlogon

- ◆ Registry Entries for Fonts

- ◆ Registry Entries for Printing

- ◆ CurrentControlSet\Select Subkey

- ◆ CurrentControlSet\Control Subkeys

- ◆ CurrentControlSet\Services Subkeys

- ◆ Registry Entries for Microsoft Mail

- ◆ Registry Entries for Program Manager

- ◆ Registry Entries for User Preferences

- ◆ Registry Entries for Subsystems

Note For Registry value entries relating to network services, such as Remote Access Services, net logon, and TCP/IP, see Chapter 5, "Examining Network Settings in Windows NT Registry." If you run Windows NT on a NetWare network, see Chapter 12 "Integrating NetWare with Windows NT Server" in *Windows NT 4 Professional Reference* published by New Riders. That chapter also gives you an excellent tutorial of how to use NetWare on a Windows NT network.

The format for each entry appears as follows:

◆ **Value Entry Name.** Description of value entry, possible values, and data type. Also included is the subkey in which the value entry appears. (Data Type)

Registry Value Entries for Software

For Registry information about the software installed on the local computer, look in the HKEY_LOCAL_MACHINE\SOFTWARE subkey for the manufacturer and version of the software. Each application has its own subkey (for Win32 applications) here for information specific to the local computer. The settings contained in these subkeys contain information provided by the manufacturer.

You can look in the HKEY_CURRENT_USER\Software*manufacturer_name* subkey for application information for the user currently logged on. These settings include user preferences, display options, and other specific settings that users can control for an application.

Registry Value Entries for Winlogon

Windows NT Settings that control the way in which the logon process behaves are contained in the following Registry subkey:

HKEY_LOCAL_MACHINE\SOFTWARE\Microsoft\Windows NT\CurrentVersion\Winlogon

The following value entries are found in this subkey:

◆ **AutoRestartShell.** Specifies that the Windows NT shell restarts. (REG_SZ)

◆ **AutoAdminLogon.** Enables the automatic logon feature. Add the DefaultUserName and DefaultPassword value entries to use this feature. By default, this value entry is not added to the Registry. Use the value of 1 to enable this feature, bypassing the Ctrl+Alt+Del process during system startup. (REG_SZ)

◆ **DefaultDomainName.** Includes the name of the last domain the user logged on to. (REG_SZ)

◆ **DefaultPassword.** Includes the password for the user listed under DefaultUserName when you enable the AutoAdminLogon feature. By default, this value entry is not included in the Registry. (REG_SZ)

◆ **DefaultUserName.** Includes user name of the last person who logged on to that computer. (REG_SZ)

◆ **LegalNoticeCaption.** Includes the caption of the message box that displays if you configure a legal notice to display at boot up. (REG_SZ)

◆ **LegalNoticeText.** Includes the text that displays if you configure a legal notice to display at boot up. (REG_SZ)

◆ **PowerdownAfterShutdown.** Instructs Windows NT to power down the computer after the user shuts down Windows NT. (REG_SZ)

◆ **ReportBookOk.** Disables the automatic startup acceptance after an initial logon when set to 0. (REG_SZ)

◆ **Shell.** Specifies the shell application that runs at startup. The default is EXPLORE.EXE. (REG_SZ)

◆ **ShutdownWithoutLogon.** Enables you to shutdown Windows NT at the Welcome dialog box.

◆ **System.** Includes system programs that WinLogon runs. (REG_SZ)

◆ **Userinit.** Specifies programs that Winlogon runs when a user logs on. (REG_SZ)

◆ **VmApplet.** Specifies the VM applications that run at logon time. (REG_SZ)

Registry Value Entries for Log Off and Shut Down

You can find Registry values for settings Windows NT uses for logging off and shutting down the system in the following subkey:

HKEY_LOCAL_MACHINE\SOFTWARE\Microsoft\Windows NT\Current Version\ Shutdown

The following value entries are available for this subkey:

◆ **LogoffSettting.** Specifies the logoff network selections on the Logoff dialog box. The default is 0. (REG_DWORD)

◆ **ShudownSetting.** Specifies the shutdown selections on the Shutdown dialog box. The default is 0. (REG_DWORD)

The following list summarizes each of the values you can select for the LogoffSetting and ShutdownSetting value entries:

0 displays the Logoff command

1 displays the Shutdown command

2 displays the Shutdown and Restart command

3 displays the Shutdown and Power Off command, if your hardware supports it

Registry Value Entries for Fonts

Although the Font application in the Control Panel is helpful for installing and viewing your fonts, the Registry can be used to examine and troubleshoot possible problems associated with fonts. The Registry includes six font subkeys in the following Registry subkey:

HKEY_LOCAL_MACHINE\SOFTWARE\Microsoft\Windows NT\CurrentVersion\

These subkeys include the following:

◆ FontCache

◆ FontDPI

◆ Font Drivers

◆ Fonts

◆ FontSubstitutes

◆ GRE_Initialize

The Font Drivers subkey might be empty unless you use an external font driver, such as the Adobe Type Manager. The Fonts subkey is a list of the installed fonts on your system. The following sections describe the value entries located in the other font Registry subkeys.

FontCache Registry Value Entries

The FontCache subkey includes value entries that define parameters for font caching. The value entries in the FontCache subkey can greatly influence the amount of memory used by the system. The value entries are as follows:

- **MaxSize.** Includes the maximum amount of address space (in kilobytes) set aside for a font cache. The default is 0x80. (REG_DWORD)

- **MinIncrSize.** Includes the minimum amount of memory (in kilobytes) incremeted when a font cache increases. The default is 0x4. (REG_DWORD)

- **MinInitSize.** Includes the minimum amount of memory (in kilobytes) initially set aside per font cache. The default is 0x4. (REG_DWORD)

FontDPI Entries

The FontDPI subkey defines the default number of dots per inch (DPI) for font display settings. The following value entry are included in this subkey.

- **LogPixels.** Specifies system resources for font display settings, including system font size and toolbar font size.

FontSubstitutes

The FontSubstitutes show the font values that include substitute settings. In some cases, a font you have installed should be used when it encounters a font in a document or application. This increases the likelihood that the application or document will display as close to the original as possible.

In this subkey, Windows NT lists the alternate font name to use, an equal sign, and the actual font name. The following is an example:

```
Time: REG_SZ: Times New Roman
```

GRE_Initialize

The Registry includes information for character-based applications (such as many MS-DOS applications) in the GRE_Initialize subkey. The following are the value entries found in this subkey:

- **FIXEDFON.FON.** Instructs Windows NT which fixed-width font to use for character-based applications. The default is VGAFIX.FON. (REG_SZ)

◆ **FONTS.FON.** Instructs Windows NT which font to use as the default system font for character-based applications. The default is VGASYS.FON. (REG_SZ)

◆ **OEMFONT.FON.** Instructs Windows NT which font to use as the default OEM or console font. The default is VGAOEM.FON. (REG_SZ)

Registry Value Entries for Printing

You can find printing information in the Registry in a couple of different places. For hardware information about Windows NT print processes and drivers, see the following subkey:

HKEY_LOCAL_MACHINE\SYSTEM\CurrentControlSet\Control\Print

The Registry contains printer information in the preceding subkey. For information on the print spooler folder, see the following subkey:

HKEY_LOCAL_MACHINE\SYSTEM\CurrentControlSet\Control\Print\Printers

For printing information for users, see the following subkey:

HKEY_CURRENT_USER\Printers

The following are value entries in the Print subkey:

◆ **BeepEnabled.** Enables beeping for remote print jobs that receive an error and the print job is retried. The default is 0, which disables the beep. (REG_DWORD)

◆ **NoRemotePrinterDrivers.** Specifies the remote printer drivers Windows NT uses, such as Windows NT Fax Driver. (REG_SZ)

◆ **PortThreadPriority.** Sets the port thread priority, which outputs to the printer. The default is 0. (REG_DWORD)

◆ **PriorityClass.** Sets spooler class priority. The default is 0, which sets the class priority for servers to 9 and 7 for workstations.

◆ **SchedulerThreadPriority.** Sets scheduler thread priority, which assigns print jobs to ports. The default is 0. (REG_DWORD)

The Print subkey includes the following subkeys:

◆ **Environments.** Includes information about the hardware system on which Windows NT is installed, such as PowerPC, x86, and so on. Under each subkey are specific subkeys for each installed printer on that system.

- **Monitors.** Includes subkeys for the print monitor (such as Print Manager) of the local machine.

- **Printers.** Lists the installed printers for the local computer. Under this subkey are subkey(s) for each printer, such as HP LaserJet IIP and so on. Each printer then has value entries established by both the printer manufacturer and you when you set up the printer, such as attributes, datatype, name, port, share name, and so on.

- **Providers.** Includes the information for network printer servicers. This subkey includes the LanMan Print Services subkey, which can include settings for print services and drivers that can be loaded only from a trusted print server.

CurrentControlSet\Select

Windows NT uses control sets to control the behavior of the boot process. You can find information about the control sets by looking at the value entries in the CurrentControlSet\SYSTEM\Select subkey. For more information about control sets, see the "Control Sets" section in Chapter 2, "Understanding the Windows NT Registry Structure."

Subkey: HKEY_LOCAL_MACHINE\SYSTEM\CurrentControlSet\Select

The following are possible value entries for this subkey:

- **Current.** Defines the control set that creates the CurrentControlSet subkey. (REG_DWORD)

- **Default.** Defines the default control set. (REG_DWORD)

- **Failed.** Identifies the previous control set that caused Windows NT not to properly boot and instead use the LastKnownGood control set. (REG_DWORD)

- **LastKnownGood.** Identifies control set used to successfully boot Windows NT. (REG_DWORD)

CurrentControlSet\Control Registry Value Entries

You can find specific information about the Windows control sets by viewing the value entries and data in this subkey. Control sets are used to determine how Windows NT boots.

Subkey: HKEY_LOCAL_MACHINE\SYSTEM\SYSTEM\CurrentControlSet\Control

The following are possible value entries for this subkey:

◆ **RegistrySizeLimit.** Sets the amount of disk space and paged pool the Registry uses (which determines the maximum size of the Registry). The default value for this entry is 8 MB, with a maximum size of 80 percent of the paged pool setting. (REG_DWORD)

◆ **Current User.** Shows the currently logged on user name. (REG_SZ)

◆ **SystemStartOptions.** Includes system arguments sent from firmware to the operating system. (REG_SZ)

The \CurrentControlSet\Control key contains several subkeys, including the following:

◆ **FileSystem.** Controls the way the Windows NT file system (NTFS or FAT) operates. Includes the NtfsDisable8dot3NameCreation (REG_DWORD) entry, which controls if NTFS creates short names from long file names. If set to 0 (the default), then short file names are created. The Win31FileSystem (REG_DWORD) entry under the FileSystem subkey is used to specify if you can use long filenames on a FAT file system. Set this entry to 1 to enable it.

◆ **Session Manager.** Contains three value entries to set global system variables used by the Windows NT Session Manager. The CriticalSectionTimeout (REG_DWORD) entry controls the timeout phase for deadlocks. The default value is 0x278d00. The Globalflag (REG_DWORD) entry sets the way in which Windows NT runs OS/2 applications. When set to 20100000 you disable the OS/2 subsystem. The BootExecute value entry is used to define the applications that Windows NT should run at startup. The Session Manager includes the following subkeys:

  ◆ **Enviroment.** Shows the environment variables used by the Windows NT logon and shell. The value entries in this subkey include ComSpec, Os2LibPath, Path, and WinDir.

  ◆ **DOS Devices.** Contains DOS links that Windows NT creates at boot up. Some of the default value entries (all REG_SZ) include PIPE, PRN (for LPT1), and TELNET.

  ◆ **KnownDLL.** Contains a list of the dynamic link libraries (DLLs) that are on the Windows NT system at boot up. This subkey includes an entry for each DLL in the format *DLLName* (REG_SZ). Some of the default value entries include olesvr32, advapi33, and kernel32.

◆ **Subsystems.** Shows the settings created at system startup for the Windows NT subsystem. The SystemPages value entry (REG_DWORD) sets the number of system page table entries set aside for I/O buffer mapping and system address space. The Windows value entry (REG_EXPAND_SZ) specifies the file Windows NT uses to start the Win32 subsystem. You also can use the Optional value entry (REG_EXPAND_SZ) to list subsystems that load when the user runs an application that needs the specified subsystem.

◆ **Memory Management.** Contains the value entries listed in table A.1 to control memory paging in Windows NT.

◆ **WOW.** Includes configuration information about how 16-bit applications run under Windows NT, including Windows 3.x and MS-DOS applications. Table A.2 lists value entries in this subkey.

TABLE A.1
Memory Management Registry Value Entries

Name	Description
IoPageLockLimit	Sets the number of bytes Windows NT can load for I/O operations. If set to 0, Windows NT uses 512 KB, which is the default. (REG_DWORD)
LargeSystemCache	Determines whether Windows NT uses the system-cache working set or the processes working set. (REG_DWORD)
NonPagedPoolSize	Sets the maximum nonpaged pool size. The default is 0; the maximum is 80 percent of the installed physical RAM. (REG_DWORD)
PagedPoolSize	Sets the maximum paged pool size. The default is 0x3000000(which sets the size to 32 MB). (REG_DWORD)
PagingFiles	Sets page file information. (REG_MULTI_SZ)

Tip

The PagingFiles entry is set by using the System application in Control Panel. By default, the setting is C:\PAGEFILE.SYS 27.

TABLE A.2
WOW Registry Value Entries

Name	Description
CmdLine	Describes the configuration setting for the command line when you run a MS-DOS-based application.
LPT_timeout	Specifies amount of time after an application quits using the LPT port that Windows NT closes and clears it. (REG_SZ)
Size	Sets the amount of memory Windows NT allocates to each MS-DOS application running. Set the value to 0 for the default setting in the PIF file to be used. (REG_SZ)
Wowcmdline	Lists the configuration of the command line. These switches can be used: -a to instruct commands to pass to VDM; -f to instruct the directory to locate NTVDM.EXE; -m to hide the VDM console window; and -w to use the WOW VDM. (REG_EXPAND_SZ)
Wowsize	Specifies amount of memory for a VDM session on RISC-based computers. Wowsize is not available for an x86 computer. (REG_SZ)

CurrentControlSet\Services Registry Value Entries

The Services subkey is used to store information about file system drivers, Win32 drivers, and various device drivers. The Services subkey contains information about each service running under Windows NT. This subkey is located in the HKEY_LOCAL_MACHINE\SOFTWARE subkey. To locate many of the drivers used by Windows NT, look under the following subkey:

HKEY_LOCAL_MACHINE\SYSTEM\CurrentControlSet\Services

 Note Built-in network services in Windows NT, such as the Alerter and Browser services, can be found in the HKEY_LOCAL_MACHINE\SOFTWARE\Microsoft\Windows NT\CurrentVersion subkey in the Registry.

The following are possible value entries for this subkey:

◆ **Serial.** Defines settings you must enter manually for serial devices. The ForceFifoEnable entry enables you to set the FIFO buffer (set the value to 1). (REG_DWORD)

◆ **Mouse and Keyboard Drivers.** Displays settings for mouse and keyboard drivers. Microsoft Bus-type mouse drivers are located in the HKEY_LOCAL_MACHINE\SYSTEM\CurrentControlSet\Services\Busmouse\Parameters subkey and include the MouseDataQueueSize and SampleRate entries. The MouseDataQueueSize sets the amount of mouse events that Windows NT buffers in nonpaged pool. The SampleRate is used for sampling rates on a bus mouse device.

For a PS/2 type mouse device, Windows NT uses the i8042prt driver located under the HKEY_LOCAL_MACHINE\SYSTEM\CurrentControlSet\Services\i8042prt\Paramaters subkey. Table A.3 lists the value entries in this subkey.

TABLE A.3
PS/2 Type Mouse Driver Registry Entries

Name	Description
KeyboardDataQueueSize	Sets the amount of keyboard events Windows NT buffers in nonpaged pool. The default is 0x64 (100). (REG_DWORD)
MouseDataQueueSize	Sets the amount of mouse events Windows NT buffers in nonpaged pool. The default is 0x64 (100). (REG_DWORD)
PollStatusIterations	Sets the number of times Windows NT checks for interrupt verification. If maximum number is reached, Windows NT may report an interrupt problem. The default is 1. If you think there is a problem, check to see if the Numlock key still works. If it does, the interrupt is working fine and there might be another problem with the keyboard. (REG_DWORD)
PollingIterations	Shows how many times Windows NT polls the hardware before failing. If you have device drive problems with a device, set this value to a higher number if you receive errors about a device operation timing out. The default is 0x400. (REG_DWORD)

continues

TABLE A.3, CONTINUED
PS/2 Type Mouse Driver Registry Entries

Name	Description
PollingIterationsMaximum	Shows the maximum number of times Windows NT polls the hardware before failing when using an AT keyboard. The default is 0x2EE0. (REG_DWORD)
ResendIterations	Sets the number of times Windows NT attempts to initialize a hardware device before failing. The default is 0x3. (REG_DWORD)
SampleRate	Sets the mouse sample rate. The default is 0x3C, or 60 Hz). (REG_DWORD)

◆ **Microsoft InPort Bus Mouse Port Driver.** Specifies settings for the Microsoft Inport bus mouse located in the HKEY_LOCAL_MACHINE\SYSTEM\ CurrentControlSet\Services\Inport\Parameters subkey. The HzMode value (REG_DWORD) is used to set the sampling rate (the default is 0x2, or 50Hz). The MouseDataQueueSize value (REG_DWORD) sets the number of mouse events Windows NT buffers in nonpaged pool. The default is 0x64 (100). The SampleRate value (REG_DWORD) sets the Inport bus mouse sampling rate, which has a default of 0x32 (or 50Hz).

◆ **Microsoft Serial Mouse Port Driver.** Specifies the configuration information for a Microsoft serial mouse. These settings are in the HKEY_LOCAL_ MACHINE\SYSTEM\CurrentControlSet\Services\Sermouse]Parameters subkey. This subkey contains the MouseDataQueueSize and SampleRate value entries, as described in the preceding bulleted item.

◆ **Mouse Class Driver.** Specifies the mouse class device driver configuration. You can locate this information in the HKEY_LOCAL_ MACHINE\SYSTEM\ CurrentControlSet\Services\Mouclass\Parameters subkey. The MouseData QueueSize value (REG_DWORD) can be set here.

◆ **Keyboard Class Driver.** Specifies the keyboard class driver configuration. You can locate this information in the HKEY_LOCAL_MACHINE\SYSTEM\ CurrentControlSet\Services\Kbdclass\Parameters subkey. The KeyboardData QueueSize entry sets the number of keyboard events Windows NT buffers in nonpaged pool. The default is 0x64 (100). (REG_DWORD)

◆ **SCSI Miniport Driver.** Defines configuration settings for basic SCSI miniport drivers. You can find this value in the HKEY_LOCAL_MACHINE\SYSTEM\ CurrentControlSet\Services subkey. The DisbleDisconnects value entry (REG_DWORD) enables you to disable disconnects for your SCSI device. The default is 1. The DisableMultipleRequests value entry (REG_DWORD) instructs the SCSI miniport driver not to send multiple requests to a SCSI device. The default is 1. The DisableSynchronousTransfers value entry (REG_DWORD) enables you to disable synchronous data transfers on a SCSI bus. The default is 1. The DisableTaggedQueuing value entry (REG_DWORD) is used with SCSI-II devices to enable you to disable tagged command queuing on a host adapter. The default is 1. The DriveParameter value entry (REG_SZ) is used to specify the IRQ number of the SCSI host adapter.

◆ **Video Device Driver.** Contains value entries for Windows NT video device drivers. You can find the value entries shown in table A.4 in the HKEY_LOCAL_MACHINE\SYSTEM\CurrentControlSet\Services subkey.

TABLE A.4
Video Device Driver Registry Entries

Name	Description
DefaultSettings.BitsPerPel	Sets the number of bits per pixel for a video driver. (REG_DWORD)
DefaultSettings.Interlaced	When set to 1, instructs video driver to interlaced mode. (REG_DWORD)
DefaultSettings.Vrefresh	Specifies video refresh rate in Hertz (Hz). (REG_DWORD)
DefaultSettings.Xresolution	Sets video driver width setting in number of pixels. (REG_DWORD)
DefaultSettings.Yresolution.	Sets video driver height setting in number of pixels. (REG_DWORD)

Note You can find OpenGL (open graphics library) value entries in the HKEY_LOCAL_ MACHINE\Software\Microsoft\WindowsNT\CurrentVersion\OpenGLDrivers subkey.

Microsoft Mail Registry Value Entries

When Microsoft Mail installs under Windows NT, configuration settings are added to the Registry. Any settings created for Microsoft Mail from a previous installation are added to the Registry from the MSMAIL.INI file. After you install Microsoft Mail, run the Mail application in Control Panel to make any changes to the way Microsoft Mail works. When the Mail dialog box appears, click on the profile you want to edit, click on Properties, select Microsoft Mail from the Services tab, and click on Properties. You can find Microsoft Mail Registry value entries in the following subkey:

HKEY_CURRENT_USER\Software\Microsoft\Mail

Tip   You also can find information about the Microsoft Mail configuration in the %*SystemRoot*%\SYSTEM32\MAPISVC.INF file. The Windows Messaging subsystem information in Windows NT 4 can be located in the HKEY_CURRENT_USER\ Software\Microsoft\Windows Messaging Subsystem\Profiles*user_name*.

The following subkeys are located in \Microsoft\Mail subkey for Microsoft Mail settings.

Microsoft Mail Subkey

This subkey contains information on the Microsoft Mail, Mail transport, and name service configurations. You also can find the mailbox server path in this subkey as well. The following list summarizes the value entries in this subkey:

- ◆ **CheckLatencyInterval.** Specifies the length of time for the latency interval for spooling activities. (REG_SZ).

- ◆ **DemosEnabled.** If you have mail demos, you can place a Demos command on the Help menu in Microsoft Mail. To enable this, enter a 1. (REG_SZ)

- ◆ **ExportMmffile.** Specifies path to a Microsoft Mail folder (MMF) that was last exported. (REG_SZ)

- ◆ **FixedFont.** Specifies the body text font and font size for Microsoft Mail. The default is 9 point Courier New. (REG_SZ)

- ◆ **ForceScanInterval.** Sets the time (in seconds) for mail spooler latency checking. (REG_SZ)

- ◆ **GALOnly.** Sets the Global Address Book to display when this value entry is set to 1. (REG_SZ)

- ◆ **IdleRequiredInterval.** Specifies the mail spooler latency checking time (in seconds) for allowing foreground work to process uninterrupted by background work. (REG_SZ)

◆ **Lang.** Specifies Japanese if not set to USA. (REG_SZ)

◆ **LocalMMF.** Sets path of user's MMF file (mail message file) when user initially runs Microsoft Mail. (REG_SZ)

◆ **Login.** Specifies the default user name that appears in the Mail Sign In dialog box. (REG_SZ)

◆ **MailBeep.** Sets the sound file used to announce a new mail message is received. Must be set to the path of a WAV file. (REG_SZ)

◆ **MailTmp.** Sets the folder for Mail to temporarily store attached files. (REG_SZ)

◆ **MAPIHELP.** Sets the path for the help file associated with MAPI functions. (REG_SZ)

◆ **MigrateIni.** Denotes if Windows NT should use settings in Microsoft Mail INI files. The default setting is 1, which enables this setting. (REG_SZ)

◆ **MigrateIniPrint.** Denotes if Windows NT should use settings in Microsoft Mail INI files for printing configurations. The default setting is 1, which enables this setting. (REG_SZ)

◆ **NetBios.** Specifies if Windows NT sends a message to a NetBIOS computer that a mail message has been sent to that machine. (REG_SZ)

◆ **NewMsgsAtStartup.** Sets Microsoft Mail to check for new mail messages when the user launches Mail. (REG_SZ)

◆ **NextOnMoveDelete.** Specifies Microsoft Mail to display the next message after a user moves or deletes a message. Set this value to 1 to enable it. (REG_SZ)

◆ **NormalFont.** Specifies the default font to display Microsoft Mail messages. The default is Helvetica (Helv) 10 point. (REG_SZ)

◆ **NoServerOptions.** Specifies if users can set MMMF file path properties. Set this value entry to 1 to enable this setting. (REG_SZ)

◆ **OfflineMessages.** Specifies the path for storing mail messages in a folder other the post office. (REG_SZ)

◆ **OldStorePath.** Specifies the path of a file you are in the process of moving. Windows NT removes this entry at the completion of the move. (REG_SZ)

◆ **Password.** Specifies the logon password. If left blank, you need to provide a password each time you log on. (REG_SZ)

◆ **PollingInterval.** Specifies interval that Microsoft Mail waits to check for new mail messages on the server. (REG_SZ)

◆ **Printing.** Specifies default printer used by Microsoft Mail. (REG_SZ)

◆ **PumpCycleInterval.** Specifies the time interval for a mail spooler to check for new mail. This can be set to occur more than once per minute or at an interval other the PollingInterval time set by the user.

◆ **ReplyPrefix.** Specifies that original message content is included with new message, but is denoted by a prefix character, such as <<. (REG_SZ)

◆ **ScanAgainInterval.** Specifies the spooler latency checking interval if spooler must perform actions associated with higher priority tasks. (REG_SZ)

◆ **Security.** Specifies that you must reenter a password each time the Mail window is changed from an icon view to a window view. (REG_SZ)

◆ **ServerPassword.** Specifies the server password for a server established in the ServerPath value entry. (REG_SZ)

◆ **ServerPath.** Sets the postoffice folder path. This entry includes one of three different formats: *pathname*; *server_name\share_name\path password*; and *server_name/ share_name:path*. (REG_SZ)

Stop Do not include a password in the ServerPath value entry if you specify one in the Security value entry.

◆ **SharedExtensionsDir.** Specifies the path for shared Mail extensions. (REG_SZ)

◆ **SharedFolders.** Specifies the path for shared Mail folders. (REG_SZ)

◆ **SpoolerBackoffInterval.** Sets the time (in milliseconds) for mail spooler to wait between a failed attempt and a new attempt. This setting is used for mail server problems when the server is running, such as file problems. (REG_SZ)

◆ **SpoolerReconnectInterval.** Sets the time (in seconds) for mail spooler to wait between a failed attempt and a new attempt. This setting is used for mail server problems when the server has problems or not logged onto the network. (REG_SZ)

- ◆ **WG.** Denotes version of Microsoft Mail as the one provided with Windows NT. (REG_SZ)

- ◆ **Window.** Denotes the window position of the Microsoft Mail main window. (REG_SZ)

Address Book Subkey

The Address Book subkey contains configuration information about the user's Address Book, including the default address directory. You can find this subkey in the Registry as follows:

HKEY_CURRENT_USER\Software\Microsoft\Mail\Address Book

Microsoft Mail File (MMF) Subkey

This subkey contains configuration information about the MMF file, which automatically compresses the Microsoft Mail message file. If you enable this feature, Windows NT compresses the MMF during idle processor time to help you regain disk space. The path for this Registry subkey is as follows:

HKEY_CURRENT_USER\Software\Microsoft\Mail\MMF

The following are value entries associated with the MMF subkey:

- ◆ **Kb_Free_Start_Compress.** Specifies the amount of free space (in kilobytes) in a message file that is to be detected before the background compression begins. (REG_SZ)

- ◆ **Kb_Free_Stop_Compress.** Specifies the amount of free space (in kilobytes) in a message file when the background compression should stop. (REG_SZ)

- ◆ **No_Compress.** Denotes that background compression is turned on or off. Set this value to 0 to enable background compression. (REG_SZ)

- ◆ **Percent_Free_Start_Compress.** Specifies the amount of free space (in percentage of total file size) in a message file when background compression starts. The default is 10 percent. (REG_SZ)

- ◆ **Percent_Free_Stop_Compress.** Specifies the amount of free space (in percentage of total file size) in a message file when background compression stops. The default is 5 percent. (REG_SZ)

- ◆ **Secs_Till_Fast_Compress.** Specifies when the background compression fast mode or slow mode is to be used. Background compression starts in slow mode, changes to fast mode after the number of seconds you denote here passes, and then returns to slow mode after any user activity on the computer. The default is 600 seconds of inactivity. (REG_SZ)

Microsoft Schedule+ Entries

This key defines the appearance and behavior of Microsoft Schedule+, which is available with Microsoft Exchange and previous versions of Windows NT. You can find the following value entries in this subkey:

HKEY_CURRENT_USER\Software\Microsoft\Schedule+\MicrosoftSchedule+

- ◆ **CopyTime.** Sets the time interval (in minutes) for Schedule+ to copy an online CAL file to a local CAL file during idle processor time. The default is 15 minutes. (REG_SZ)

- ◆ **CreateFileFirstTime.** Denotes if Schedule+ creates an online calendar file for a first time user. The default is 0, which does not create an online calendar. (REG_SZ)

- ◆ **PollTime.** Sets time (in centiseconds) for Schedule+ to check the server of schedule file changes. The default is 6000 centiseconds, which is one minute. (REG_SZ)

- ◆ **ReminderPollTime.** Sets the time (in minutes) for Schedule+ to poll the server for alarm changes. Specifies the frequency for polling the server for alarm changes. The default is 15 minutes. (REG_SZ)

- ◆ **UpdatePostOfficeTime.** Sets time (in centiseconds) for Schedule+ to poll the server post office when a change is made. The default is 6000 centiseconds, which is one minute. (REG_SZ)

User Preferences Registry Value Entries

The following sections describe Registry value entries that pertain to user preferences, such as desktop settings, keyboard configurations, and more.

Tip Use the Windows NT Control Panel, Administrative Tools (Common), the System Policy Editor, and other tools to make user preferences changes before modifying the Registry settings shown here.

The value entries in the following sections are located in the HKEY_CURRENT_USER subkey for the user currently logged on. For default user settings, look in the HKEY_USERS\.DEFAULT subkey.

Console Value Entries for Users

The Console subkey includes font, cursor, and screen control values in the HKEY_CURRENT_USER\Console Registry subkey. The following are value entries included in this subkey:

- ◆ **FullScreen.** Specifies screen mode. To set to full screen mode, use 1. Use 0 for window mode. The default is 0 (0x0). (REG_DWORD)

- ◆ **HistoryBufferSize.** Sets buffer size for number of commands stored in history buffer. The default is 0x32. (REG_DWORD)

- ◆ **NumberOfHistoryBuffers.** Sets number of history buffers associated with console. The default is 0x4. (REG_DWORD)

- ◆ **QuickEdit.** Sets quick edit mode. The default is 0, which disables quick edit. (REG_DWORD)

- ◆ **ScreenBufferSize.** Sets console screen buffer size. The default is 0x00190050. (REG_DWORD)

- ◆ **WindowSize.** Sets console window size. The default is 0x00190050. (REG_DWORD)

Desktop Value Entries for Users

The Windows NT Desktop subkey includes value entries that determine the appearance of the screen background and the position of windows and icons on the screen. You can find these entries in the following Registry subkey:

HKEY_CURRENT_USER\Control Panel\Desktop

The Desktop subkey contains the following entries:

- ◆ **BorderWidth.** Specifies the window border widths for windows you can resize. This settings affects how fast windows repaint on your screen. For the narrowest margin use 1; for widest use 49. The default is 3. (REG_SZ)

- ◆ **CoolSwitch.** Specifies that the user can use the Alt+Tab task switching feature. The default is 1, which turns it on. (REG_SZ)

- ◆ **CursorBlinkRate.** Specifies cursor blink rate in milliseconds. The default is 530 milliseconds. (REG_SZ)

- ◆ **ScreenSaveActive.** Specifies whether a screen saver turns on when the display has been inactive for a specified amount of time. The default is 0, which disables the screen saver feature. (REG_SZ)

◆ **ScreenSaveTimeOut.** Sets the amount of time before a screen saver turns on when the display has been inactive for the specified amount of time. The default is 900 seconds. (REG_SZ)

◆ **TileWallpaper.** Sets the way in which wallpaper displays on the desktop. Use 1 to tile the wallpaper and 0 to center it. The default is 0. (REG_SZ)

Keyboard Value Entries for Users

The Keyboard subkey in the Registry determines the keyboard configuration for the selected computer. You can find this subkey in the following location:

HKEY_CURRENT_USER\Control Panel\Keyboard

Note You can find Registry settings for a user's keyboard layout in the HKEY_ CURRENT_USER\Control Panel\Keyboard Layout subkey. These settings are based on HKEY_LOCAL_MACHINE\SYSTEM\CurrentControlSet\Control\NLS\ KeyboardLayout subkey.

The following value entries appear in this subkey:

◆ **KeyboardDelay.** Specifies keyboard repeat rate. In general, 0 represents 250 milliseconds, and 3 represents 1 second, with a 20 percent accuracy. Default is 1. (REG_SZ)

◆ **KeyboardSpeed.** Specifies how quickly a character repeats on the display when you hold down the character's key. Generally, 0 represents 2 per second, and 31 represents 30 per second. Default is 31. (REG_SZ)

Mouse Value Entries for Users

User's mouse configuration information is stored in the following subkey in the Registry:

HKEY_CURRENT_USER\Control Panel\Mouse

The following value entries are located in this subkey:

◆ **ActiveWindowTracking.** Enables the active window tracking feature, which displays a line on-screen as you move the mouse. The default is 0, which turns off this feature. (REG_SZ)

◆ **DoubleClickSpeed.** Specifies the double-click rate in milliseconds. The default is 686 milliseconds. (REG_SZ)

◆ **MouseSpeed.** Specifies the relationship between the mouse and cursor movement when the MouseThreshold1 or MouseThreshold2 value entry is met. When set to 0, there is no acceleration. For twice the normal cursor speed when the movement surpasses the Mouse Threshold values, set this value to 1. For accelerations of twice the normal speed of MouseThreshold1, and four time the speed of MouseThreshold2, set this value to 2.

◆ **MouseThreshold1 and MouseThreshold2.** Specify the maximum number of pixels the mouse moves between mouse interrupts before the system alters mouse and cursor movement relationship based on the MouseSpeed setting. The defaults are MouseThreshold1=6 and MouseThreshold2=10. (REG_SZ)

◆ **SnapToDefaultButton.** Specifies that the mouse cursor jumps to the default button in a dialog box. The default is 0, which disables this feature. (REG_SZ)

◆ **SwapMouseButtons.** Changes the left and right mouse buttons. Use 1 to swap the buttons. The default is 0. (REG_SZ)

Network Entries for Users

You can find user preference information in the Registry at the following location. The information found in this subkey is used by Windows NT administrative tools, such as User Manager for Domains, Event Viewer, and Server Manager.

HKEY_LOCAL_MACHINE\SOFTWARE\Microsoft\Windows NT\CurrentVersion\ Network\Shared Parameters

◆ **Slow Mode.** Includes information about the servers and domains that are on a low-speed connection.

The Perfmon subkey contains the DataTimeOut value entries under the HKEY_CURRENT_USER\SOFTWARE\Microsoft\Perfmon subkey. This entry determines the amount of time the Performance Monitor waits for thread information on a remote computer. The default is 20000 milliseconds. (REG_DWORD)

Program Manager Entries for Users

You can find Program Manager Registry information in the Registry at the following subkey. These settings are useful if you use the Program Manager interface that Windows NT 3.x used.

HKEY_CURRENT_USER\Software\Microsoft\Windows NT\CurrentVersion\ Program Manager\

In this subkey, you have the following subkeys:

◆ Common Groups

◆ Restrictions

◆ Settings

◆ UNICODE Groups

The value entries in the Restrictions subkey are as follows:

◆ **EditLevel.** Enables you to set restrictions on what users can change in the Windows NT environment, such as adding, deleting, or moving program groups, and changing program item information. The default is 0, which does not impose any user-level restrictions. (REG_DWORD)

◆ **NoClose.** Disables the shutdown commands in Windows NT. The default is 0, which does not disable this feature. (REG_DWORD)

◆ **NoFileMenu.** Disables the File menu on Program Manager. (REG_DWORD)

◆ **NoRun.** Removes the Run command from the File menu on Program Manager. (REG_DWORD)

◆ **NoSaveSettings.** Enables you to turn off the save settings on Exit command in the Options menu on Program Manager. (REG_DWORD)

◆ **Restrictions.** Enables or disables the restrictions you set up. (REG_DWORD)

The Settings subkey includes the following value entries:

◆ **AutoArrange.** Sets Program Manager to automatically arrange the icons in the program groups. (REG_DWORD)

◆ **CheckBinaryTimeout.** Sets the auto-check delay time and turns on and off the Run in Separate Memory Space option. (REG_DWORD)

◆ **CheckBinaryType.** Turns on or off the binary type feature. (REG_DWORD)

◆ **display.dr.** Specifies the video driver setting. (REG_SZ)

◆ **MinOnRun.** Sets Program Manager to display as an icon when you execute a program. The default is 1, which minimizes Program Manager. (REG_DWORD)

◆ **SaveSetttings.** Sets Windows NT to save settings when you exit Program Manger. The default is 1, which enables this feature. (REG_DWORD)

◆ **Window.** Defines the on-screen placement of the Program Manager window. The default is 68 63 636 421 1. The final 1 indicates that the window is maximized. (REG_SZ)

Recovery Value Entries for Users

You can find the Registry value entries that set how Windows NT is to behave during a system STOP error (also called a system crash) in the following subkey:

HKEY_LOCAL_MACHINE\SYSTEM\CurrentControlSet\Control\CrashControl

The value entries you are likely to find under this subkey are as follows:

◆ **AutoReboot.** Instructs Windows NT to automatically reboot the computer. (REG_DWORD)

◆ **CrashDumpEnabled.** Enables you to send debugging information to a log file when a STOP error occurs. The default is 1, which enables this feature. (REG_DWORD)

◆ **LogEvent.** Instructs Windows NT to write events to a system log. The default is 1 (enabled) for Windows NT Server and 0 (disabled) for Windows NT Workstation. (REG_DWORD)

◆ **Overwrite.** Instructs Windows NT to write over an existing log file when set to 1. The default for Windows NT Server is 1 and 0 for Windows NT Workstation. (REG_DWORD)

◆ **SendAlert.** Specifies if an alert is sent to the administrator in the event of a crash. The default is 1 (enabled) for Windows NT Server and 0 (disabled) for Windows NT Workstation. (REG_DWORD)

Windows Value Entries for Users

You can find user settings from the WIN.INI file in the following Registry subkey:

HKEY_CURRENT_USER\Software\Microsoft\Windows NT\CurrentVersion\Windows

◆ **Documents.** Lists only those file extensions for documents not listed in the Extensions subkey. (REG_SZ)

◆ **DosPrint.** Instructs Windows NT to use DOS interrupts for printing. The default is No. (REG_SZ)

◆ **ErrorMode.** Specifies the way in which Windows NT controls error messages. (REG_DWORD)

◆ **load.** Instructs Windows NT which applications to run as icons at startup. The default is to have no applications listed. (REG_SZ)

◆ **NetMessage.** Specifies to Windows NT whether a message is displayed if the correct network is running, or if a network is not running that is configured to run. The default is No, for no message. (REG_SZ)

◆ **NullPort.** Lists the null ports that run under Windows NT.

◆ **Programs.** Lists application extensions (such as EXE, BAT, and COM) that Windows NT handles as applications. (REG_SZ)

◆ **run.** Instructs Windows NT which applications to run at startup. The default is to have no applications listed. (REG_SZ)

Registry Value Entries for Windows NT Subsystems

The Windows NT Registry contains subkeys for controlling the way in which Windows NT subsystems run applications. These subsystems include the following:

◆ **Windows.** Instructs Windows NT how to run Windows 3.x applications.

◆ **WOW.** Includes settings from the SYSTEM.INI file from Windows 3.x.

◆ **OS/2.** Includes settings for running OS/2 1.0 applications on Windows NT.

The Windows subsystem information is found in the following subkey:

HKEYLOCALMACHINE/SOFTWARE\Microsoft\Windows NT\CurrentVersion\ Windows

It contains the following value entries:

◆ **AppInit_DLLs.** Instructs that all of the specified DLLs are to be attached to all Windows-based applications. (REG_SZ)

◆ **DeviceNotSelected Timeout.** Sets the time (in seconds) the system waits for a device to be turned on, such as a printer. The default is 15 seconds. (REG_SZ)

◆ **Spooler.** Sets the application to use the Print Manager. If set to Yes, the application uses it. If set to No, does not use it. The default is Yes. (REG_SZ)

◆ **swapdisk.** Specifies the swap disk path for Windows 3.x applications to use. By default, the folder specified in the TEMP environment is used. Or, if the TEMP environment is not established, the boot directory of the hard disk is used, such as C:\. (REG_SZ)

◆ **TransmissionRetryTimeout.** Sets the time (in seconds) that the application retries a failed transmission by Print Manager. The default is 45 seconds. (REG_SZ)

The OS/2 version 1 software Registry value entries are located under the following subkey:

HKEY_LOCAL_MACHINE\SOFTWARE\Microsoft\OS/2 Subsystem for NT\1.0

The OS/2 Subsystem for NT\1.0 subkey can contain many subkeys and value entries. Initially, the config.sys and os2.ini are the only subkeys available. Under the config.sys subkey are the following value entries:

◆ **config.sys.** Contains a sample of what the OS/2 subkeys can include. (REG_MULTI_SZ)

◆ **Flags.** Includes any system flags for the OS/2 subsystem. (REG_DWORD)

Tip   You can disable the OS/2 subsystem in Windows NT by changing the GlobalFlag setting in the HKEY_LOCAL_MACHINE\SYSTEM\CurrentControlSet\Control\ Session Manager subkey to **20100000**.

Finally, the WOW subsystem is located in the following subkey:

HKEY_LOCAL_MACHINE\SOFTWARE\Microsoft\WindowsNT\CurrentVersion\ WOW

The individual settings for this subkey are contained in the SYSTEM.INI file and are discussed in detail in Chapter 3, "Understanding the Role of Initialization Files in the Windows NT Registry."

About the Software on the CD-ROM

Included with this book is a CD-ROM that includes applications to help you view and modify the Windows NT Registry. To use any of the files provided on the CD-ROM, create a folder on your Windows NT system and copy the selected application and any corresponding files to the new folder. The easiest way to do this is to open Explorer, create a main folder called REG-TOOL or something similar, and then copy the entire folder for the application you want to use.

All of the applications included are either shareware or freeware. If you like the application and want to continue using it, read the accompanying help files or licensing agreements to find out how to register and, in some cases, pay for the license to continue using the product. The programs included on the *Windows NT Registry Troubleshooting* CD-ROM are not registered versions.

 Stop Although the utilities included on the enclosed CD-ROM have been tested to function as stated in the product literature, you might experience problems using them on your system. For this reason, always make a back up of your Registry before using these utilities. You also should back up your entire system periodically in case you need to reinstall some or all of your files.

The following sections provide a general description of each utility and a short overview of the type of tasks you can perform with each. For specific information about installing and using each utility, see the help files and instructions that accompany each utility.

Somarsoft Utilities

The enclosed CD-ROM includes four separate utilities from Somarsoft, which include the following:

- ◆ **DumpReg.** Enables you to display Registry values in a window, like the one shown in figure B.1. By default, you can select to display the HKEY_LOCAL_ MACHINE, HKEY_USERS, or HKEY_CURRENT_USER hives. You also can filter the data that displays, such as displaying only those items that match certain criteria. DumpReg also enables you to view and sort Registry information according to the modification time. With DumpReg, you can search, view, and print Registry data, but you cannot modify Registry settings. DumpReg is located in the DUMPREG folder on the *Windows NT Registry Troubleshooting* CD-ROM.

- ◆ **DumpAcl.** Enables you to view the Access Control List (ACL) in Windows NT for users and groups (see fig. B.2). DumpAcl provides a list of the permissions and audit settings for the Registry, file system, printers, and shares. You might want to use DumpAcl to determine which Registry keys have auditing and security permissions applied to them. By viewing the DumpAcl report, you can quickly see if a key or file has a security or auditing permission setting. DumpAcl is located in the DUMPACL folder on the *Windows NT Registry Troubleshooting* CD-ROM.

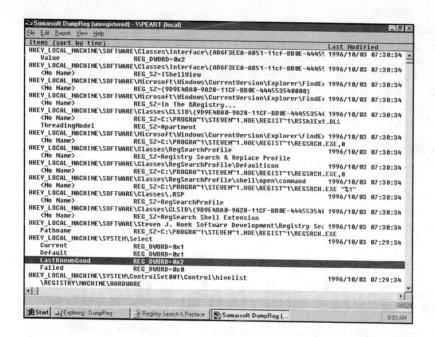

Figure B.1

DumpReg is an alternative to the Windows NT Registry Editor to view Registry values.

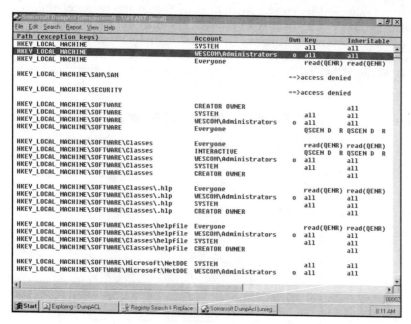

Figure B.2

DumpAcl can be used to view which Registry keys are set up with auditing or security permissions.

◆ **DumpEvt.** Enables you to dump the Windows NT event log into a file to import into a database. You can import the event log into Microsoft Access or SQL Server databases to create reports, run queries, and view event logs in easy to read format. DumpEvt is ideal for auditing Registry activities on networks in which event logs become too large to view daily with the Event Viewer. After you dump the event log, you also can clear it using DumpEvt. DumpEvt is located in the DUMPEVT folder on the *Windows NT Registry Troubleshooting* CD-ROM.

◆ **RegEdit.** Enables you to find and edit specific Registry keys in Windows NT. RegEdit is a Dynamic Link Library (DLL) file you use with Visual Basic or Visual Basic for Excel 95 to modify all Windows NT user profiles at once. This enables you to make global changes to several user profiles with a single VB or VBA program, rather than editing individual Registries for all users. RegEdit is located in the RGEDIT folder on the *Windows NT Registry Troubleshooting* CD-ROM.

Registry Search and Replace V. 2.0

This utility enables you to search for a specific Registry setting in Windows NT and replace the current value with a new one. With Registry Search and Replace, you enter search data and select search criteria on the General tab (see fig. B.3). You then can set advanced settings to isolate your search to specific types of information to find—values or data. You also can select options to search for data types (REG_SZ, REG_EXPAND_SZ, and REG_MULTI_SZ), hives, and whether the Registry is local or remote.

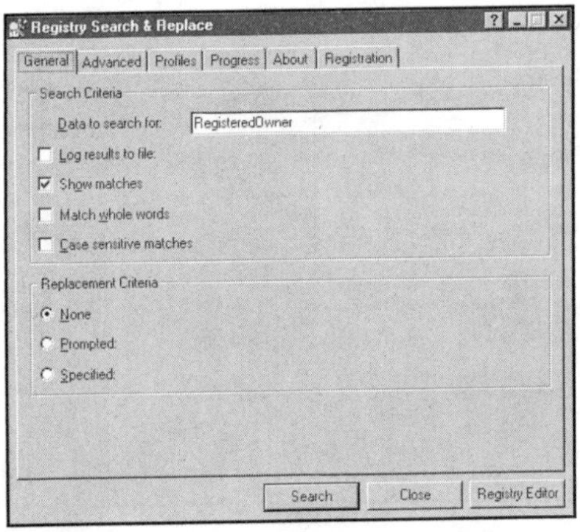

Figure B.3

Registry Search and Replace simplifies the task of locating and modifying Registry settings.

Registry Search and Replace is located in the REGSRCH folder on the *Windows NT Registry Troubleshooting* CD-ROM.

Registry Class Browser

The Registry Class Browser utility enables you to display each CLSID (Class ID) on you system. CLSID subkeys are located in the HKEY_CLASSES_ROOT subkey. With Registry Class Browser, you can display and print details for each class, including key, data type, and value. You also can get the class name and class ID for each class. Figure B.4 shows an example of the Dial-Up Phonebook class.

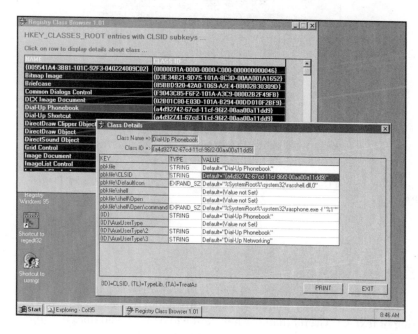

Figure B.4

To quickly obtain the class name and class ID for Windows NT classes, use the Registry Class Browser.

Registry Class Browser is located in the REGCL101 folder on the *Windows NT Registry Troubleshooting* CD-ROM.

Registry Surfer

Registry Surfer is used to search key names, values, and value data in the Registry. You can specify to find whole words only, match case, and run minimized as an icon during the search procedure. Once Registry Surfer locates the matching data, you can view and print the information (see fig. B.5).

Figure B.5

Registry Surfer is an easy-to-use utility to view and print Registry data.

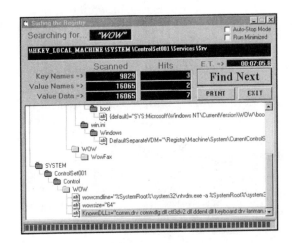

Registry Surfer is located in the REGSURF folder on the *Windows NT Registry Troubleshooting* CD-ROM.

CC Grep

Grep is a Unix command that enables you to search for keywords in a file. With CC Grep (see fig. B.6), you can search an exported Registry file to find a specific word, phrase, or string of text. CC Grep is handy when Notepad or WordPad does not find the string or data you are looking for in an exported Registry file.

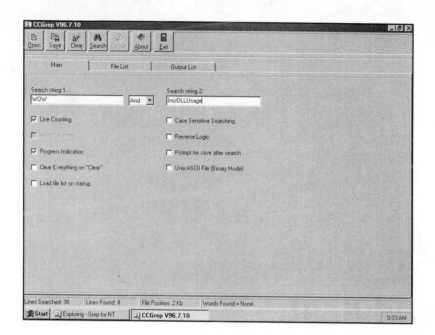

Figure B.6

You can use CC Grep to locate search strings in exported Registry files.

CC Grep is located in the CCGREP folder on the *Windows NT Registry Troubleshooting* CD-ROM.

Finding More Information

There are two fundamental reasons why the Registry poses so many problems. First, it is a difficult system to understand. It is full of arbitrary and intimidating information that is not designed for everyone to tinker with. Second, not much information has been written about it. Microsoft technical support refuses to answer questions about the Registry.

This appendix is designed to help you locate other Registry sources if you need to supplement the information in this book.

Microsoft Download Service

The Microsoft Download Service is an electronic bulletin board you can contact with a modem that contains support files, device drivers, and utilities that were not included on the Windows NT disks. The phone number is 206-936-6735. To access the service, you need a modem that is set to 8 data bits, 1 stop bit, and no parity. You also need a communications program, such as HyperTerminal.

The cost to you is the amount of long-distance charges you spend hooking up. If you are downloading small drivers and documents, the call is worth the price. Sometimes Microsoft includes beta software on the site that you can download (if you are an approved beta site tester). When you first call in, you'll need to answer some standard questions, and then you can move on.

If you are member of CompuServe, you can access the Microsoft Download Service from there by typing in **GO MSDL**.

Microsoft's Online Presence

Microsoft is making huge strides into different parts of the online community. It has a huge presence on the World Wide Web, has Usenet newsgroups devoted to Windows NT, and has various mailing lists to which you can subscribe. Microsoft also has its own commercial online service, the Microsoft Network, but much of that content is being moved to the World Wide Web. You won't find a better round-table discussion than what takes place in Microsoft's various Usenet newsgroups. Many times you can find out specific answers to problems you've been struggling with for days or weeks.

The following is a quick look at how to find out what Microsoft offers at each of the online services:

◆ **World Wide Web.** Connect to http://www.microsoft.com.

◆ **E-mail.** To subscribe to the monthly WinNews newsletter, send an e-mail message to enews@microsoft.nwnet.com. Include the words **subscribe winnews** in your message body. Nothing else. Also, do not include a subject for the message. For developer information, you can send e-mail to devwire@microsoft.nwnet.com with "Subscribe DevWire" in the message body.

◆ **FTP through the Internet.** Connect to ftp.microsoft.com and access the / PerOpSys/Win_News directory.

◆ **America Online.** Use the keyword winnews to locate the WinNews area.

◆ **CompuServe.** GO WINNEWS.

◆ **GEnie.** Check the WinNews area under the Windows 95 RTC.

◆ **Prodigy.** jump winnews.

◆ **Microsoft Network (MSN).** On Microsoft menu, select Windows NT and click WINNEWS. You also can access the Microsoft Knowledge Base on MSN.

Microsoft Knowledge Base and Developer's Knowledge Base

The Microsoft Knowledge Base (MSKB) is a source for a broad range of technical knowledge about Microsoft products. The following are some general topics:

◆ Answers to frequently asked questions

◆ Technical articles

◆ Bug lists and fixes

◆ Listings of downloadable files

◆ Technical documentation updates

◆ Microsoft Developer Knowledge Base that includes programming information

The Knowledge Base is available in a variety of sources, including the Microsoft Developer Network CD and the Microsoft TechNet CD. These are subscription-based technical products sent to subscribers on a regular basis.

You also can find the Knowledge Base on the World Wide Web at http:// www.microsoft.com/kb (see fig. C.1).

Figure C.1

The Knowledge Base includes answers to many of your problems.

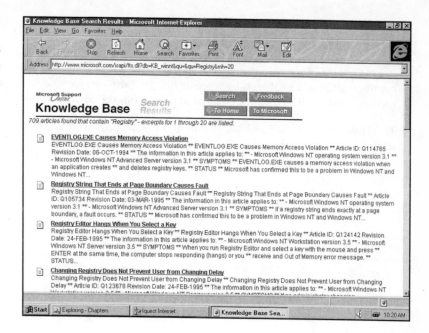

The Knowledge Base is also found on CompuServe, the Microsoft Network, and the Microsoft Download Service.

Microsoft TechNet

TechNet is a CD-ROM subscription service designed for people who support users of Microsoft products, administer networks, and must remain current with topics. The TechNet package contains two CDs and is updated monthly. For information about subscribing, call 800-344-2121.

Microsoft Developer Network

The Microsoft Developer Network is a three-tiered subscription service designed for programmers. It includes updates to development tools and programming information distributed on CD-ROM, a printed newsletter, and access to World Wide Web content. Call 800-759-5474 for information about subscribing to this service.

Microsoft FastTips

Microsoft FastTips is an automated, toll-free service that provides quick answers to common technical problems by voice or fax. You also can use the FastTips service to receive fax or mail delivery of popular articles from the Microsoft Knowledge Base.

To get the most out of FastTips, you should first acquire a "map" of the system and a technical library catalog of topics. To access FastTips or receive a map and catalog, call the FastTips number listed for your product of interest, as shown in table C.1.

TABLE C.1
FastTips Numbers

Product	Number
Desktop applications	(800) 936-4100
Microsoft home products	(800) 936-4100
Personal operating systems	(800) 936-4200
Development tools products	(800) 936-4300
Business systems	(800) 936-4400

Troubleshooting Specific Windows 95 Problems in the Registry

I n Chapter 7, "Administering Remote Registries from Windows NT," you learn how the Windows 95 Registry is different from the Windows NT Registry, as well as how to use the Registry to find specific entries and values. You also learn how to use some of the other tools Windows 95 provides to let you configure and troubleshoot your Windows 95 installation, including the System Policy Editor and user profiles.

As a network administrator there comes a point, however, when you have to go straight to the source and edit some Windows 95 Registry settings directly. This might be due to bugs in the software, hidden features that only the application programmer is aware of, or a new way of using an old feature. You'll find in this appendix a collection of specific problems users have encountered in Window 95 clients.

In this appendix, you learn the following:

◆ How to modify Registry settings relating to networking problems

◆ How to modify Registry settings relating to Internet problems

◆ How to modify Registry settings to customize the Windows 95 environment

Internet and Networking Issues

One of the more complicated aspects of any computing environment is getting two machines communicating with one another. Invariably you'll have problems. When you start adding to the number of PCs that must interconnect, problems really start surfacing. Finally, when you throw in the massive network of the Internet, with its TCP/IP requirements and loads of traffic, you might need some help adjusting some of Windows 95's settings. This section looks at some of the problems users have encountered.

Stop Before you make any changes to the Windows 95 Registry, make a backup copy of the SYSTEM.DAT and USER.DAT files. These are hidden files stored in the Windows 95 folder that contain all the Registry settings. Also, you should understand how to use the Windows 95 Registry Editor (REGEDIT.EXE), as discussed in Chapter 7, "Administering Remote Registries from Windows NT."

Also, to edit a remote or local Windows 95 Registry, you must be logged on to the network from a Windows 95 machine. You cannot make changes to a Windows 95 Registry from a Windows NT computer. In this chapter, when the instruction reads to open or start the Registry Editor, it is implied to mean the Windows 95 Registry (REGEDIT.EXE).

Renaming a Windows 95 User upon Logon

If you want to have a user name appear when a network logon dialog box displays, use these instructions. What this will do is display the user name instead of the user's real name. The name that appears in the logon dialog box is the one assigned to the user policy.

1. Open the Registry Editor and locate the HKEY_CURRENT_USER\
   Remote access\Profile*net_name* subkey. The *net_name* parameter in this case is
   the name of your connection.

2. In the right pane, edit the User value to reflect the name you want to appear when the logon dialog box displays.

3. Shut down and restart Windows 95.

Enabling Routing in Windows 95

You will not find a routing protocol in the Microsoft TCP/IP version in Windows 95. To enable static routine in Windows 95, you'll need to change or add the EnableRouting= value to the HKEY_LOCAL_MACHINE\System\CurrentControlSet\Services\VxD\MSTCP subkey.

The default for this value is 0. Change the value to 1 to enable it.

Adding SNMP Communities

To add Simple Network Management Protocol (SNMP) communities on your system, open the Registry Editor and locate the HKEY_LOCAL_MACHINE\System\CurrentControlSet\Services\SNMP\Parameters\TrapConfiguration key. Next, create a new key and input a name that you want as a new community.

Create new string values for each console to which the SNMP sends traps. Value names need to be numerical starting at 1 and increasing, such as 2, 3, and so on. The value data you input is the IP or IPX address of the SNMP console to which traps are sent.

Shut down and restart Windows 95.

Removing Remote Agents

The Network option in the Control Panel gives you easy access to removing network service agents. Normally, you modify policies in the System Policy Editor to turn off services.

For the SNMP agent and some others, you must go directly into the Registry to remove them. You can find these agents in the HKEY_LOCAL_MACHINE\Software\Microsoft\Windows\CurrentVersion\RunServices and \Run subkeys.

Resetting DNS Lookup Time for WINS

You can reset the time allotted for a Domain Name Service (DNS) lookup when you are attached to the World Wide Web. Many Web sites are so busy that DNS lookup times are too short to allow for traffic congestion. You can change the NameSrvQueryTimeout value entry to give you more DNS lookup time. This only works if you are using the Microsoft WINS service. It does not work with regular DNS.

Disabling DNS for WINS Resolution

You can use the Registry to disable the DNS for WINS resolution in Windows 95. The default setting for this in Windows 95 is on. By disabling the NetBIOS name resolution on a DNS system, you can still keep other DNS functionality. To do this, use the following instructions:

1. Open the Registry Editor and locate the HKEY_LOCAL_MACHINE\ System\CurrentControlSet\Services subkey.

2. Next, drill down to the \VxD\MSTCP key.

3. Change EnableDNS value entry from 1 to 0. This turns off the enable DNS feature.

4. Shut down and restart Windows 95.

Handling Problems with Sending Mail and News

If you encounter problems in Windows 95 with sending mail, posting newsgroup items, or uploading via FTP, look to the Registry for answers.

1. Open the Registry Editor and locate HKEY_LOCAL_MACHINE\ System\CurrentControlSet\Services\VxD\MSTCP.

2. Set the PMTUBlackHoleDetect value entry to 0 or 1. The default is 0.

3. Set the PMTUDiscovery value entry to 0 or 1, which is the default. This setting specifies whether Microsoft TCP/IP will do a path MTU discovery.

4. Shut down and restart Windows 95.

Note   The PMTUBlackHoleDetect value determines whether the stack attempts to detect MTU routers that do not send back ICMP fragmentation messages.

You can find more out about the MTU discovery by reading the Internet RFC 1191 document.

Removing the Network Neighborhood Icon

You can use the System Policy Editor to hide the Network Neighborhood icon from selected users' desktops. When you remove the icon, you do not affect any of the actual networking components that you've configured.

To do this, use the following steps:

1. Start the System Policy Editor.

2. Select Open, Registry.

3. Double-click on the Local User icon.

4. Select Shell.

5. Select Restrictions.

6. Select Hide Network Neighborhood.

When the specified user logs on the next time, the Network Neighborhood will not display on the desktop.

Looking at Hostname Resolution Order

The default hostname resolution order is shown in the Registry key HKEY_LOCAL_ MACHINE\System\CurrentControlSet\Services\VxD\MSTCP\ServiceProvider. The following values are the default settings in Windows 95:

LocalPriority=499

HostsPriority=500

DNSPriority=2000

NetbtPriority=2001

Tip When you look at these values, the lower number sets a higher priority for name resolution. These settings are used for 16-bit Windows Sockets. These Sockets need to rely on the resolvers that are expected to take the least amount of time.

Importing Large Keys into the Registry

Besides being very difficult to work with, the real-mode Registry Editor has trouble importing large keys. The following two error messages might display if you import a Registry file while running REGEDIT.EXE at the DOS prompt:

```
Unable to open registry (14) - SYSTEM.DAT
```

or

```
Error accessing the registry: The file may not be complete.
```

If you look at the HKEY_CLASSES_ROOT key of the Registry, you'll notice a lot of entries within that hierarchy. This is primarily due to the number of applications you have installed (or have ever installed) under Windows 95. According to Microsoft, the only way to work around this problem is to try not to use the real-mode Registry Editor.

You might also export branches of the Registry periodically so that you break up the file into its component pieces. This way, when you use REGEDIT.EXE in real-mode, you can use the *filename1* switch to import a single branch into the Registry.

Importing REG Files into Windows 95

You can double-click on a REG file in Windows 95 (as well as in Windows 3.x) to place the settings in the REG file into the Registry. Sometimes, however, the Windows 95 Registry does not interpret this information correctly and adds a new value based on this data, rather than update an existing value.

The reason this happens is due to a difference in the REG file and the Registry value. As a quirk, if one of the values—either the REG file value or the Registry value—contains a trailing space that the other one does not, Windows 95 automatically creates a new value.

To get around this, before you double-click on the REG file in Explorer, open the file in Notepad and compare it to the existing setting in the Registry. If there is a difference, modify the key values in the REG file. These values must match exactly or the update will not be successful.

Dealing with File Type Associations that Don't Work

If you experience problems associating a file type with an application, particularly if that file type was previously defined, you might have to use a work-around. To associate a file type, use the File Types dialog box (see fig. D.1). If that association doesn't take effect, return to the File Types dialog box and delete the old association completely. Next, add a new association.

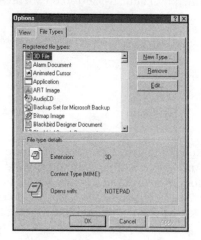

Figure D.1

The File Types dialog box is used to change file associations.

You also can open the Registry Editor and search on the file extension, such as JPG. The values for the extensions are stored in the HKEY_LOCAL_MACHINE\ Software\Microsoft\Windows\CurrentVersion\Extensions subkey. Make sure the value entries are set correctly for that file type. If not, change them appropriately and restart Windows.

Installing NICs Not Listed

You might need to install a NDIS 2 network interface card (NIC) that is not supported by Windows 95. Windows 95 might not include an option to choose your card when you run install the card. Also, Windows 95 might not include an OEMSETUP.INF file.

To start, make sure you have the device driver for the card. You might be able to obtain it from the Microsoft Web site or off CompuServe. If you can't find it there, contact the manufacturer. Start the installation process as normal by running the Network option from the Control Panel and selecting the Adapter option. When you need to select the driver type, select Real Mode (16-bit) NDIS driver.

When you get to the point where Windows 95 prompts you to shut down and restart the computer, don't do that yet.

You need to manually configure resource settings in the PROTOCOL.INI file that the installation wizard creates. You'll find the PROTOCOL.INI file in the Windows 95 directory. The INI file will have only two lines in it so far:

```
[]
DriverName=
```

Notice how the IRQ, DMA channel, I/O address, and so on are absent. You'll add these in the file. You'll need to include the following type of data:

```
[card_name]
DriverName=name_of_driver
transceiver=type_of_transceiver
iochrdy=Late
ioaddress=IOPortaddress
irq=valid_irq
```

Once you create the INI file, you need to insert the name of the card into the Registry. Locate the HKEY_LOCAL_MACHINE\Software\Microsoft\Windows\currentVersion\Network\Real Mode Net key. Add the string value netcard to this subkey. The value will be *DriverName*.DOS, where *DriverName* is the name of your card's driver. After you edit the Registry, open the AUTOEXEC.BAT file and include the following line:

```
C:\WINDOWS\NET START
```

This command loads the NDIS 2 NIC, protocol drivers, and binds them together. Save the BAT file. Shut down and restart Windows 95.

Handling Problems from Installing Plus! Internet Components

If you rushed out and bought the wonderful Microsoft Plus! Companion for Windows 95 to get the Internet connectivity features, you might be surprised that you may not be able to install it. A few instances where you might not be able to install the Internet JumpStart Kit include when you install the Internet Explorer from an online service or if you purchased Windows 95 from an OEM vendor.

In these cases, a Registry key is enabled that prevents Plus! from installing the Internet components. To enable these components, use the following steps:

1. Open the Registry Editor and locate the HKEY_LOCAL_MACHINE\Software\Microsoft\Internet Explorer\Iver subkey.

2. Delete the Iver key.

3. Shut down and restart Windows 95.

Note As you use the Internet Explorer, you'll gather Internet shortcuts. These are commonly referred to as bookmarks, but Microsoft has to start new trends all the time. These shortcuts are stored in the Favorites folder, which is located in the Registry at the following location:

HKEY_CURRENT_USER\Software\Microsoft\Windows\CurrentVersion\Explorer\Shell Folder

Shortcuts and Time Savers

It seems like everyone is too busy to get their jobs done. With the work piling up on your desk and the phone ringing off the hook, you need to squeeze every ounce of efficiency out of Windows and your applications. This section looks at some of the ways you can modify Registry settings to do just that.

Adding to the Context Menu

Providing the capability to use the right mouse button has to be one of the best new features in Windows 95. Although third-party mouse manufacturers sometimes included software to enable this feature in Windows 3.x, the right mouse button could only perform small tasks like double-clicking automatically when you single clicked the button. With Windows 95, the right mouse button offers an entire new world of convenient options with only a quick click of the mouse.

By default, Windows 95 places several items on the context menu when you right click. Some of these options are handy (Send To a floppy drive, for instance), while others are less appealing (such as create a new wave sound). You can modify this list of options by modifying the Registry.

1. Start by opening the application you want to add to the context menu, such as Microsoft Word 95. Next, create an empty document and save it with a file name of your choice (but keep its standard, registered file extension). You can set template values and so forth if you want to create a specific type of document. You can use the document template for your company letterhead, for instance.

2. Close the document and copy the file into the \WINDOWS95\SHELLNEW folder, which is hidden.

3. In the Registry Editor, open the HKEY_CLASSES_ROOT key and search on the file extension type of the document you just created. For the Word example, for instance, search using *.DOC searching parameter.

Tip

Make sure the Keys option in the Look at section of the Find dialog box is marked. Otherwise you might end up editing the wrong key value.

4. Under the subkey for that extension, insert a new key and name it ShellNew. Next, add a string value with the name "FileName". Figure D.2 shows what this looks like.

Figure D.2

Remember that the quotation marks are added automatically around the string value.

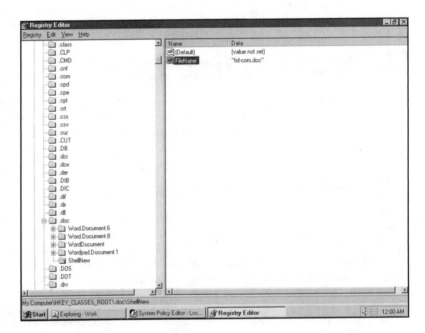

5. Double-click on the value and insert the filename and extension of the document you created in step 1 in the Edit String dialog box. The Registry takes care of location the path for the file, so you can simply enter the document name.

6. Exit the Registry, and shut down and restart Windows 95.

When you return, the context menu will have a brand new item that you can quickly click on to start the document of your choice.

Note

Is there a context menu option that includes an option to the application you want, but you want to change the default document? No problem. Just find the extension and ShellNew value for the application. Change the FileName value to the name of the new document you created in step 1.

Viewing Unregistered File Types

Associating file types is a convenient way to open and work with certain files. Some file types, however, should not have regular file types associated with them, such as system files that you don't want to open in an application or text editor. You can, though, create a handy tool that enables you to quickly view unregistered file types.

1. Open the Registry Editor and find the HKEY_CLASSES_ROOT\Unknown\shell.

2. Add a new key named **OpenNote**.

3. Add another new key named **command** under the OpenNote key.

4. Change the value entry for the (Default) entry to point to the path and file name of the application you want to use as the default viewer. You might want to use a text editor like Notepad in this case.

5. Add %1 after the path and file name. If, for example, you use Notepad your syntax in the value data area would be "**c:\windows95\notepad.exe %1**".

Shut down and restart Windows 95 to try out your new tool. Every time Windows 95 encounters a file of a type it doesn't recognize, Windows will automatically open it in Notepad for you.

Configuring Windows To Open on Command

When browsing folders, many users have Windows 95 set to use a single window that changes when they open a new folder. The alternative is to open a new window for each folder. If you want to copy or move files around, you might want to quickly open a separate window for a folder.

You can add an Open New Window option on the context menu by using these steps:

1. Start the Registry Editor and locate the HKEY_CLASSES_ROOT\Directory\Shell subkey.

2. Create a new key called **opennew**.

   Set the (Default) value to **Open New &Window**. The ampersand character (&) denotes that the next character is to be the Windows accelerator key.

4. Add another key beneath the opennew key and call it **command**.

5. Set the (Default) value to **explorer %1**.

Shut down and restart Windows 95. When you highlight a folder, you can right-click and select Open New Window to create a new window that lists the contents of the selected folder.

Modifying the Double-Click Sensitivity

If the range of motion for a double-click on your mouse is not enough, change it.

1. Locate the HKEY_CURRENT_USER\Control Panel\Desktop Registry subkey.

2. Add two new string values called DoubleClickHeight and DoubleClickWidth.

3. Insert value data in the data dialog box for each value. The values will be denoted in terms of pixels, so don't make them very large.

Shut down and restart Windows 95. You might want to experiment with these settings a couple of times to get the feel just right.

Turning Off Desktop Icons

If you want to turn off all the icons on your desktop, you need to use the System Policy Editor. (Besides limiting which icons a user can access, this also has the benefit of turning off the CD AutoPlay feature.) Next, use these steps:

1. Select Local User.

2. Select the Shell policy and Restrictions option.

3. Select Hide all items on Desktop.

When you restart Windows 95 the next time and log on under this user name, you will not see icons.

Adding a Cascading Control Panel to Start Menu

How many clicks does it take to activate the Network program in the Control Panel? One, two...too many.

If you're like many users, you spend a better part of your day monkeying around with several Control Panel items. You can speed up the time it takes to access these items by placing the Control Panel options right in the Start menu. Use the following instructions:

1. Create a new folder in the Start Menu folder. The Start Menu folder can be found in the Windows 95 folder.

2. Name the folder this:

   `Control Panel.{21EC2020-3AEA-1069-A2DD-08002B30309D}`

3. After you enter this value and press Enter, you'll get a new folder in the Start Menu named Control Panel. A cascading menu also appears, which contains all the Control Panel items in it.

In the long string you entered above, the period between "Control Panel" and the number creates a Registry entry for this item. You now can look in the Registry for this new subkey and value.

Tip You can add the Printers and Dial-Up Networking folders to the Start menu using these values:

Dial Up Networking:

`Dial Up Net.{992CFFA0-F557-101A-88EC-00DD010CCC48}`

Printers:

`Printers.{2227A280-3AEA-1069-A2DE-08002B30309D}`

Setting Default Actions for Any File Type

To create a right-click menu option that will react to any file type, whether it is registered or not, use these steps:

1. Create a new Text Document on the desktop.

2. Name the text document All.Reg.

3. Enter the following data into the new document:

```
REGEDIT4
[HKEY_CLASSES_ROOT\*]
"EditFlags"=hex:02,00,00,00
[HKEY_CLASSES_ROOT\Unknown]
"EditFlags"=hex:02,00,00,00
```

4. Select Merge by right-clicking on the new document.

5. Open the Explorer.

6. Select the View, Options menu.

7. Click on the File Types tab.

In the File Types list you should see an asterisk, and then further down the list you should see an Unknown file type.

Disabling Window Animations

Have you noticed how Windows 95 likes to animate the window of an application when you maximize or minimize it? This seems to be one of those Macintosh features that someone at Microsoft thought was cute. For most users, especially those using slow video cards with slow repaint rates, it gets annoying.

Turn it off by using the following steps:

1. Start the Registry Editor and locate the HKEY_CURRENT_USER\Control Panel\Desktop\WindowMetrics subkey.

2. Add a new string value with the name MinAnimate.

3. Double-click on the new value entry and enter the new string value as 0 for off, and 1 for on. You'll want 0 to turn off the Window animation.

Shut down and restart Windows 95. Now when you minimize or maximize a window it displays in a smooth fashion, without the jerkiness in it.

Refreshing Screen Automatically

When you use the Explorer or My Computer and add or delete folders or files, you need to press F5 for the changes to show up. For users not accustomed to this refresh requirement, or if you get tired of hitting the F5 key every few seconds, enable the automatic refresh feature. Use the following steps:

1. Open the HKEY_LOCAL_MACHINE\System\CurrentControlSet\Control\ Update Registry subkey.

2. Double-click on the UpdateMode entry in the right pane of the Registry Editor (see fig. D.3).

3. Edit the DWORD hexadecimal value to a setting that is between 1 and 7.

4. Click on OK and restart Windows.

When you make changes in the Explorer or other parts of Windows that require you to press F5 for a refresh, Windows 95 handles it automatically.

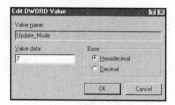

Figure D.3

You can increase the refresh rate of Windows 95 using this Registry key.

Removing System Icons

You might find it valuable to remove icons for system devices, such as hard drives and the like. You can keep these items off the desktop by modifying the Registry. Use the following steps:

1. Locate the subkey for the resource you want to remove, such as Inbox. The subkey for this is HKEY_CLASSES_ROOT\CLSID\{00020D-75-0000-0000-C000-000000000046}\ShellFolder.

2. In the right pane, delete the Attributes value.

3. Press F5 to refresh the Registry.

Shut down and restart Windows 95.

Summary

This appendix showed you some common configuration and setup changes you can make using the Registry Editor in Windows 95. If you are responsible for managing Windows 95 clients on a Windows NT network, you should find this appendix handy at times to make your Windows 95 clients run more efficiently or to customize the way they look or behave.

To find out more information about the Windows 95 Registry, read Chapter 7, "Administering Remote Registries from Windows NT," or pick up a copy of *Windows 95 Registry Troubleshooting*, published by New Riders. You also can find troubleshooting articles in the Microsoft Knowledge Base at http://www.microsoft.com/kb on the World Wide Web.

Index

REGISTRATION CARD

Windows NT Registry Troubleshooting

Name _____ Title _____

Company _____ Type of business _____

Address _____

City/State/ZIP _____

Have you used these types of books before? ☐ yes ☐ no

If yes, which ones? _____

_____

How many computer books do you purchase each year? ☐ 1–5 ☐ 6 or more

How did you learn about this book? _____

Where did you purchase this book? _____

Which applications do you currently use? _____

_____

Which computer magazines do you subscribe to? _____

_____

What trade shows do you attend? _____

_____

Comments: _____

_____

_____

Would you like to be placed on our preferred mailing list? ☐ yes ☐ no

☐ **I would like to see my name in print!** You may use my name and quote me in future New Riders products and promotions. My daytime phone number is: _____

New Riders Publishing 201 West 103rd Street ◆ Indianapolis, Indiana 46290 USA

Fax to 317-581-4670

Fold Here

BUSINESS REPLY MAIL
FIRST-CLASS MAIL PERMIT NO. 9918 INDIANAPOLIS IN

POSTAGE WILL BE PAID BY THE ADDRESSEE

NEW RIDERS PUBLISHING
201 W 103RD ST
INDIANAPOLIS IN 46290-9058